18th Workshop on Multiword Expressions (MWE 2022)

Held at LREC 2022

Marseille, France
20 – 25 June 2022

Editors:

Archna Bhatia
Paul Cook
Shiva Taslimipoor
Marcos Garcia
Carlos Ramisch

ISBN: 978-1-7138-6128-7

Printed from e-media with permission by:

Curran Associates, Inc.
57 Morehouse Lane
Red Hook, NY 12571

Some format issues inherent in the e-media version may also appear in this print version.

Association for Computational Linguistics
209 N. Eighth Street
Stroudsburg, Pennsylvania 18360

Phone: 1-570-476-8006
Fax: 1-570-476-0860

acl@aclweb.org

Additional copies of this publication are available from:

Curran Associates, Inc.
57 Morehouse Lane
Red Hook, NY 12571 USA
Phone: 845-758-0400
Fax: 845-758-2633
Email: curran@proceedings.com
Web: www.proceedings.com

LREC 2022 Workshop
Language Resources and Evaluation Conference
20-25 June 2022

18th Workshop on Multiword Expressions
MWE 2022

PROCEEDINGS

Editors:
Archna Bhatia, Paul Cook, Shiva Taslimipoor, Marcos Garcia and
Carlos Ramisch

Proceedings of the LREC 2022 workshop on 18th Workshop on Multiword Expressions (MWE 2022)

Edited by: Archna Bhatia, Paul Cook, Shiva Taslimipoor, Marcos Garcia and Carlos Ramisch

ISBN: 979-10-95546-90-0
EAN: 9791095546900

For more information:
European Language Resources Association (ELRA)
9 rue des Cordelières
75013, Paris
France
http://www.elra.info
Email: lrec@elda.org

Introduction

The 18th Workshop on Multiword Expressions (MWE 2022)[1] took place on a hybrid (on-site/remote) format on June 25, 2022 in Marseille (France), in conjunction with the 13th Edition of the Language Resources and Evaluation Conference (LREC 2022). MWE 2022 was organized and sponsored by the Special Interest Group on the Lexicon (SIGLEX) of the Association for Computational Linguistics (ACL).

Multiword expressions (MWEs) are word combinations which exhibit lexical, syntactic, semantic, pragmatic and/or statistical idiosyncrasies, such as by and large, hot dog, pay a visit and pull one's leg. The notion encompasses closely related phenomena: idioms, compounds, light-verb constructions, phrasal verbs, rhetorical figures, collocations, institutionalised phrases, etc. Their behaviour is often unpredictable; for example, their meaning often does not result from the direct combination of the meanings of their parts. Given their irregular nature, MWEs often pose complex problems in linguistic modelling (e.g. annotation), NLP tasks (e.g. parsing), and end-user applications (e.g. natural language understanding and MT), hence still representing an open issue for computational linguistics.

For almost two decades, modelling and processing MWEs for NLP has been the topic of the MWE workshop organised by the MWE section of SIGLEX in conjunction with major NLP conferences since 2003. Impressive progress has been made in the field, but our understanding of MWEs still requires much research considering its need and usefulness in NLP applications. For this 18th edition of the workshop, we identified three topics on which contributions are particularly encouraged:

- MWE processing in low-resource languages: The PARSEME shared tasks, among others, have fostered significant progress in MWE identification, providing datasets that include low-resource languages, evaluation measures and tools that now allow fully integrating MWE identification into end-user applications. A few efforts have recently explored methods for automatic interpretation of MWEs. Pursuing similar efforts on understanding MWEs in low-resource languages is beneficial. there are some recent efforts on processing of MWEs in low-resource languages. Resource creation and sharing should be pursued in parallel to the development of methods able to capitalize on small datasets.

- MWE identification and interpretation in pre-trained language models: Most current MWE processing is limited to their identification and detection using pre-trained language models, but we lack understanding about how MWEs are represented and dealt with therein. Now that NLP has shifted towards end-to-end neural models like BERT, capable of solving complex end-user tasks with little or no intermediary linguistic symbols, questions arise about the extent to which MWEs should be implicitly or explicitly modelled in such models.

- MWE processing to enhance end-user applications: As underlined by the MWE 2021 call for papers, MWEs gained particular attention in end-user applications, including MT, simplification, language learning and assessment, social media mining, and abusive language detection. We believe that it is crucial to extend and deepen these first attempts to integrate and evaluate MWE technology in these and further end-user applications.

We received 23 submissions of original research papers (12 long and 11 short). We selected 15 papers (9 long and 6 short), 10 presented orally and 5 as posters. The overall acceptance rate was 65%. As a novelty in this edition, we also called for non-archival submissions of abstracts (describing preliminary results, work in progress, or abstract of papers recently submitted or published at other venues), considered for

[1]https://multiword.org/mwe2022/

presentation but not included in the proceedings. We received 7 non-archival submission, from which we selected 5 for presentation.

Moreover, we organised a joint session with the workshop of the Special Interest Group on Under-resourced Languages, SIGUL 2022, to foster future synergies that could address scientific challenges in the creation of resources, models and applications to deal with multiword expressions and related phenomena in low-resource scenarios, in accordance with one of our special topics in MWE 2022.

In addition to the oral and poster sessions, the workshop featured two invited talks, given by Sabine Schulte im Walde (University of Stuttgart, Germany) and by Steven Bird (Charles Darwin University, Australia).

We are grateful to the paper authors for their valuable contributions, the members of the Program Committee for their thorough and timely reviews, all members of the organizing committee for the fruitful collaboration, and to all the workshop participants for their interest in this event. Our thanks also go to the LREC 2022 organizers for their support, to SIGLEX for their endorsement, and to SIGUL for their efforts and interest in organising the MWE-SIGUL joint session.

Archna Bhatia, Paul Cook, Shiva Taslimipoor, Marcos Garcia, Carlos Ramisch

Organizers

Program Chairs

Archna Bhatia – Florida Institute for Human & Machine Cognition
Paul Cook – University of New Brunswick – Faculty of Computer Science
Shiva Taslimipoor – University of Cambridge – NLIP Group

Publication Chair

Marcos Garcia – Universidade de Santiago de Compostela – CiTIUS Research Centre

Communication Chair

Carlos Ramisch – Aix Marseille University – TALEP Research Group

Program Committee

Tim Baldwin, University of Melbourne (Australia)
Verginica Barbu Mititelu, Romanian Academy (Romania)
Francis Bond, Palacký University (Czech Republic)
Claire Bonial, U.S. Army Research Laboratory (USA)
Tiberiu Boroș, Adobe (Romania)
Marie Candito, Université Paris Cité (France)
Anastasia Christofidou, Academy of Athens (Greece)
Ken Church, Baidu (USA)
Matthieu Constant, Université de Lorraine (France)
Monika Czerepowicka, University of Warmia and Mazury (Poland)
Myriam de Lhonneux, University of Copenhagen (Denmark)
Gaël Dias, University of Caen Basse-Normandie (France)
Gülşen Eryiğit, Istanbul Technical University (Turkey)
Meghdad Farahmand, University of Geneva (Switzerland)
Christiane Fellbaum, Princeton University (USA)
Joaquim Ferreira da Silva, New University of Lisbon (Portugal)
Aggeliki Fotopoulou, Institute for Language and Speech Processing/RC "Athena" (Greece)
Voula Giouli, Institute for Language and Speech Processing (Greece)
Stefan Th. Gries, UC Santa Barbara (USA) & JLU Giessen (Germany)
Uxoa Iñurrieta, University of the Basque Country (Spain)
Diptesh Kanojia, Surrey Institute for People-Centred AI, University of Surrey (UK)
Ioannis Korkontzelos, Edge Hill University (UK)
Cvetana Krstev, University of Belgrade (Serbia)
Eric Laporte, Gustave Eiffel University (France)
Timm Lichte, University of Tübingen (Germany)
Irina Lobzhanidze, Ilia State University (Georgia)
Teresa Lynn, ADAPT Centre (Ireland)
Gunn Inger Lyse Samdal, University of Bergen (Norway)
Stella Markantonatou, Institute for Language and Speech Processing (Greece)
Yuji Matsumoto, RIKEN Center for Advanced Intelligence Project (Japan)

Jan Odijk, University of Utrecht (Netherlands)
Haris Papageorgiou, Institute for Language and Speech Processing (Greece)
Yannick Parmentier, Université d'Orléans (France)
Pavel Pecina, Charles University (Czech Republic)
Ted Pedersen, University of Minnesota (USA)
Scott Piao, Lancaster University (UK)
Alain Polguère, Université de Lorraine (France)
Livy Real, americanas s.a. (Brazil)
Fatiha Sadat, Université du Québec à Montréal (Canada)
Magali Sanches Duran, University of São Paulo (Brazil)
Sabine Schulte im Walde, University of Stuttgart (Germany)
Matthew Shardlow, Manchester Metropolitan University (UK)
Ivelina Stoyanova, Bulgarian Academy of Sciences (Bulgaria)
Pavel Straňák, Charles University (Czech Republic)
Stan Szpakowicz, University of Ottawa (Canada)
Carole Tiberius, Dutch Language Institute (Netherlands)
Beata Trawinski, Leibniz Institute for the German Language (Germany)
Zdeňka Urešová, Charles University (Czech Republic)
Ruben Urizar, University of the Basque Country (Spain)
Lonneke van der Plas, University of Malta (Malta)
Veronika Vincze, Hungarian Academy of Sciences (Hungary)
Martin Volk, University of Zürich (Switzerland)
Zeerak Talat, Digital Democracies Institute, Simon Fraser University (Canada)
Marion Weller-Di Marco, Ludwig Maximilian University of Munich (Germany)
Jelena Mitrović, University of Passau (Germany)
Petya Osenova , Bulgarian Academy of Sciences (Bulgaria)
Ashwini Vaidya, Indian Institute of Technology, Delhi (India)

Table of Contents

Conference Program

9:00–9:10	***Opening***
9:10–10:30	**Session 1: Oral presentations**
9:10–9:25	*A General Framework for Detecting Metaphorical Collocations* Marija Brkić Bakarić, Lucia Načinović Prskalo and Maja Popović
9:25–9:40	*Improving Grammatical Error Correction for Multiword Expressions* Shiva Taslimipoor, Christopher Bryant and Zheng Yuan
9:40–9:50	*Native and Non-native Speakers' Idiom Production: What Can Read Speech Tell Us?* (non-archival paper) Jing Liu and Helmer Strik
9:50–10:10	*An Analysis of Attention in German Verbal Idiom Disambiguation* Rafael Ehren, Laura Kallmeyer and Timm Lichte
10:10–10:30	*Support Verb Constructions across the Ocean Sea* Jorge Baptista, Nuno Mamede and Sónia Reis
10:30–11:00	*Coffee break*
11:00–12:00	**Session 2: Invited Talk #1** *Figurative Language in Noun Compound Models across Target Properties, Domains and Time* Sabine Schulte im Walde
12:00–13:00	**Session 3: Oral presentations**
12:00–12:20	*A Matrix-Based Heuristic Algorithm for Extracting Multiword Expressions from a Corpus* Orhan Bilgin
12:20–12:40	*Multi-word Lexical Units Recognition in WordNet* Marek Maziarz, Ewa Rudnicka and Łukasz Grabowski
12:40–13:00	*Automatic Detection of Difficulty of French Medical Sequences in Context* Anaïs Koptient and Natalia Grabar
13:00–14:00	*Lunch break*
14:00–15:00	**Session 4: Poster Session (joint with SIGUL)** *Annotating "Particles" in Multiword Expressions in te reo Māori for a Part-of-Speech Tagger* Aoife Finn, Suzanne Duncan, Peter-Lucas Jones, Gianna Leoni and Keoni Mahelona *Metaphor Detection for Low Resource Languages: From Zero-Shot to Few-Shot Learning in Middle High German* Felix Schneider, Sven Sickert, Phillip Brandes, Sophie Marshall and Joachim Denzler *Automatic Bilingual Phrase Dictionary Construction from GIZA++ Output* Albina Khusainova, Vitaly Romanov and Adil Khan *A BERT's Eye View: Identification of Irish Multiword Expressions Using Pre-trained Language Models* Abigail Walsh, Teresa Lynn and Jennifer Foster *Enhancing the PARSEME Turkish Corpus of Verbal Multiword Expressions* Yagmur Ozturk, Najet Hadj Mohamed, Adam Lion-Bouton and Agata Savary

	German Light Verb Constructions in Business Process Models (non-archival paper) Kristin Kutzner and Ralf Laue
	BPE beyond Word Boundary: How NOT to Use Multi Word Expressions in Neural Machine Translation (non-archival paper) Avijit Thawani and Dipesh Kumar
15:00–16:00	**Session 5: Invited Talk #2 (joint with SIGUL)**
	Multiword Expressions and the Low-Resource Scenario from the Perspective of a Local Oral Culture Steven Bird
16:00–16:30	*Coffee break*
16:30–17:40	**Session 6: Oral Presentations**
16:30–16:40	*Compound-internal Anaphora: Evidence from Acceptability Judgements on Italian Argumental Compounds* (non-archival paper) Irene Lami and Joost van de Weijer
16:40–16:50	*Light Verb Constructions in Corpora of Historical English* (non-archival paper) Eva Zehentner
16:50–17:05	*Sample Efficient Approaches for Idiomaticity Detection* Dylan Phelps, Xuan-Rui Fan, Edward Gow-Smith, Harish Tayyar Madabushi, Carolina Scarton and Aline Villavicencio
17:05–17:20	*mwetoolkit-lib: Adaptation of the mwetoolkit as a Python Library and an Application to MWE-based Document Clustering* Fernando Rezende Zagatti, Paulo Augusto de Lima Medeiros, Esther da Cunha Soares, Lucas Nildaimon dos Santos Silva, Carlos Ramisch and Livy Real
17:20–17:40	*Handling Idioms in Symbolic Multilingual Natural Language Generation* Michaelle Dubé and François Lareau
17:40–18:00	**MWE Community Discussion**

Figurative Language in Noun Compound Models across Target Properties, Domains and Time

Sabine Schulte im Walde
Institute for Natural Language Processing
University of Stuttgart
sabine.schulte-im-walde@ims.uni-stuttgart.de

Abstract

A variety of distributional and multi-modal computational approaches has been suggested for modelling the degrees of compositionality across types of multiword expressions and languages. As the starting point of my talk, I will present standard variants of computational models that have been proven successful in predicting the compositionality of German and English noun compounds. The main part of the talk will then be concerned with investigating the general reliability of these standard models and discussing implications for gold-standard datasets: I will demonstrate how prediction results vary (i) across representations, (ii) across empirical target properties, (iii) across compound types, (iv) across levels of abstractness, and (v) for general- vs. domain-specific language. Finally, I will present a preliminary quantitative study on diachronic changes of noun compound meanings and compositionality over time.

Proceedings of the 18th Workshop on Multiword Expressions (MWE 2022) n@LREC2022, page 1
Marseille, 25 June 2022.

Multiword Expressions and the Low-Resource Scenario from the Perspective of a Local Oral Culture

Steven Bird
Charles Darwin University
steven.bird@cdu.edu.au

Abstract

Research on multiword expressions and on under-resourced languages often begins with problematisation. The existence of non-compositional meaning, or the paucity of conventional language resources, are treated as problems to be solved. This perspective is associated with the view of Language as a lexico-grammatical code, and of NLP as a conventional sequence of computational tasks. In this talk, I share from my experience in an Australian Aboriginal community, where people tend to see language as an expression of identity and of 'connection to country'. Here, my early attempts to collect language data were thwarted. There was no obvious role for tasks like speech recognition, parsing, or translation. Instead, working under the authority of local elders, I pivoted to language processing tasks that were more in keeping with local interests and aspirations. I describe these tasks and suggest some new ways of framing the work of NLP, and I explore implications for work on multiword expressions and on under-resourced languages.

Proceedings of the 18th Workshop on Multiword Expressions (MWE 2022) n@LREC2022, page 2
Marseille, 25 June 2022.

A General Framework for Detecting Metaphorical Collocations

Marija Brkić Bakarić **Lucia Načinović Prskalo** **Maja Popović**

Faculy of Informatics and Digital Technologies, University of Rijeka
Radmile Matejcic 2, 51000 Rijeka, Croatia
{mbrkic, lnacinovic}@uniri.hr

ADAPT Centre, School of
Computing Dublin City University,
Ireland
maja.popovic@adaptcentre.ie

Abstract

This paper aims at identifying a specific set of collocations known under the term metaphorical collocations. In this type of collocations, a semantic shift has taken place in one of the components. Since the appropriate gold standard needs to be compiled prior to any serious endeavour to extract metaphorical collocations automatically, this paper first presents the steps taken to compile it, and then establishes appropriate evaluation framework. The process of compiling the gold standard is illustrated on one of the most frequent Croatian nouns, which resulted in the preliminary relation significance set. With the aim to investigate the possibility of facilitating the process, frequency, logDice, relation, and pretrained word embeddings are used as features in the classification task conducted on the logDice-based word sketch relation lists. Preliminary results are presented.

Keywords: metaphorical collocations, classification, gold standard, significant relations, evaluation framework

1. Introduction

This paper is concerned with defining a framework for detecting metaphorical collocations. Since manually annotating corpus is extremely time-consuming and tedious, a combination of computational-linguistic and theoretical-semantic approaches is applied. The aim is to explore different patterns involved in the formation of metaphorical collocations in Croatian and discover possibilities of their automatic extraction. The final goal of this research is to create multilingual inventories of metaphorical collocations extracted from comparable corpora.

In generic terms, collocations imply awareness of common, conventional use. Metaphorical collocations form a very specific subset of lexical collocations. They are interesting in terms of cross-language comparison, since an in-depth analysis might provide universal formation patterns.

In metaphorical collocations, the base, which is usually a noun, retains its basic meaning. The collocate, on the other hand, is used in its secondary meaning, which is a consequence of the lexicalized (not spontaneous, vanished) metaphor (Stojić & Košuta, 2021a). Idiosyncrasy that is present with collocations is even more present in the case of metaphorical collocations. If we compare equivalents in Croatian, English, and German regarding the concept of a "long-time bachelor", it is evident that the collocates are represented by different images, i.e., "time" in English, "bark" in Croatian (*okorjeli neženja*), and "carved in flesh" in German (*eingefleischther Junggeselle*). In English, a temporal dimension is present. In Croatian and German, on the other hand, a spatial dimension can be observed, i.e., its properties of thickness and depth, respectively (Geld & Stanojević, 2018). The same extra-linguistic reality is lexicalized in different ways, thus indicating arbitrariness. However, the lexicalization is driven by a metaphorical mechanism in both cases. This leads to a conclusion that the process of making a relation between the base and its collocate might be following the same pattern. In this paper we focus on the Croatian language formation patterns.

Manual or semi-automatic compilation of language resources is extremely time-demanding, and thus expensive. Each time a method is modified, or a new method is tested, a new round of evaluation has to be performed, resulting in a huge waste of resources.

This paper presents an approach to developing the gold standard of metaphorical collocations. The approach is described in detail in section 2, in which a general evaluation framework is also proposed. Section 3 describes the subset of the gold standard involving the most frequent noun in the Croatian language. The related work on the existing collocation extraction studies, with a particular focus on Croatian is presented in Section 4. Section 5 presents some preliminary results obtained by approaching the task as a classification task. Concluding remarks are given in the final section of this paper.

2. Framework

Prior research has shown that nouns usually form the base of metaphorical collocations and that they retain their meaning, while the change in meaning usually manifests itself in the collocate. Due to that, we first compile the list of the most frequent nouns. The manual processing is therefore done in order of frequency (Stojić & Košuta, 2021b). The procedure proposed for compiling the gold standard can be outlined by the following steps:

1. Precise specification of the task
2. Selection of a suitable source corpus
3. Profiling
    a. Establishing the collocation profile of the most frequent noun based on a selected metric
    b. Exhaustive search
4. Determining fertile grammatical relations.

After the selection of a suitable source corpus, the collocation profile of the most frequent noun is established, and fertile grammatical relations are determined based on an exhaustive search.

The semantic analysis of the collocates performed in the second phase of the third step gives insight into semantic shifts and reveals language formation patterns in the language of interest, which might eventually lead to accepting the hypothesis about the universality of the process.

Steps 3-4 are repeated until a predefined number of nouns has been processed, each time taking into account the next

Proceedings of the 18th Workshop on Multiword Expressions (MWE 2022) n@LREC2022, pages 3–8

most frequent noun. If convergence has not been reached, the predefined number of nouns is enlarged. The point of convergence is reached when there are no new grammatical relations added to the list of fertile relations. Since we aim at doing a cross-language comparison, as a follow-up, steps 2-4 are conducted separately for each language. In our case, these are defined on the basis of available linguists employed for the task, and include English, Croatian, German, and Italian. However, step 3a is adapted to allow for direct comparisons. The list of the most frequent nouns is therefore taken to be the intersection of the nouns that appear in all four lists. The rank is determined by our base language, which is taken to be Croatian, but the nouns found in these lists are mostly the same, with minor differences in their respective ranks. In this paper, the presented results are limited to the most frequent Croatian noun *godina* ("year") for which the required output from the linguists has been obtained.

The output of the procedure described above is a list of metaphorical collocations, which will be used as our gold standard in evaluating different automatic extraction methods. Under the limitations set by our gold standard, beside a potential linguistic filter, we introduce additional constraint related to filtering the obtained candidate lists based on the available, i.e., processed, nouns which represent the nodes or the base words of the metaphorical collocations. This will allow us to compute precision and recall. As an additional verification step, which is also used for enlarging the gold standard with new base words and their collocates, we propose extracting the list of candidates not found in the manually processed lists and asking linguists to check for metaphorical collocations. If new collocates are determined, they are added to the gold standard, and the evaluation procedure is re-run. This is done to make the gold standard unbiased towards the measure used for the preliminary extraction.

From the joint discussions in which linguistic experts for all four languages participated, it could be concluded that the task of determining metaphorical collocations is quite subjective. Therefore, the experts held several discussion sessions prior to performing analysis and compiling the final list of metaphorical collocations per each language, up until they felt confident enough that they could differentiate between different types of collocations and thus extract metaphorical collocations. Two linguists per language participated in the task and the final lists comprise only collocations for which both linguists agreed to be metaphorical.

3. Processing the most frequent Croatian noun

In this section we provide details on the procedure applied in analysing the most frequent Croatian noun.

3.1 Corpus

Since our base language for exploring different patterns involved in the formation of metaphorical collocations is Croatian, the first corpus we process is the Croatian Web Corpus (Ljubešić & Erjavec, 2011), which consists of texts collected from the Internet and contains over 1.2 billion words. The hrWaC corpus is PoS tagged with MULTEXT-East Croatian POS tagset version 5 (Erjavec & Ljubešić, 2016). Considering the source of the corpus, it comes as no surprise that misspellings or non-standard language variants are infiltrated into the word sketch results. Additionally, due to the statistical nature of the tools employed in the pre-processing phase, there are also cases of incorrect lemmas and incorrect part-of-speech (POS) tags.

3.2 Measure

A measure used for identifying collocations (step 3a that is concerned with establishing the collocation profile of the most frequent noun) that is used in this research is the measure logDice implemented in Sketch Engine[1]. More details about logDice can be found in (Rychlý, 2008), and about its Sketch Engine implementation in (Kilgarriff et al., 2015). It is based on the frequencies of the base word and its collocate, and on the frequency of the whole collocation (co-occurrence of the base and the collocate). Since logDice is not affected by the size of the corpus, it can be used to compare scores between different corpora. The equation for calculating the logDice score is given in (1).

$$logDice(w_1, R, w_2) = 14 + \log_2 \frac{2 \times ||w_1, R, w_2||)}{||w_1, R, *|| + ||*, R, w_2||} \quad (1)$$

3.3 Relations

Sketch Engine relies on the language-dependent pattern matching grammars defined within the system that allow the system to automatically identify possible relations of words to the keyword, in our case *godina*. This makes the relations highly likely to contain false positives, but also to miss some collocations. However, for the purpose of this research, we find all these issues to be minor, as the candidate lists undergo additional inspection by linguists. For the word *godina,* Sketch Engine generates a total of 21 grammatical relations: *kakav?, oba_u_genitivu, u_genitivu_n, a-koga-čega, n-koga-čega, koga-što, particip, prijedlog, infinitive, koga-čega, s_prilogom, a-koga-što, a-komu-čemu, komu-čemu, glagol_ispred_prijedloga, prijedlog-iza, veznik, koordinacija, imenica_iza_prijedloga, biti_kakav?* and *subjekt_od.* There are 1,747 unique collocates dispersed over different grammatical relations, out of a total of 5,019 collocation candidates. Since the focus of this research are lexical collocations, only those grammatical relations with auto-semantical lexemes are considered relevant, i.e., ***kakav?*** (descriptive), *oba_u_genitivu* (an adjective and a noun both in genitive), *u_genitivu-n* (a noun in genitive), ***n-koga-čega*** (two nouns—one in genitive), *a-koga-čega* (an adjective in nominative and a noun in genitive), ***koga-što*** (accusative), ***subjekt_od*** (subject of), ***particip*** (participle), ***biti_kakav?*** (be like what). Exact rules for the listed relations can be found in Sketch Engine. Approximate descriptions are given in brackets. The relations shown in bold are taken to form the final significance set (Stojić & Košuta, 2021b), as elaborated in more detail in the upcoming subsection.

[1] SketchEngine (https://www.sketchengine.eu/)

3.4 Annotation

During the annotation task, the annotators process relations one by one, by analysing the obtained collocations and, if necessary, corpus examples of its use (Stojić & Košuta, 2021b). They label whether a candidate is a collocation, and additionally, whether it is a metaphorical collocation. There is an additional field in which the annotators can leave comments. That field is mostly used for trying to distinguish between different concepts and processes involved in the formation of metaphorical collocations, such as terms, metonymy, lexicalized metaphor, and personification. Over 80% of the metaphorical collocations belonging to the relation *subject_od* are labelled as personification. Regarding the relation *n-koga-čega*, there is approximately equal ratio between terms and metaphors, with the number of terms slightly superior. The relations such as *kakav?*, *koga-što*, *particip*, and *biti_kakav* have over 60% of metaphorical collocations labelled as resulting from the metaphorization process. The relation *kakav* comprises also a substantial number of terms.

The total number of candidates processed is 673. Among these candidates, there are 202 collocations, while 194 of these collocations are labelled as metaphorical collocations. Around 25% of the collocations in the relations *kakav?* and *biti_kakav* overlap. Moreover, almost 100% of the collocations in the relations *kakav?* and *oba_u_genitivu* overlap, which is why the latter is excluded from the final relation significance set. In the relation *u_genitivu-n* the keyword is a collocate and not the base, so it is considered irrelevant. The relation *a-koga-čega* is also irrelevant because it does not reflect collocations but independent lexemes. Furthermore, there are 25 metaphorical collocations detected by chance while examining contexts in the relation *biti_kakav*[2]. The detailed statistics is shown in Table 1. The extracted significance set of relations consists of patterns comprising the base, which is a noun, and another noun (N), an adjective (A), or a verb (V). However, scatterplots show no discernible patterns which could be used for the identification of metaphorical collocations neither on the basis of their logDice scores nor on the basis of the collocation frequency.

Relation	# of cands	# of colls	# of m_colls	Ratio of m_colls
kakav?	99	54	54	55%
n-koga-čega	100	41	38	41%
koga-što	100	41	41	41%
particip	100	16	11	11%
subjekt_od	100	30	30	30%
biti_kakav?	74	20	20	55%
Total	673	202	194	29%

Table 1: The annotated dataset

4. Related work

To our knowledge, there are no studies on the extraction of metaphorical collocations. In this section we, therefore, tackle recent work on the extraction of collocations in general, and the related work for the language involved, namely Croatian.

The most extensive empirical evaluation which includes 84 automatic collocation extraction methods can be found in (Pecina, 2005). Another comprehensive evaluation of lexical association measures (AMs) and their combination is presented in (Pecina, 2010). Linear logistic regression, linear discriminant analysis, support vector machines and neural networks are used to learn a ranker based on 82 association scores and all perform better than the individual AMs. Principal component analysis shows that the number of model variables can be significantly reduced.

A more recent study covering 13 corpora, eight context sizes, four frequency thresholds, and 20 AMs against two different gold standards of lexical collocations is presented in (Evert et al., 2017). The results show that the optimal choice of an AM depends strongly on the particular gold standard used. With respect to the corpora, larger corpora of the same kind perform better, which is in line with the positive effects observed by (Pecina, 2010). However, the authors in (Evert et al., 2017) acknowledge that clean, balanced corpora are better than large, messy Web corpora of the same size. Additionally, they find that even measures that highly correlate sometimes achieve substantially different evaluation results.

Recently, approaches based on word embeddings have started to gain popularity. A comparison between a supervised machine learning approach and a heuristic-based approach is presented in (Ljubešić et al., 2021). Regarding the rankings of collocates, a supervised machine-learning approach produces more relevant results than the approach based on heuristics. Furthermore, the word embeddings approach, which encodes distributional semantics of words, is a more useful source of information for the ranking of candidates than logDice, which encodes frequency information. An approach for identifying candidates of monolingual collocations using syntactic dependencies followed by the process of creating bilingual word-embeddings and a strategy for discovering collocation equivalents between languages is shown in (Garcia et al., 2017). A distributional semantics-based model that classifies collocations with respect to broad semantic categories is proposed in (Wanner et al., 2017).

As far as Croatian is concerned, there are several papers dealing with collocation extraction in general. For example, (Petrovic et al., 2006) explore four different association measures (PMI, Dice coefficient, Chi-squared test and Log-likelihood ratio) on Croatian legal texts. They use a linguistic filter and take into account AN and NN for bigrams and ANN, AAN, NAN, NNN, NXN for trigrams, where A stands for adjectives, N for nouns, and X for others. The results show that PMI measure performs the best.

A language and collocation type independent genetic programming approach for evolving new association measures is presented in (Šnajder et al., 2008). An evolved measure performs at least as good as any AM included in the initial population. Most of the best evolved AMs take into account the POS information.

(Seljan & Gašpar, 2009) conduct automatic term and collocation extraction based on the parallel English-

[2] Duplicate candidates are excluded from the figures in Table 1.

Croatian corpus of legal texts using two statistically based tools and applying a post-processing linguistic filter. The frequency of syntactic patterns in the automatically obtained lists is in agreement with the manually compiled, and contains AN, NN and NPN

Authors in (Karan, Šnajder and Bašić 2012) are the first one to treat collocation extraction in Croatian as a classification problem. They apply several classification algorithms including decision trees, rule induction, Naive Bayes, neural networks, and Support Vector Machines (SVM). Features classes used include word frequencies, AMs (Dice, PMI, $\chi 2$), and POS tags. SVM classifier performs the best on bigrams and the decision tree on trigrams. The features that contribute most to the overall performance are PMI, semantic relatedness, and features representing a subset of POS tags. Experiments are conducted on a manually annotated set of bigrams and trigrams sampled from a newspaper corpus. The results of F1 measure go up to 80%.

In (Hudeček & Mihaljević, 2020), collocation extraction is based on the use of the Sketch Engine Word Sketch tool on the Croatian Web Repository Online Corpus and Croatian Web Corpus corpora. The results are filtered to include only frequent collocations with a typical syntactic construction.

Similarly, in this research we start with the word sketches generated by Sketch Engine. Next, we analyse the performance of the selected classification algorithms in the task of making the resulting candidate list more meaningful. By applying a classifier to the resulting candidate lists, we can facilitate the process of manual analysis.

5. Preliminary results

Naïve Bayes (NB) is extremely fast classification algorithm and has shown to work quite well in some real-world situations despite its oversimplifying assumptions (Witten et al., 2017). Hence, we take it to be our baseline and compare it to a tree based C4.5, and to more complex Support Vector Machines (SVM) and MultiLayer Perceptron (MLP).

C4.5 algorithm (Quinlan, 1993) is a descendant of ID3. It is a classification algorithm in the form of decision tree in which a splitting criterion known as the gain ratio is used. Decision nodes specify tests carried out at individual attribute values, and contain one branch for each possible outcome, while leaf nodes indicate class. An instance is classified by starting at the root of the tree and moving downwards until a leaf is encountered.

The kernel-based SVMs (Vapnik, 1995) are among the most popular models in Natural Language Processing applications. SVMs capture all features and their interdependencies. In this paper we use the sequential minimal optimization algorithm for training a support vector classifier using polynomial kernels.

MLP is a classifier based on artificial neutral networks. We experiment with several configurations and present results obtained with three hidden layers with 5, 10, and 20 neurons, respectively, and with the learning rate set to 0.3, momentum rate to 0.2, the number of training epochs to 500, and the number of consecutive increases of error allowed for validation testing before training terminates to the value of 20.

In this paper the labelled instances are obtained by manually annotating word sketches from Sketch Engine. Each instance is represented by a vector of feature values. We perform experiments on two sets of features. The first one contains collocation frequency, logDice, and relation (f=3). The second one additionally contains pretrained word embeddings of collocates (Grave et al., 2018), making a total of 303 features (f=303). Word embeddings are added to capture both the semantic and syntactic meanings of words, since they are trained on large datasets. At this point, we do not take into account the word embedding of the base word *godina*, as no other base words have been processed.

Prior to running classification, we pre-process our dataset. We remove instances that do not have valid lemmas due to lemmatization errors. Additionally, we remove duplicate lemmas that are found across several grammatical relations and keep instances with the highest frequencies. However, we do this separately for positively and for negatively labelled instances.

We set 42 as the seed value for the random number generator and run a stratified 10-fold cross validation repeated 10 times. We test whether different algorithms perform significantly better or worse when the feature set is expanded with word embeddings.

Precision (the share of correctly classified positive instances among all positive instances in the system output) and recall (the share of correctly identified positive instances among all instances that should have been identified as positive) are used to evaluate the classification. We also report F-measure scores. Recall results are given in Table 2, precision scores in Table 3, and F-measure scores in Table 4.

When only three features are taken into account, NB is the best performing algorithm at 5% significance level regarding recall, and the worst regarding precision. At the same time, its recall score is severely affected by expanding the feature set by word embeddings. For the other three classifiers, there are no statistically significant differences between their individual recall scores on the two feature sets. The difference in the recall and precision scores between SVM and MLP with f=303 is statistically significant. Regarding F-measure, no statistically significant differences can be observed between the four algorithms when f=3. However, when f=303, NB is outperformed by the other three algorithms.

Recall	f=3	f=303
NB	**0.94***	0.40
C4.5	0.81	0.79
SVM	0.78	**0.80***
MLP	0.80	0.76

Table 2: Recall of the selected algorithms

Precision	f=3	f=303
NB	0.68	0.72
C4.5	0.73	0.77
SVM	0.74	0.74
MLP	0.75	**0.78***

Table 3: Precision of the selected algorithms

F-measure	*f*=3	*f*=303
NB	**0.78**	0.50
C4.5	0.77	**0.78**
SVM	0.76	0.77
MLP	0.77	0.77

Table 4: F-measure of the selected algorithms

If we take into account the fact that metaphorical collocations for the Croatian headword *year* ("year") account for barely 30% of the candidate list obtained through Sketch Engine based on the logDice score, we find these preliminary results promising. However, our current dataset only contains collocates of the most frequent noun. In what way these results will be affected when we expand the dataset remains to be seen.

6. Conclusion

Association measures such as logDice rely exclusively on co-occurrence statistics, which is hardly enough for collocations in the broad meaning, let alone for the subtype of metaphorical collocations. This work is done with the aim to determine a way to encode the relation that refers to collocates contributing the semantic feature to their respective base words, i.e., a metaphor.

In this research we propose a procedure for compiling the gold standard of metaphorical collocations and establish the general evaluation framework for our future work.

Manual processing of the base words and their candidate lists of collocates is extremely time-demanding. Up to this point, linguists have only completed the processing of the most frequent Croatian noun *godina*. Therefore, this paper presents work in progress. The analysis performed is done using the Word Sketch function of the Sketch Engine,, which is based on the logDice score. Through the analysis, six significant grammatical relations are determined. The final relation significance set might be updated as new base words and their collocates are added to the gold standard. The compilation of the gold standard will be performed for a predefined number of base words under the condition that the final relation significance set reached convergence. The relation significance set will allow us to introduce a meaningful linguistic filter to different extraction methods, either as a pre-processing or a post-processing step.

From the experiment presented in this paper, it is evident that collocate embeddings strongly affect the performance of NB in most metrics. However, regarding the other three algorithms, statistically significant differences are obtained only in precision and recall scores between SVM and MLP with *f*=303.

In the follow-up we plan to test different AMs and machine learning algorithms in order to detect methods that are most helpful in automating the procedure of extracting metaphorical collocations. Comparison between different methods might be beneficial for other Slavic languages.

The final goal of this research is to create parallel inventories of metaphorical collocations that are extracted from comparable corpora in Croatian, German, English, and Italian. Due to unpredictability inherent in collocations in general, tasks such as machine translation would highly benefit from such lists.

7. Acknowledgements

This work has been fully supported by Croatian Science Foundation under the project "Metaphorical collocations – Syntagmatic word combinations between semantics and pragmatics" (IP-2020-02-6319).

8. Bibliographical References

Erjavec, T., & Ljubešić, N. (2016). MULTEXT-East Morphosyntactic Specifications, Version 5. Http://Nl.Ijs.Si/ME/Vault/V5/Msd/Html/Msd-Hr.Html.

Evert, S., Uhrig, P., Bartsch, S., & Proisl, T. (2017). E-VIEW-alation-a Large-scale Evaluation Study of Association Measures for Collocation Identification. In *Proceedings of ELex*, pages 531–549.

Garcia, M., García-Salido, M., & Alonso-Ramos, M. (2017). Using bilingual word-embeddings for multilingual collocation extraction. In *Proceedings of the 13th Workshop on Multiword Expressions*, pages 21–30. http://universaldependencies.org/

Geld, R., & Stanojević, M. M. (2018). Strateško konstruiranje značenja riječju i slikom : Konceptualna motivacija u ovladavanju jezikom. Srednja Europa.

Grave, E., Bojanowski, P., Gupta, P., Joulin, A., & Mikolov, T. (2018). Learning Word Vectors for 157 Languages. In *Proceedings of the International Conference on Language Resources and Evaluation* (LREC 2018), pages 3483–3487. https://fasttext.cc/

Hudeček, L., & Mihaljević, M. (2020). Collocations in the Croatian Web Dictionary - Mrežnik. *Slovenščina 2.0: Empirical, Applied and Interdisciplinary Research*, 8(2), 78–111. https://doi.org/10.4312/slo2.0.2020.2.78-111

Karan, M., Šnajder, J., & Bašić, B. D. (2012). Evaluation of Classification Algorithms and Features for Collocation Extraction in Croatian. In *Proceedings of the Eighth International Conference on Language Resources and Evaluation (LREC'12)*, pages 657–662. http://www.lrec-conf.org/proceedings/lrec2012/pdf/796_Paper.pdf

Kilgarriff, A., Baisa, V., Bušta, J., Jakubíček, M., Kovář, V., Michelfeit, J., & Rychlý, P. (2015). Statistics used in the Sketch Engine. https://doi.org/10.1007/s40607

Ljubešić, N., & Erjavec, T. (2011). hrWaC and slWac: Compiling Web Corpora for Croatian and Slovene. In *International Conference on Text, Speech and Dialogue*, pages 395–402. https://doi.org/10.1007/978-3-642-23538-2_50

Ljubešić, N., Logar, N., & Kosem, I. (2021). Collocation ranking: frequency vs semantics. *Slovenscina 2.0*, 9(2), 41–70. https://doi.org/10.4312/slo2.0.2021.2.41-70

Pecina, P. (2005). An Extensive Empirical Study of Collocation Extraction Methods. In *Proceedings of the ACL Student Research Workshop*, pages 13–18.

Pecina, P. (2010). Lexical association measures and collocation extraction. *Language Resources and Evaluation*, 44(1–2), 137–158. https://doi.org/10.1007/s10579-009-9101-4

Petrovic, S., Snajder, J., Dalbelo Basic, B., & Kolar, M. (2006). Comparison of Collocation Extraction Measures for Document Indexing. *Journal of Computing and Information Technology*, 14(4), 321. https://doi.org/10.2498/cit.2006.04.08

Rychlý, P. (2008). A Lexicographer-Friendly Association Score. In *Recent Advances in Slavonic Natural Language Processing*, pages 6–9.

Seljan, S., & Gašpar, A. (2009). First Steps in Term and Collocation Extraction from English-Croatian Corpus. In *Proceedings of 8th International Conference on Terminology and Artificial Intelligence*.

Šnajder, J., Dalbelo Bašić, B., Petrović, S., & Sikirić, I. (2008). Evolving new lexical association measures using genetic programming. In *Proceedings of ACL-08: HLT,* pages 181–184.

Stojić, A., & Košuta, N. (2021a). Istraživanje metaforičkih kolokacija - teorijska osnova i prijedlog modela opisa. *Linguistica,* 61(1), 81–91. https://doi.org/10.4312/linguistica.61.1.81-91

Stojić, A., & Košuta, N. (2021b). Izrada inventara metaforičkih kolokacija u hrvatskome jeziku i njihova obrada sa semantičkoga i pragmatičkoga aspekta. Fluminensia, 34(1) (u rukopisu).

Vapnik, V. N. (1995). The Nature of Statistical Learning Theory. Springer Sceience + Business Media, LLC.

Wanner, L., Ferraro, G., & Moreno, P. (2017). Towards distributional semantics-based classification of collocations for collocation dictionaries. *International Journal of Lexicography*, 30(2), 167–186. https://doi.org/10.1093/ijl/ecw002

Improving Grammatical Error Correction for Multiword Expressions

Shiva Taslimipoor[1] **Christopher Bryant**[1] **Zheng Yuan**[2,1]
[1] ALTA Institute, Department of Computer Science and Technology, University of Cambridge, U.K.
{firstname.lastname}@cl.cam.ac.uk
[2] Department of Informatics, King's College London, U.K.
zheng.yuan@kcl.ac.uk

Abstract

Grammatical error correction (GEC) is the task of automatically correcting errors in text. It has mainly been developed to assist language learning, but can also be applied to native text. This paper reports on preliminary work in improving GEC for multiword expression (MWE) error correction. We propose two systems which incorporate MWE information in two different ways: one is a multi-encoder decoder system which encodes MWE tags in a second encoder, and the other is a BART pre-trained transformer-based system that encodes MWE representations using special tokens. We show improvements in correcting specific types of verbal MWEs based on a modified version of a standard GEC evaluation approach.

Keywords: Multiword Expressions, Grammatical Error Correction

1. Introduction

Second language learners make various kinds of errors in their writing. State-of-the-art Grammatical Error Correction (GEC) systems attempt to correct these errors primarily using neural machine translation technology (Yuan and Briscoe, 2016). These systems are often biased towards correcting the most common error types, however, such as determiner, preposition and spelling errors. Learners can nevertheless also be more creative in generating semantically incorrect phrases such as *by the other side* or *in the other hand* rather than *on the other hand*, or *dream becomes true* instead of *dream comes true*.

Multiword expressions (MWEs), which are combinations of two or more words with syntactic and semantic idiosyncratic behaviours (Sag et al., 2002), are known to be challenging for language learners (Christiansen and Arnon, 2017; Meunier and Granger, 2008). However, like most machine translation (MT) systems, current GEC systems do not take them into consideration. One important challenge involved in the natural language understanding of these expressions is that their meaning deviates from the meaning of their constituent words. Shwartz and Dagan (2019) show that even the state-of-the-art contextualised word representation models have problems in detecting such meaning shifts and their performance is far from that of humans.

Previous studies pointed to the importance of MWEs in GEC. In particular, Mizumoto et al. (2015) merged the tokens in a MWE into a single unit and then applied phrase-based MT and reported a generally better performance for their GEC system that took MWEs into consideration. It has also been reported that such errors are related to learners' L1 (Nesselhauf, 2003). In line with this, Dahlmeier and Ng (2011) use L1-induced paraphrases to correct learners' erroneous use of collocations. Other works focusing on correcting collocation errors made by language learners include the studies by Kochmar (2016). She focused on adjective-noun and verb-object combinations and extracted the meaning representations of the combinations using models of compositional semantics in order to distinguish between the representations of the correct and incorrect content word combinations.

In this work, we deal with all types of MWEs which are difficult to correct based solely on standard contextualised information/embeddings. Specifically, we add MWE information to existing GEC systems in order to investigate how they can improve performance.

Contributions: We propose two different approaches to encode MWE information in existing GEC systems: 1) We augment an encoder-decoder transformer-based GEC model with a separate encoder which encodes MWE tags, and 2) We add special MWE tokens around automatically-detected MWEs in the input to help the encoder-decoder model learn a special representation for them. We show improvements in the performance of the two GEC systems especially in correcting specific types of verbal MWE errors.

2. Grammatical Error Correction

Most recent work on GEC treats the task as a monolingual machine translation problem from 'incorrect' to 'correct' English (Felice et al., 2014; Yuan and Briscoe, 2016; Grundkiewicz et al., 2019; Stahlberg and Kumar, 2021; Yuan et al., 2021). Specifically, given a corpus of parallel erroneous and grammatical sentences, the task is to generate corrected sentences from the erroneous sentences. Alternatively, another recent promising approach treats the task as a sequence labelling problem where each token label represents an edit in the sentence (e.g. KEEP, DELETE, REPLACE) (Awasthi et al., 2019; Omelianchuk et al., 2020; Stahlberg and Kumar, 2020).

Proceedings of the 18th Workshop on Multiword Expressions (MWE 2022) n@LREC2022, pages 9–15

In this paper, we employ two different Transformer-based NMT systems (Vaswani et al., 2017) for GEC: 1) An encoder-decoder GEC system based on Yuan et al. (2021) and 2) A strong BART-based GEC system (Katsumata and Komachi, 2020). The main advantage of the first system is that it includes multi-encoders for representing different features. In particular, while Yuan et al. (2021) used the additional encoder to include features from grammatical error detection, we use the extra encoder to incorporate MWE tags into the model (see Section 4.2). In contrast, the main advantage of the second system is that it is a strong baseline GEC system that simply fine-tunes BART on in-domain GEC data (and hence does not rely on additional techniques such as re-ranking or ensembling) to produce results that are competitive with the state of the art. We add special tokens for MWEs to the data to allow the model to explicitly encode MWEs (Section 4.3).

3. Multiword Expression Identification

As far as we are aware, no dataset in GEC has been explicitly annotated with MWE information; i.e. we do not know which tokens comprise ungrammatical/grammatical MWEs in both the original and the corrected text. Since this information is necessary in an MWE-aware GEC system, we derive these labels automatically.

Our MWE identification system is a transformer-based pre-trained language representation model which we fine-tune for sequence tagging. The model is similar to MTLB-STRUCT (Taslimipoor et al., 2020) with the difference that we use ELECTRA rather than BERT and perform single-task learning for which they reported better performance than for multi-task training in most languages. ELECTRA (Clark et al., 2020) is a variation of BERT (Devlin et al., 2019) that is pre-trained to discriminate between original and replaced tokens rather than generate masked tokens, on the data. In order to predict various types of MWEs including noun compounds, e.g. *customer service*; set phrases, e.g. *as well, so far*; and idioms, e.g. *go the extra mile*, we fine-tune our system on a combination of the STREUSLE dataset (Schneider et al., 2014) and the English side of the PARSEME dataset (Ramisch et al., 2018). The newest version of STREUSLE, as used by Liu et al. (2021), contains more detailed/fine-grained tags for verbal MWEs (following Savary et al. (2017)). Both these datasets are tagged following a variation of IOB labeling (Inside, Outside, Beginning) where *O* indicates that the token is not part of an MWE, *B* indicates the token is the beginning of a new MWE and *I* indicates that the token is a continuation of an MWE. *B*, and *I* tags in these datasets are followed by the type of MWE.

For evaluating our MWE identification system, we follow Liu et al. (2021) and report standard STREUSLE evaluation metrics for MWEs and also

	MWE LinkAvg			Verbal MWE-based		
	P	R	F_1	P	R	F_1
# Gold	433.5			66		
Liu et al. (2021)	82.0	64.3	72.0	-	-	63.9
Our system	**90.7**	**66.8**	**76.7**	**65.2**	**68.2**	**66.7**

Table 1: Overall performance of the MWE identification system on STREUSLE test set.

PARSEME MWE-based metrics for verbal MWEs on the STREUSLE test set. Table 1 shows that our ELECTRA-based system outperforms the BERT-based system used by Liu et al. (2021).

The MWE tags for English contain lexical category labels from STREUSLE including ADJ (adjective), ADV (adverb), DET (determiner) which are in line with Universal part-of-speech tags, AUX (auxiliary), DISC (discourse/pragmatic expression), N (noun, common or proper), P (single-word or compound adposition), PP (prepositional phrase MWE), and PRON (non-possessive pronoun, including indefinites like someone) which indicate the holistic grammatical status of strong multiword expressions plus the verbal MWE tags as follows:

- IAV (Inherently adpositional verbs, also called prepositional verbs e.g. *come accross*),
- LVC.full (light verb constructions in which the verb is semantically totally bleached, e.g. *make a decision*),
- VID (verbal expressions that have fully idiomatic interpretations, e.g., *go bananas*),
- VPC.full (fully non-compositional verb particle constructions, in which the particle totally changes the meaning of the verb, e.g. *give up*),
- VPC.semi (semi non-compositional verb particle constructions, in which the particle adds a partly predictable meaning to the verb, e.g. *eat up*)

Since verbal MWEs are often more challenging for learners (Siyanova and Schmitt, 2007), we particularly focus on this subset of MWE tags in our evaluation.

4. Experiments

4.1. MWE-Augmented GEC Data

Having built a system to annotate MWEs, we apply it to several popular GEC corpora, including the public FCE (Yannakoudakis et al., 2011), NUCLE (Dahlmeier et al., 2013) and W&I (Bryant et al., 2019). Specifically, we annotate the original, uncorrected side of the parallel data with MWE information and convert the annotations into two different formats for our experiments, as explained below.

4.2. Experiment 1: Using MWE in Multi-encoder GEC

Following the work of Yuan and Bryant (2021; Yuan et al. (2021), we incorporate additional MWE information into GEC by introducing a second encoder to

S	This	reminds	me	of	a	trip	that	I	have	been	to	.
3-class	O	O	O	O	O	O	O	O	O	B	I	O
23-class	O	O	O	O	O	O	O	O	O	B-V	I-V	O
T	This	reminds	me	of	a	trip	that	I	have	been	on	.

Table 2: An example sentence with MWE tags at different levels of granularity. 3-class: Begin, Inside, Outside; 23-class: Begin-Verb, Inside-Verb.

the standard Transformer encoder-decoder model. The original Transformer encoder reads the source sentence S_{src} and learns a vector representation c_{src} as before. An additional encoder is introduced to process any auxiliary MWE tags S_{mwe} and compute another representation c_{mwe} in parallel. The decoder now includes a new MWE multi-head attention which attends directly to the MWE encoder representation c_{mwe}, and a linear gating mechanism that combines the source multi-head attention and the new MWE multi-head attention.

A two-step training strategy is employed to train the new GEC model. In the first step, we follow the standard encoder-decoder model training procedure and train a sequence-to-sequence model on parallel Cambridge Learner Corpus (CLC) data (Nicholls, 2003) without MWE information using Fairseq (Ott et al., 2019). In the second step, we fine-tune this model using the auxiliary MWE-tagged data at different levels of granularity. Specifically, the model is fine-tuned on the MWE-tagged FCE, NUCLE and W&I training data where each token is tagged with a coarse (IOB) or fine-grained (IOB+type) MWE labels (Table 2).

4.3. Experiment 2: MWE Marker Tokens

Inspired by Baldini Soares et al. (2019) who used 'entity markers' as special tokens to mark the beginning and end of named entities, we similarly use special tokens to mark the spans of MWEs. This allows us to encode a representation of an MWE as a special unit. We augment our GEC training data with two reserved special tokens [MWE] and [/MWE] to mark the beginning and end of each MWE, respectively, as determined by the MWE identification system (Section 3), in both the original and corrected sides of the texts. We follow two scenarios for marking MWEs in parallel GEC data:

1. We predict MWEs in the *original* text and map the special tokens to the equivalent positions in the *corrected* text.
2. We predict MWEs in the *corrected* text and map the special tokens to the equivalent positions in the *original* text.

In the first case, we simply annotate the texts in the original (source) side with automatically identified MWE tags and use the GEC alignment algorithm ERRANT (Bryant et al., 2017) to automatically find the corresponding spans in the corrected (target) texts. This scenario represents the realistic use-case since we are always given the original text to be corrected. The disadvantage of this approach, however, is that the MWE identification system may not be very accurate since it is trained on native texts with no errors yet applied to ungrammatical text.

In the second case, we hence annotate MWEs in the corrected side, where they are more likely to be well-formed, and again find the equivalent spans in the original text using ERRANT. In contrast with the first case, the disadvantage of this second approach is that we do not have access to the corrected text in the realistic use-case even though the identified MWEs may be more reliable. We nevertheless explore this scenario for comparison with the first scenario. Figure 1 shows an example of a parallel sentence pair with marked MWEs. [1]

Model: Encoder-decoder	P	R	$F_{0.5}$
baseline	57.95	31.22	49.48
MWE-augmented [3-class]	57.80	33.60	50.53
MWE-augmented [23-class]	58.53	33.98	**51.14**

Table 3: Overall performance of the encoder-decoder GEC systems on BEA dev set.

Model: BART	P	R	$F_{0.5}$
baseline	56.08	37.73	51.11
MWE-augmented (1)	56.88	35.36	50.71
MWE-augmented (2)	57.21	36.71	**51.46**

Table 4: Overall performance of the BART GEC system fine-tuned on raw and MWE-tagged W&I data.

S: they also [MWE] made talks [/MWE] and presentations about the earth 's problems
T: they also [MWE] give talks [/MWE] and presentations about the earth 's problems

Figure 1: A sentence pair with marked MWEs.

In this experiment, we use a pre-trained BART model which we fine tune on the MWE-annotated W&I training corpus (Bryant et al., 2019). Katsumata and Komachi (2020) have shown that this model produces competitive results with the state of the art in GEC. Our addition of explicit MWE markers helps the model to better encode representations of MWEs.

4.4. Evaluation

We first report the general performance of our GEC systems with and without incorporating MWE tags in

[1] This example is the same in both scenarios, however, there are also cases where MWEs on one side are aligned with non-MWEs on the other side.

	MWE type	#	Baseline GEC P	R	$F_{0.5}$	MWE-augmented GEC P	R	$F_{0.5}$
Encoder-decoder	V.IAV	41	60.7	41.5	55.6	55.2	39.0	51.0
	V.LVC.full	55	34.6	16.4	28.3	45.8	20.0	**36.4**
	V.VID	47	55.6	21.3	42.0	62.5	21.3	**45.1**
	V.VPC.full	25	38.5	20.0	32.5	54.6	24.0	**43.5**
	V.VPC.semi	12	50.0	25.0	41.7	60.0	25.0	**46.9**
BART GEC	V.IAV	41	57.7	36.6	51.7	56.7	41.5	**52.8**
	V.LVC.full	55	43.3	23.6	37.1	42.9	21.8	35.9
	V.VID	47	55.6	21.3	42.0	78.6	23.4	**53.4**
	V.VPC.full	25	31.6	24.0	29.7	41.7	40.0	**41.3**
	V.VPC.semi	12	50.0	16.7	35.7	50.0	8.3	25.0

Table 5: GEC performance for different types of verbal MWEs.

terms of precision (P), recall (R) and $F_{0.5}$ using the ERRANT evaluation framework. $F_{0.5}$, which weights precision twice as much as recall, has been the most common evaluation metric for GEC since the CoNLL-2014 shared task (Ng et al., 2014).

Table 3 shows the overall performance of the encoder decoder GEC system (Experiment 1) in different settings: baseline (no MWE information), MWE-augmented [3-class] (auxiliary IOB MWE labels), MWE-augmented [23-class] (auxiliary IOB+type MWE labels). We can see that adding MWE information improves GEC system performance.

Table 4 shows the overall performance of the BART model (Experiment 2) fine-tuned on the standard W&I GEC data compared to the models trained on the MWE tagged data in scenarios 1 (where we predict MWEs in the original side) and 2 (where we predict MWEs in the corrected side). Overall, we see a slight improvement on the $F_{0.5}$ performance only in the case of MWE-augmented model (2).

4.5. Fine-grained analysis

We furthermore analyse the performance of our GEC models for specific types of MWEs. In particular, we aim to determine whether our systems are able to detect and correct incorrect usages of MWEs by learners. In order to perform this evaluation, we annotate our system output with MWE tags using the MWE identification system (Section 3) and find the overlap between MWE spans and ERRANT edit spans to determine which hypothesis edits involve MWEs. In this way, we can compare how our system performs on MWE errors irrespective of other errors. We particularly focus on verbal MWE errors.

Table 5 shows the results for both experiments. We focus on five types of verbal MWEs present in the corrected side of the data (V.IAV, V.LVC.full, V.VID, V.VPC.full, and V.VPC.semi) and compare the performance of the two GEC systems (encoder-decoder and BART) with or without MWE-augmentation. We focus on the 23-class MWE augmentation for the encoder-decoder system and scenario 2 for the BART system. In Table 5, we can see that GEC performance improves for four out of five verbal MWE types when we use MWE-augmented systems for the encoder-decoder GEC method and for three out of five verbal MWE types when we use setting 2 of the BART system. The highest improvement is in the case of VPC.full and VID, and the BART model results in more improvement (11.6 compared to 11 for VPC.full and 11.4 compared to 3.1 for VID). The BART system being unsuccessful in the case of V.LVC.full might be due to the fact that LVCs can have multiple arbitrary words in between their canonical form components (e.g. ***make** a very good **decision***). The marking system cannot differentiate them and considers words in between the MWE components as part of the MWE span which brings some noisy information to the system.

4.6. Discussion

In Table 6, we show two examples of sentences containing MWE errors corrected by each system. In the first example, none of the baseline systems were successful, but both MWE-augmented systems managed to correct the VPC *sign up*. In the second example, only the MWE-augmented BART system managed to correct the idiom *get to know*. This perhaps suggests the multi encoder-decoder system, which only uses MWE tags as token-level features, finds it hard to learn the notion of relationships between the components of the expression. The fact that we incorporate labels in the IOB labelling format combined with the MWE types helps the system have more informative features. However, the system still lacks direct linking information between MWE components. The BART system, on the other hand, has a different perspective and works with the text span representations that are encoded by special tokens. However it also treats all MWEs as continuous spans of texts of the same type and adds some arbitrary words in between their components. This is not favourable in the case of more structurally flexible MWEs such as LVCs. Non of the systems are yet successful in correcting more conceptual errors, for example in replacing *end up with* with *bring an end to* in the erroneous sentence, *'cars don't need necessarily to end up with the public transport'*.

	sentence
Original	*the course was fantastic and I am looking forward to signing it again next year .*
enc-dec	
baseline	the course was fantastic and I am looking forward to signing it again next year .
MWE-augmented	the course was fantastic and I am looking forward to **signing up** for it again next year .
BART	
baseline	the course was fantastic and I am looking forward to signing it again next year .
MWE-augmented	the course was fantastic and I am looking forward to **signing up** for it again next year .
Original	*it could allow you to communicate with people , know different cultures ...*
enc-dec	
baseline	it could allow you to communicate with people , know different cultures ...
MWE-augmented	it could allow you to communicate with people , know different cultures ...
BART	
baseline	it could allow you to communicate with people , know different cultures ...
MWE-augmented	it could allow you to communicate with people , **get to know** different cultures ...

Table 6: Example sentences with MWEs corrected by the encoder-decoder (enc-dec) and the BART MWE-augmented systems.

5. Conclusions

In this paper, we propose incorporating MWE information into two different GEC systems in order to improve GEC for MWEs which are challenging for language learners. The experiments show that the additions help GEC in the case of more conventional MWEs, like verbal idioms and verb particle constructions. More research is needed to improve GEC for more syntactically-flexible MWE types which allow arbitrary words in between their components. Our system relies on the performance of MWE detection systems as no GEC data is annotated for MWE type errors. This makes it more difficult for automatically correcting conceptual errors made by learners. Future work in this area benefits from more detailed annotation of learner errors related to their understanding of MWEs.

6. Bibliographical References

Awasthi, A., Sarawagi, S., Goyal, R., Ghosh, S., and Piratla, V. (2019). Parallel iterative edit models for local sequence transduction. In *Proceedings of the 2019 Conference on Empirical Methods in Natural Language Processing and the 9th International Joint Conference on Natural Language Processing (EMNLP-IJCNLP)*, pages 4260–4270, Hong Kong, China, November. Association for Computational Linguistics.

Baldini Soares, L., FitzGerald, N., Ling, J., and Kwiatkowski, T. (2019). Matching the blanks: Distributional similarity for relation learning. In *Proceedings of the 57th Annual Meeting of the Association for Computational Linguistics*, pages 2895–2905, Florence, Italy, July. Association for Computational Linguistics.

Bryant, C., Felice, M., and Briscoe, T. (2017). Automatic annotation and evaluation of error types for grammatical error correction. In *Proceedings of the 55th Annual Meeting of the Association for Computational Linguistics (Volume 1: Long Papers)*, pages 793–805, Vancouver, Canada, July. Association for Computational Linguistics.

Bryant, C., Felice, M., Andersen, Ø. E., and Briscoe, T. (2019). The BEA-2019 shared task on grammatical error correction. In *Proceedings of the Fourteenth Workshop on Innovative Use of NLP for Building Educational Applications*, pages 52–75, Florence, Italy, August. Association for Computational Linguistics.

Christiansen, M. H. and Arnon, I. (2017). More than words: The role of multiword sequences in language learning and use. *Topics in Cognitive Science*, 9(3):542–551.

Clark, K., Luong, M.-T., Le, Q. V., and Manning, C. D. (2020). ELECTRA: Pre-training Text Encoders as Discriminators Rather Than Generators. In *International Conference on Learning Representations.*

Dahlmeier, D. and Ng, H. T. (2011). Correcting semantic collocation errors with L1-induced paraphrases. In *Proceedings of the 2011 Conference on Empirical Methods in Natural Language Processing*, pages 107–117, Edinburgh, Scotland, UK., July. Association for Computational Linguistics.

Dahlmeier, D., Ng, H. T., and Wu, S. M. (2013). Building a large annotated corpus of learner English: The NUS corpus of learner english. In *Proceedings of the Eighth Workshop on Innovative Use of NLP for Building Educational Applications*, pages 22–31, Atlanta, Georgia, June. Association for Computational Linguistics.

Devlin, J., Chang, M.-W., Lee, K., and Toutanova, K. (2019). BERT: Pre-training of deep bidirectional transformers for language understanding. In *Proceedings of the 2019 Conference of the North American Chapter of the Association for Computational Linguistics: Human Language Technologies, Volume 1 (Long and Short Papers)*, pages 4171–4186, Minneapolis, Minnesota, June. Association for Computational Linguistics.

Felice, M., Yuan, Z., Andersen, Ø. E., Yannakoudakis, H., and Kochmar, E. (2014). Grammatical error correction using hybrid systems and type filtering. In *Proceedings of the Eighteenth Conference on Computational Natural Language Learning: Shared Task*, pages 15–24, Baltimore, Maryland, June. Association for Computational Linguistics.

Grundkiewicz, R., Junczys-Dowmunt, M., and Heafield, K. (2019). Neural grammatical error correction systems with unsupervised pre-training on synthetic data. In *Proceedings of the Fourteenth Workshop on Innovative Use of NLP for Building Educational Applications*, pages 252–263, Florence, Italy, August. Association for Computational Linguistics.

Katsumata, S. and Komachi, M. (2020). Stronger baselines for grammatical error correction using a pretrained encoder-decoder model. In *Proceedings of the 1st Conference of the Asia-Pacific Chapter of the Association for Computational Linguistics and the 10th International Joint Conference on Natural Language Processing*, pages 827–832, Suzhou, China, December. Association for Computational Linguistics.

Kochmar, E. (2016). Error detection in content word combinations. Technical report, University of Cambridge, Computer Laboratory.

Liu, N. F., Hershcovich, D., Kranzlein, M., and Schneider, N. (2021). Lexical semantic recognition. In *Proceedings of the 17th Workshop on Multiword Expressions (MWE 2021)*, pages 49–56, Online, August. Association for Computational Linguistics.

Meunier, F. and Granger, S. (2008). *Phraseology in foreign language learning and teaching*. John Benjamins Publishing.

Mizumoto, T., Mita, M., and Matsumoto, Y. (2015). Grammatical error correction considering multiword expressions. In *Proceedings of the 2nd Workshop on Natural Language Processing Techniques for Educational Applications*, pages 82–86, Beijing, China, July. Association for Computational Linguistics.

Nesselhauf, N. (2003). The Use of Collocations by Advanced Learners of English and Some Implications for Teaching. *Applied Linguistics*, 24(2):223–242, 06.

Ng, H. T., Wu, S. M., Briscoe, T., Hadiwinoto, C., Susanto, R. H., and Bryant, C. (2014). The conll-2014 shared task on grammatical error correction. In *Proceedings of the Eighteenth Conference on Computational Natural Language Learning: Shared Task*, pages 1–14.

Nicholls, D. (2003). The cambridge learner corpus: Error coding and analysis for lexicography and ELT. In *Proceedings of the Corpus Linguistics 2003 conference*, pages 572–581.

Omelianchuk, K., Atrasevych, V., Chernodub, A., and Skurzhanskyi, O. (2020). GECToR – grammatical error correction: Tag, not rewrite. In *Proceedings of the Fifteenth Workshop on Innovative Use of NLP for Building Educational Applications*, pages 163–170, Seattle, WA, USA → Online, July. Association for Computational Linguistics.

Ott, M., Edunov, S., Baevski, A., Fan, A., Gross, S., Ng, N., Grangier, D., and Auli, M. (2019). fairseq: A fast, extensible toolkit for sequence modeling. In *Proceedings of the 2019 Conference of the North American Chapter of the Association for Computational Linguistics (Demonstrations)*, pages 48–53, Minneapolis, Minnesota, June. Association for Computational Linguistics.

Ramisch, C., Cordeiro, S. R., Savary, A., Vincze, V., Barbu Mititelu, V., Bhatia, A., Buljan, M., Candito, M., Gantar, P., Giouli, V., Güngör, T., Hawwari, A., Iñurrieta, U., Kovalevskaitė, J., Krek, S., Lichte, T., Liebeskind, C., Monti, J., Parra Escartín, C., QasemiZadeh, B., Ramisch, R., Schneider, N., Stoyanova, I., Vaidya, A., and Walsh, A. (2018). Edition 1.1 of the PARSEME shared task on automatic identification of verbal multiword expressions. In *Proceedings of the Joint Workshop on Linguistic Annotation, Multiword Expressions and Constructions (LAW-MWE-CxG-2018)*, pages 222–240, Santa Fe, New Mexico, USA, August. Association for Computational Linguistics.

Sag, I. A., Baldwin, T., Bond, F., Copestake, A., and Flickinger, D. (2002). Multiword expressions: A pain in the neck for nlp. *Lecture Notes in Computer Science*, 2276:1–15.

Savary, A., Ramisch, C., Cordeiro, S., Sangati, F., Vincze, V., QasemiZadeh, B., Candito, M., Cap, F., Giouli, V., Stoyanova, I., and Doucet, A. (2017). The PARSEME shared task on automatic identification of verbal multiword expressions. In *Proceedings of the 13th Workshop on Multiword Expressions (MWE 2017)*, pages 31–47, Valencia, Spain, April. Association for Computational Linguistics.

Schneider, N., Onuffer, S., Kazour, N., Danchik, E., Mordowanec, M. T., Conrad, H., and Smith, N. A. (2014). Comprehensive annotation of multiword expressions in a social web corpus. In *Proceedings of the Ninth International Conference on Language Resources and Evaluation (LREC'14)*, pages 455–461, Reykjavik, Iceland, May. European Language Resources Association (ELRA).

Shwartz, V. and Dagan, I. (2019). Still a pain in the neck: Evaluating text representations on lexical composition. *Transactions of the Association for Computational Linguistics*, 7:403–419, March.

Siyanova, A. and Schmitt, N. (2007). Native and nonnative use of multi-word vs. one-word verbs. 45(2):119–139.

Stahlberg, F. and Kumar, S. (2020). Seq2Edits: Sequence transduction using span-level edit operations. In *Proceedings of the 2020 Conference on Empirical*

Methods in Natural Language Processing (EMNLP), pages 5147–5159, Online, November. Association for Computational Linguistics.

Stahlberg, F. and Kumar, S. (2021). Synthetic data generation for grammatical error correction with tagged corruption models. In *Proceedings of the 16th Workshop on Innovative Use of NLP for Building Educational Applications*, pages 37–47, Online, April. Association for Computational Linguistics.

Taslimipoor, S., Bahaadini, S., and Kochmar, E. (2020). Mtlb-struct@ parseme 2020: Capturing unseen multiword expressions using multi-task learning and pre-trained masked language models. In *Proceedings of the Joint Workshop on Multiword Expressions and Electronic Lexicons*, pages 142–148.

Vaswani, A., Shazeer, N., Parmar, N., Uszkoreit, J., Jones, L., Gomez, A. N., Kaiser, L. u., and Polosukhin, I. (2017). Attention is all you need. In I. Guyon, et al., editors, *Advances in Neural Information Processing Systems 30*, pages 5998–6008. Curran Associates, Inc.

Yannakoudakis, H., Briscoe, T., and Medlock, B. (2011). A new dataset and method for automatically grading ESOL texts. In *Proceedings of the 49th Annual Meeting of the Association for Computational Linguistics: Human Language Technologies*, pages 180–189, Portland, Oregon, USA, June. Association for Computational Linguistics.

Yuan, Z. and Briscoe, T. (2016). Grammatical error correction using neural machine translation. In *Proceedings of the 2016 Conference of the North American Chapter of the Association for Computational Linguistics: Human Language Technologies*, pages 380–386, San Diego, California, June. Association for Computational Linguistics.

Yuan, Z. and Bryant, C. (2021). Document-level grammatical error correction. In *Proceedings of the 16th Workshop on Innovative Use of NLP for Building Educational Applications*, pages 75–84, Online, April. Association for Computational Linguistics.

Yuan, Z., Taslimipoor, S., Davis, C., and Bryant, C. (2021). Multi-class grammatical error detection for correction: A tale of two systems. In *Proceedings of the 2021 Conference on Empirical Methods in Natural Language Processing*, pages 8722–8736, Online and Punta Cana, Dominican Republic, November. Association for Computational Linguistics.

An Analysis of Attention in German Verbal Idiom Disambiguation

Rafael Ehren[1], Laura Kallmeyer[1], Timm Lichte[2]
[1]Heinrich Heine University, [2]University of Tübingen
{ehren,kallmeyer}@phil.hhu.de, timm.lichte@uni-tuebingen.de

Abstract

In this paper we examine a BiLSTM architecture for disambiguating verbal potentially idiomatic expressions (PIEs) as to whether they are used in a literal or an idiomatic reading with respect to explainability of its decisions. Concretely, we extend the BiLSTM with an additional attention mechanism and track the elements that get the highest attention. The goal is to better understand which parts of an input sentence are particularly discriminative for the classifier's decision, based on the assumption that these elements receive a higher attention than others. In particular, we investigate POS tags and dependency relations to PIE verbs for the tokens with the maximal attention. It turns out that the elements with maximal attention are oftentimes nouns that are the subjects of the PIE verb. For longer sentences however (i.e., sentences containing, among others, more modifiers), the highest attention word often stands in a modifying relation to the PIE components. This is particularly frequent for PIEs classified as literal. Our study shows that an attention mechanism can contribute to the explainability of classification decisions that depend on specific cues in the sentential context, as it is the case for PIE disambiguation.

Keywords: verbal idiomatic multi-word expressions, attention models, explainable AI

1. Introduction

Due to the success of the Transformer architecture (Vaswani et al., 2017), attention is one of the most popular concepts in Deep Learning right now. In NLP, BERT-based (Devlin et al., 2019) architectures are so dominant, that it seems to have given rise to the new field of 'BERTology' (Rogers et al., 2020; Søgaard, 2021), where researchers try to explore, what BERT learns about language. But it is not only the performance, which makes attention so popular, but also the fact that it gives us a certain degree of explainability, as attention weights potentially reveal what influences a model the most during a decision. However, it is currently the subject of lively debate how great this potential actually is (cf. Section 2).

In this work, we use attention in order to gain some insights into what contextualizing deep learning architectures are capable of learning when performing the task of disambiguating potentially idiomatic expressions (PIEs). PIE disambiguation is a subtask of multi word expression (MWE) identification. PIEs are potentially idiomatic, i.e., they can have a literal or an idiomatic reading like *rock the boat* ('cause trouble'):

(1) If you want that promotion, you should stop rocking the boat. IDIOMATIC

(2) They rocked the boat and fell into the freezing cold river. LITERAL

Example (1) shows a sentence containing an idiomatic usage of the PIE type, i.e. an instance of the verbal idiom (VID) type, while (2) contains an instance of its literal counterpart[1]. PIEs are challenging for NLP applications, because it is not enough to map a string to a certain VID type. To correctly disambiguate a PIE instance we have to take the context into account as well as its form, since VIDs are often subject to morhposyntactic restrictions (e.g. *kick the bucket* is not readily passivisable: **the bucket was kicked*).

In this paper, we use an established architecture for PIE disambiguation in German, based on Ehren et al. (2020), and investigate which elements of the sentential context of a PIE are crucial for deciding whether it is literal or not. More concretely, we investigate syntactic features and relations to the PIE components of those elements that are particularly indicative for literalness and idiomaticity. To this end, we propose an attention-based architecture capable of revealing which part of the context has the strongest influence on the model's classification decisions. More concretely, we stack an attention mechanism on top of the BiLSTM architecture proposed by Ehren et al. (2020) (cf. Section 4). Our architecture is applied to German verbal idioms, using the data from Ehren et al. (2020) (cf. Section 3). We opted for the former architecture instead of a BERT-based one for the sake of simplicity, comparability and greater transparency.

Our results, presented in Section 7, support the view that attention can be leveraged to make neural-network models more "explainable", as we can statistically corroborate our impression that the attention model often puts its focus on tokens that seem to be most crucial also for the human classifier. At the same time, the difficulties of the classifier with the peculiarities of the minority class becomes evident. To our knowledge, this is the first study of its kind, particularly in the area of idiom identification.

[1]The term PIE was coined by Haagsma et al. (2019) and it allows to encompass the literal and idiomatic usage at the same time.

Proceedings of the 18th Workshop on Multiword Expressions (MWE 2022) n@LREC2022, pages 16–25

2. Related Work

Attention-based models, especially BERT, have been used in the task of PIE classification (as well as many other NLP tasks) with considerable success, reaching first places in shared tasks (Taslimipoor et al., 2020; Pannach and Dönicke, 2021) or state-of-the-art results on well established data sets (Fakharian and Cook, 2021). Following the success in this and other areas of NLP, an interest in the more fine grained representational properties of these models has grown.

One way to shed more light on these models is to examine the resulting embeddings using cosine similarity. This is, for example, done in Garcia et al. (2021) for investigating the representation of compositionality in nominal compounds. Looking at pretrained embeddings from several both contextualizing and static models, they compare embeddings of compounds with the embeddings of their components, synonyms, and contexts by means of cosine similarity and find that pretrained contextualized models often do not distinguish between compositional and idiomatic compounds.

Another approach that has recently attracted a great deal of interest is to use the attention scores in attention-based models such as BERT, and to analyse the focus of attention when the model is classifying input in a certain way. An early example of such an analysis was already given by Bahdanau et al. (2016) who were the first to apply attention to a machine translation task, and who employed two-dimensional attentional heat maps to visualize the "non-monotonic" alignments between tokens of source and target language. Meanwhile, there are powerful interactive tools such as BertViz (Vig, 2019) to vizualize the attention scores of different heads and layers. At the same time, however, there is an ongoing discussion to what extent attention scores are actually useful to explain the decisions of contextualizing models (Jain and Wallace, 2019; Wiegreffe and Pinter, 2019; Bastings and Filippova, 2020; Søgaard, 2021). For example, it has been claimed by Jain and Wallace (2019) that "Attention is not Explanation". In a series of experiments on binary text classification and question answering, using BiLSTMs coupled with Bahdanau Attention, they found only a weak correlation between attention weights and other, gradient-based measures of feature importance. Furthermore, they were able to find attention distributions very different from the learned ones, which nevertheless yielded nearly identical prediction scores. From this, they conclude that attention does not provide "faithful" explanations of a model's decisions. Wiegreffe and Pinter (2019) reject the assumption that an attention distribution needs to be *exclusive* to serve as explanation. In addition, they show that even when adversarial attention distributions can be found, they do not perform as well on a simple diagnostic as their learned counterparts. They conclude that explainability depends on the definition and distinguish between plausible and faithful explanations, with the former not being invalidated by the work of Jain and Wallace (2019). We agree with Wiegreffe and Pinter (2019) that exclusivity is not a prerequisite in order for an attention distribution to serve as plausible explanation. Furthermore, like the two former works we will also use a one-layered BiLSTM as an encoder, coupled with Bahdanau attention, since Wiegreffe and Pinter (2019) established that the hidden states can still act as faithful representations of the input tokens, which is very important as we want to make claims about the influence of the different inputs. It is not clear, if this also holds for a very deep encoder like a BERT-based one. In this work, we will be contributing to the question of the usefulness of attention scores by applying a statistical and introspective analysis of the main attention to the classification of PIEs.

3. Data

We perform our experiments on the COLF-VID 1.0 (COrpus of Literal and Figurative meanings of Verbal IDioms) data set (Ehren et al., 2020), which consists of 6985 sentences drawn from newspaper texts with examples of 34 German VID types. Every instance in the corpus is annotated with one of the four labels IDIOMATIC, LITERAL, UNDECIDABLE or BOTH. Only 0.59% of the instances are given one of the latter two labels, so basically we are dealing with a binary classification task. The distribution of the remaining two labels is imbalanced as 77.55% of the instances are labeled as idiomatic, while only 21.86% are judged to be literal. An example from COLF-VID 1.0 is shown in (3):

(3) Bundesbahn will die **Notbremse ziehen**.
Federal railway wants the **emergency brake pull**.
'Federal railway wants to pull the emergency brake.'

It shows a usage case for the VID *die Notbremse ziehen* ('pull the emergency brake'⇒'put an immediate hold on something') which is labeled as IDIOMATIC.

The data is split following Ehren et al. (2020): 70% of the data are used for training, while 15% are used for the dev and the test set, respectively. Since the number of instances per PIE types in COLF-VID is highly skewed, we perform a balanced split, i.e. every split contains the same ratio of instances per PIE type.

There exist a variety of similar PIE corpora that would in principle be suitable for our proposed attention architecture, for example the MAGPIE corpus (Haagsma et al., 2020). The main reason we choose COLF-VID 1.0 is its size and relatively low idiomaticity rate, and the fact that it has been used in Ehren et al. (2020), which our attention architecture builds on. We describe our architecture in the next section.[2]

[2]Another corpus of verbal PIEs, which contains COLF-

4. System

Our system is based on the BiLSTM+MLP classifier by Ehren et al. (2020) enhanced with an attention mechanism similar to the one in Bahdanau et al. (2016). Figure 1 shows the overall architecture together with an example for the input (4):

(4) Das Konzert **fiel ins** **Wasser**.
The conert **fell into the Water**.
'The concert was cancelled.'

In a first step shown at he bottom of Figure 1, the pretrained embeddings of the input tokens are fed into a BiLSTM. The concatenated outputs of the forward and backward LSTMs give us the contextualized version of the input embeddings, which ideally should contain information about the relevant preceding and succeeding elements in the token sequence. In Ehren et al. (2020), the contextualized embeddings are then fed into a multilayer perceptron (MLP) to conduct PIE classification. However, in our model, we add an attention mechanism between the BiLSTM and the MLP.

When talking about attention mechanisms, the terms *keys*, *values* and *query* – which all denote vectors – play an important role. We can think of the query as the vector representation of the question what the model should pay attention to, while the keys are the potential candidates for receiving this attention. Since our aim is to explore which tokens in the input sequence the model focuses on the most during classification, it makes sense to use the their contextualized embeddings. Keys and values are the same in our case. The answer what should function as the query is less obvious as there exist numerous options. Because the PIE instance is the anchor point for every classification decision, we choose the average of the pretrained embeddings of the PIE's components. Now we can compute the attention scores based on the query and the keys. Given a query $q \in \mathbb{R}^q$ and a key $k_i \in \mathbb{R}^k$ we leverage the following scoring function taken from Bahdanau et al. (2016):

$$score(q, k_i) = w_v^\top \tanh(W_q q + W_k k_i) \quad (1)$$

Here, k_i is a key, and $W_q \in \mathbb{R}^{h \times q}$ and $W_k \in \mathbb{R}^{h \times k}$ represent linear transformations mapping k and q into the same space before they are added together[3]. Then, the resulting vector is put through the $tanh$ function and is multiplied with $w_v^\top$, so we receive a single score. After we computed the attention score for every key k_i we apply *softmax* in order to obtain a probability distribution $a_{0:n}$ of attention weights over all input tokens.

With $a_{0:n}$, we compute the weighted average for the contextualized embeddings $v_{0:n}$, which gives us the context vector c that represent the context of a PIE instance:

$$c = \sum_{i=0}^{n} a_i v_i \quad (2)$$

Note that all contextualized embeddings are included, even the ones representing the PIE components, although they do not really belong to the context, but form the target expression itself. One could exclude them by setting their scores to $-\infty$, which would result in their corresponding attention weights being set to zero when fed into the softmax function (as done with the padding tokens). But as addressed earlier, it might not only be the context providing clues on the correct reading, but also the PIE constituents themselves by exhibiting morphosyntactic flexibility atypical for the respective VID.

Finally, we concatenate c with q and feed it into a MLP to compute the scores for the four classes. What we expect in this example is that the contextualized representation for the token *Konzert* receives the highest attention and thus influences the context vector the most, because it is the only token in the sentence that provides information on the correct reading of the PIE instance.

5. Disambiguation experiments

Using the same hyperparameters as Ehren et al. (2020), we train our model for 30 epochs with a batch size of 32 and employ fastText embeddings (Bojanowski et al., 2016) with 300 dimensions as input. The hidden layers of the LSTMs are of size 100 which give us contextualized vectors of size 200 after concatenation. Consequently, the context vector has the same dimensionality. For the query vector, the centroid of input embeddings is used, and its concatenation with the context vector results in an input layer of size 500 for the MLP, which has one hidden layer with 100 neurons. For optimization we use cross-entropy loss and the Adam (Kingma and Ba, 2014) variant of the SGD algorithm. The implementation can be found on GitHub[4].

Table 1 shows the results on the validation and the test. We report the weighted macro average to account for the stark imbalance in classes. Since we use the same model and data set as Ehren et al. (2020), it makes sense to compare results to those achieved by the base model[5]. To our surprise, the attention model performs slightly worse than the base model with an F1 score of 87.66 against 87.99 on the validation set and 86.89 against 87.83 on the test set.

We suspect that the reason for the decrease in performance is that, by adding the attention mechanism, we introduce an additional 60.000 parameters in the form of the two weight matrices W_q and W_k (cf. Equation 1),

VID, was used in a recent shared task at KONVENS (Ehren et al., 2021).

[3]Note that k and q might already be in the same space if the contextualizations and embeddings have the same dimensionality.

[4]`https://github.com/rafehr/PIE-attention`

[5]More precisely, to the results with the model using fastText embeddings. Ehren et al. (2020) also employ word2vec and ELMo.

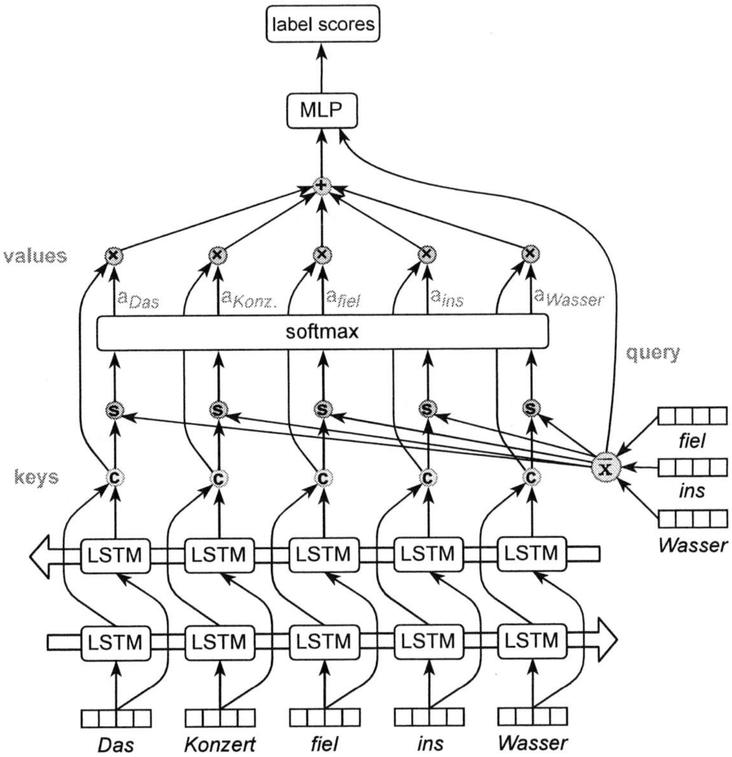

Figure 1: Architecture of the attention model.

Model	Split	Pre	Rec	F1
		Weighted macro average		
Majority baseline	Val	56.78	75.32	64.75
	Test	59.22	76.95	66.93
Ehren et al. +fastText	Val	87.86	88.14	87.99
	Test	87.45	88.29	87.83
This work	Val	87.44	87.88	87.66
	Test	86.83	86.89	86.85

Table 1: Evaluation results of the attention model on the COLF-VID 1.0 data set and comparison to baseline models

which make up the attention scoring function and were both of size 100×300. For training a model with that many parameters, our data set might be too small. This is supported by the fact that other parameter increasing measures during hyperparameter tuning like an enlargement of hidden layer size or hidden layer number all result in (far) worse performance. We refrain from more extensive hyper parameter tuning, since our focus is not on performance but on using the attention mechanism for purposes of explainability.

6. Extracting properties of tokens that receive a high attention

Our main goal is to uncover which parts of the input the model pays most attention to and what this might tell us about what it is learning in this kind of task. Therefore our architecture is designed in a way that attention scores are expected to have considerable influence on the classifier's decision: Everything the MLP sees at the end is a context vector which is composed of contextualized fastText embeddings weighted by their respective attention score.

We are particularly interested in the *maximum attention token* (MAT) of PIE contexts, i.e., the token that receives the highest attention, and we inspect the following properties of the MAT: (i) its attention weight, (ii) its POS tag, and (iii) the label of the first arc on the dependency path between the verb component (respectively the noun component) of the PIE and the MAT.

In order to gather this information, we parse the sentences using the NLP library spaCy[6], which gives a labeled dependency tree for every sentence. The POS tagging is conducted with the TreeTagger (Schmid, 1999), which uses the STTS tag set. We group the STTS POS tags into four general categories: noun (NN, NE), verb (VV*, VA*, VM*), adjective (ADJD, ADJA), and other. Note that we use the dependency

[6] `https://spacy.io/`

parses and POS tags only for the attention statistics; the PIE disambiguation classifier does not use syntactic information but acts solely on surface tokens.

Concerning the dependency labels, there are obviously cases where we do not have a direct arc between the respective PIE component and the MAT, but we always have a dependency path, provided parsing was successful. We assume that the label of the first arc on this path, starting from the PIE component, is a good choice for characterizing the relevant aspect of the dependency relationship between the two words, since it indicates the relation between the PIE component and the MAT including its dependency context. For illustration, consider Figure 2, which shows an idiomatic usage of *in der Luft hängen* ('hang in the air'⇒'be present').[7] Components of the PIE are bold, the MAT

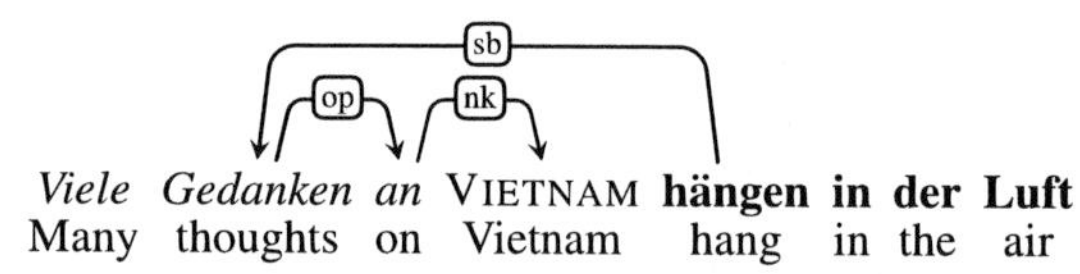

Figure 2: Subject (SB) relation between the verb and the noun phrase containing the MAT *Vietnam*

in capital letters and the rest of the sentence is in italic. There is no direct arc from the PIE verb to the MAT, but there is a path from the subject of the PIE verb to the MAT (VIETNAM), since the latter is part of a PP that modifies the subject. Thus, since the MAT is part of the subject NP, the system pays attention to some property of the subject. Such examples motivate our choice to register the first label (here SB) on the path from PIE component to MAT.

There is one more peculiarity with regard to how we register dependency relations. Very often – in 20.38% of the cases to be exact – the first arc in the (undirected) path from the PIE verb to the MAT is labeled OC for *object clause*, see for example Figure 3. Here the head

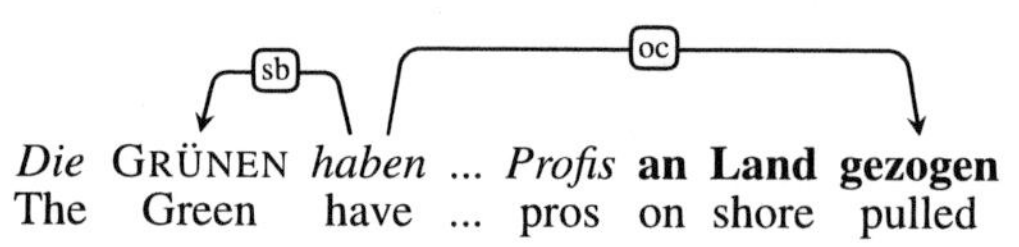

Figure 3: OC (object clause) relation between the PIE verb and the finite auxiliary verb

of the PIE verb is the auxiliary *haben* which in turn governs the subject. In such cases, we disregard the OC relations and register the label first label on the path from PIE component to MAT that is not OC (SB in this case).

[7]Another meaning of *in der Luft hängen* is 'to be uncertain'.

	FIG	LIT	overall
average MaxAttn	0.52	0.46	0.51
STD	0.2	0.18	0.2
MaxAttn on PIE verb (%)	1.23	2.92	1.6
MaxAttn on PIE noun (%)	6.51	13.75	8.11
MaxAttn on noun (%)	82.06	71.25	79.53
MaxAttn on adjective (%)	9.21	15.00	10.66
MaxAttn on verb (%)	3.56	7.5	4.43
MaxAttn on other (%)	5.16	6.25	5.38
MaxAttn on sb (%)	39.8	17.08	34.62
MaxAttn on mo (%)	25.8	41.67	29.43

Table 2: Selection of global attention statistics

7. Attention statistics

We collect the attention scores on the test set and compute statistics individually for instances where the system predicts the label FIGURATIVE (FIG) and for instances where the label LITERAL (LIT) is predicted.[8] Finally, we also perform an ablation experiment by replacing noun MATs with pronouns, in order to assess whether the system pays attention rather to grammatical functions or to semantic properties of lexical items.

7.1. Global attention statistics

Table 2 shows a selection of the global attention statistics. The first column contains the numbers for FIG, the second for LIT, and the last for FIG and LIT combined.

First, not surprisingly, for both classes, LIT and FIG, the model focuses more on content words than on function words, since the vast majority of MATs have POS tags of nouns and adjectives. However, there is a considerable difference between the two classes: LIT has a much larger preference for (adverbial/predicative) adjectives than FIG (15 % vs. 9.21 %) and a lower preference for nouns (71.25 % vs. 92.06 %).

Concerning dependency relations, in FIG sentences, subjects are more likely to contain a MAT compared to LIT. The reason might be that for the verb (without the PIE context), the literal reading is much more frequent, and in idiomatic readings, we might have subjects whose semantic properties are in contradiction to the semantic features that subjects of the literal reading usually have. Put differently, the choice of the subject filler is more marked in figurative readings than in literal ones.

This is in line with our experience when annotating PIEs, where selectional preference violation was identified as one of the key factors to inform the decision whether a PIE instance was idiomatic. The following example shows such a violation:

[8]The other two labels are barely predicted at all, so we do not include those in the statistics.

(5) But the **White House** is **playing with fire** by not complying here [...].[9]

Here the subject is an institution instead of the animate agent we would expect with the verb *play*, thus revealing the idiomatic reading.
Another salient observation is the magnitude of the attention given to the MAT by the system: the mean attention is 0.51 with a standard deviation of 0.2. This indicates that the attention is rather not distributed between multiple tokens. On the contrary, the model seems to pick one target that clearly stands out in terms of attention score, since, on average, MaxAttention differs considerably from the second highest attention score. The minority class LIT has a smaller MaxAttention than the majority class FIG, which seems to reflect the uncertainty of the classifier and the difficulties to identify clear indicators of LIT instances.
A further noticeable difference can be observed in the ratio of cases in which the MaxAttention is on PIE elements: again this could be taken to speak for the uncertainty of the classifier regarding LIT instances; or it might be the case that morphology contributes crucial indicators by deviating from the canonical form we expect in FIG instances. Note that fastText embeddings also take morphological features into account by virtue of the subword method. However, a manual inspection of the nominal PIE elements with MaxAttention failed to confirm that they are consistently morphologically non-canonical with respect to FIG usage. A more detailed investigation of why the model chooses a PIE element in some cases is left for future work.

7.2. Attention scores and sentence length

Since the features we investigated above can vary considerably depending on the size of the sentence, we also plotted them against sentence length, distinguishing again between FIG and LIT.
Figure 4 and Figure 5 show how the maximal, second highest and average attention (RestAttention, not counting maximal attention) scores develop with increasing sentence length. The solid line is the mean, while the area surrounding it represents the 95 % confidence interval. In both LIT and FIG, MaxAttention decreases with increasing sentence length, albeit Pearson's correlation coefficient is only weakly negative (overall -0.267 for sentences up to 30 tokens). Second highest attention and RestAttention remain rather stable, and in both LIT and FIG, the difference between MaxAttention and second highest attention seems pronounced, while in LIT the confidence interval almost overlaps in some areas, which is clearly not the case for FIG. Generally, second highest attention and RestAttention are relatively close. Again, the larger confidence area and the slightly (but not significantly) lower

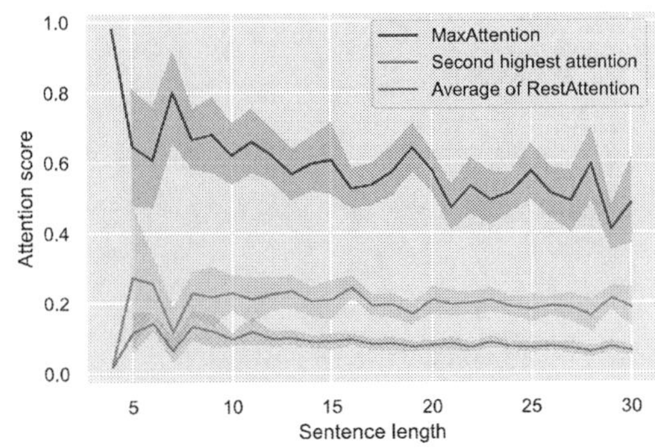

Figure 4: Attention and sentence length for FIG

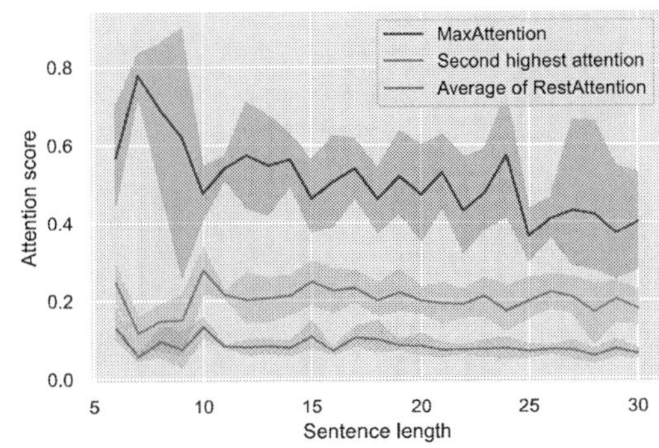

Figure 5: Attention and sentence length for LIT

MaxAttention mean for LIT seems to suggest that the classifier is struggling more to find good indicators for LIT than for FIG, regardless of the sentence size.

7.3. Syntactic features of MATs and sentence length

The development of syntactic properties of the MAT (POS tag and dependency label) is plotted against sentence length in Figure 7 for LIT and in Figure 6 for FIG. Again, we observe very different patterns in the two cases.
First, as already mentioned above in connection with Table 2, we see that MATs are more often contained in subjects (relation SB) of figurative PIEs, compared to literal PIEs; for longer sentences the difference is even more striking than the overall values from Table 2.
A second observation is that, for LIT, modifiers (relation MO) quickly become more important than subjects. Thus, for longer sentences in LIT, modifiers seem to be rather indicative for the label. And although adjectives play a larger role in LIT, especially for shorter sentences, the most frequent general POS tag for MATs is noun as can be seen from Figure 7. A manual inspection of the data suggests that nominal MATs with a modifying relation to the PIE verb are often the heads

[9] `https://www.politico.com/newsletters/playbook/2019/10/08/trump-changes-the-subject-486633`, accessed 04/11/2022

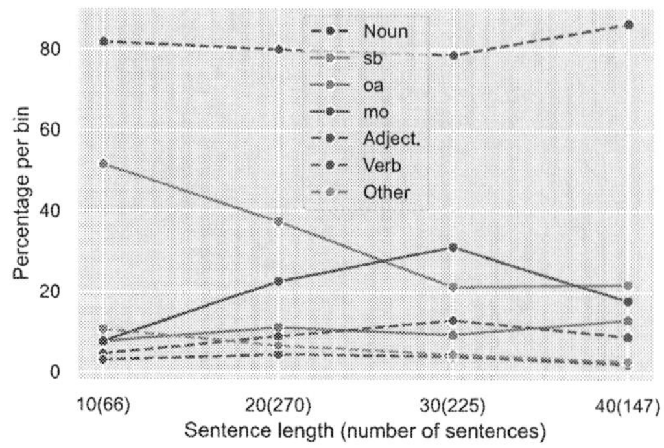

Figure 6: POS/dep. labels and sentence length for FIG

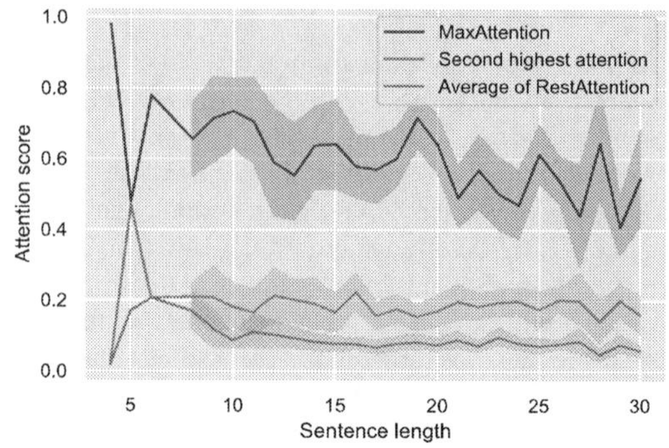

Figure 8: Attention and sentence length for FIG before pronominalization

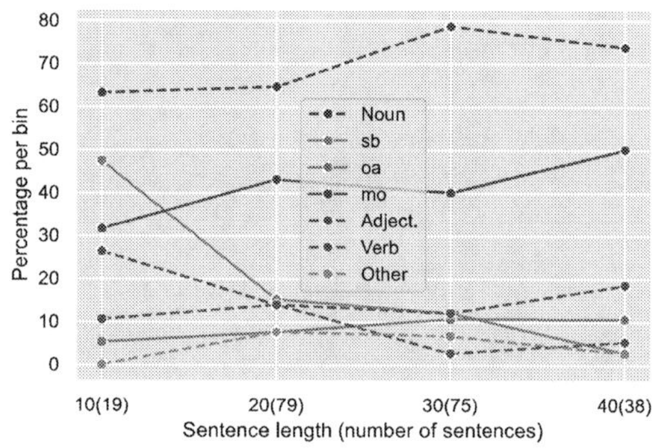

Figure 7: POS/dep. labels and sentence length for LIT

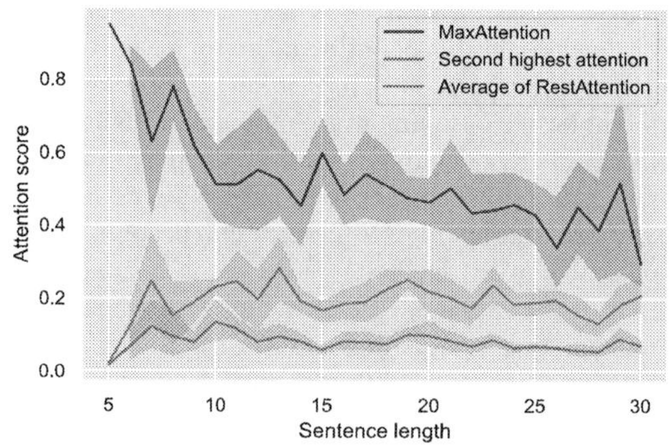

Figure 9: Attention and sentence length for FIG after pronominalization

of locative PPs.

7.4. Ablation test using pronouns

The goal of replacing MAT nouns with pronouns – while taking care that the remaining sentence is still grammatical – is to test whether it is the grammatical function which the model likes to pay attention to, or rather some token in the context of the PIE by virtue of being a content word. For this, we manipulate a subset of 474 PIE instances and compute the attention statistics as done above. Because of the increasing data sparseness, we concentrate on FIG with 339 instances and compare them with the attention scores of the unmanipulated source.

The overall attention scores for the original and manipulated FIG instances are shown in Figure 8 and Figure 9) respectively. We can observe that the MaxAttention decreases, compared to the original data, but the pattern basically remains intact.

Figure 10 and Figure 11 plot the MAT's syntactic features against sentence length for the original and pronominalized FIG instances respectively. A general observation in both cases is that, after pronominalization, nominal POS tags and SB dependencies receive less attention than before; i.e., the MaxAttention does not tend to remain on the role filled with the new pronoun (the POS tags for pronouns account for only 2.5% in total). Modifiers (MO), on the other hand, receive more frequently the highest attention, in particular for short sentences. This seems to indicate that the model pays attention to combinations of subject dependency label and content word and, in the absence of this, tends to turn to modifiers.

8. Qualitative analysis

To gain a better intuition for the attention preferences of the model, we now turn to a qualitative analysis of some of the data. We will look into examples from the perspective of an annotator in order to explore whether the systems attention falls on tokens a human would also consider important for their decision to annotate a PIE instance in a certain way. The example sentences below are equipped with a heatmap indicating the weight distribution - the higher the attention, the more intense the color.

Example (6) shows an instance of the PIE *auf dem Tisch liegen* ('lay on the table'⇒'be available/be known') with *Zahlen* ('numbers') as subject:

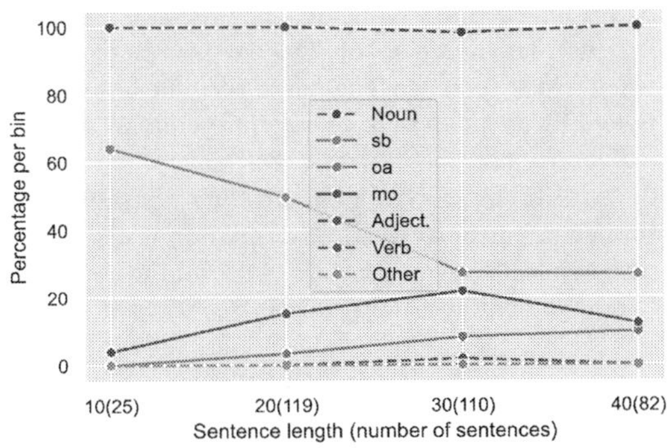

Figure 10: POS/dep. relation vs. sentence length for FIG before pronominalization

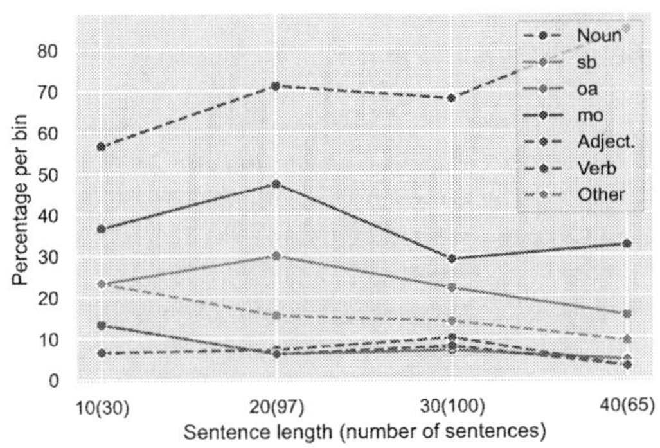

Figure 11: POS/dep. relation vs. sentence length for FIG after pronominalization

(6) *Diese Zahlen* **lagen** *am Morgen danach*
These numbers **lay** on the morning after
bereits **auf** *Erich Honeckers* **Tisch.**
already **on** Erich Honecker's **table**.
'These numbers were already reported to Erich Honecker the following morning.'

We can interpret the abstractness of the subject as an indicator for the idiomatic reading, since numbers (usually)[10] cannot be placed on a table. The model set the same focus and in four of four cases, in which *Zahlen* was the subject of *auf dem Tisch liegen*, it received the highest weight and the label *FIG* was predicted.

[10]We could of course construct a context with physical representations of numbers, but this is obviously not the case here. A bigger problem is that we can interpret it metonymically with *numbers* standing for a phyisical report lying on someone's table. But the annotators of COLF-VID did not follow this route and usually judged these type of instances to be figurative.

In (7) we have one of eight instances of the PIE *eine Brücke bauen* ('build a bridge'), where *Brücke* ('bridge') was modified with the adjective *goldene* ('golden') which gives rise to the idiomatic meaning 'give someone an easy way to retreat'.

(7) *So werden dem künftigen*
This way will be the future
Bankkunden goldene **Brücken** *bis zu*
bank customer golden **bridges** including
Zinssparen und Dispokredit **gebaut.**
interest saving and overdraft credit **built.**
'This way, golden bridges will be built for the future bank customer as far as interest savings and overdraft facilities.'

Since bridges are seldomly built from gold, the presence of the adjective is very informative to establish the correct reading. The model did pick up on that fact as *goldene* is in the top 3 of tokens with the highest attention in seven of eight cases, predicting FIG six times.
Another adjective attracting a lot of attention is *tief* ('deep'), when used adverbially with Luft holen (''take a breath'⇒'to take a break') as shown in (8).

(8) *Wer dort tief* **Luft holt,** *kann den Duft*
Who there deeply **air takes**, can the smell
des Newlands Stadium in Kapstadt
of the Newlands Stadium in Cape Town
einatmen [...] .
breathe in [...].
'If one takes a deep breath, one can breathe in the smell of the Newlands Stadium in Cape Town.'

In 9 of 12 of those cases the system gave the highest attention to *tief*, predicting the class LIT eight times. But in contrast to the examples above, it actually is not a sure sign for a literal reading, because it can just as well modify the idiomatic reading (*take a deep breath* ⇒ *take a long break*), as is represented in the test set, since 6 of the 12 instances were actually labeled as idiomatic. But since roughly 70% of instances in the training set occurring with *tief* were labeled as literal, the model reasonably predicted the label LIT.
More examples in which the model paid attention to tokens that a human annotator would also consider highly relevant for the disambiguation task can be found when examining the four literal instances of *im Blut haben* ('have in one's blood'⇒'have a predisposition for sth.') in the test set. In each of these cases, the object of the PIE, that represented a substance a person can actually have in their blood, was given the second or third highest attention (*Schadstoffe* ('pollutants'), *Cholesterinkonzentrationen* ('cholesterol concentration'), *Kokain* ('cocaine'), *Alkohol* ('alcohol')), while always predicting the correct reading.
(9) gives an example that was misclassified by the model since LIT was predicted although FIG would

have been correct.

(9) *Wer hat die größte, die schönste*
Who has the biggest, the most beautiful
Brücke gebaut?
bridge built?
'Who has established the best connection?'

However, the error is understandable; without context, a human annotator would also classify (9) as LIT, because of the attributes *größte* ('biggest') and *schönste* ('most beautiful') which modify *Brücke* ('bridge') (and which the attention model also focuses on).
Even though we could present many more of these types of examples, we of course do not claim, that our model's decisions correspond always to the way humans would decide between LIT and FIG concerning the role that the different input tokens play for this decision. There are a lot of instances to be found where the highest weights are associated with input tokens, that – from a human perspective – do not seem to be informative for the disambiguation. This is partly due to biases from training data, which distinguish of course our system from a human native speaker. But with our experiments, we were able to show two things: (1) The attention distribution is not arbitrary. This is not only supported by the statistics presented above, but also by a qualitative analysis of the data. (2) The relationship between the input and the output tends to be tangible and straightforward, i.e. a human can comprehend why the model focused on certain tokens. This is not self-evident, since with contextualizing models like a BiLSTM we cannot automatically assume that the hidden states are still faithful representations of the input tokens. It would be interesting to see whether a BERT-based encoder with its many layers would still allow for such a straightforward interpretation.

9. Conclusions

In the context of PIE disambiguation, we have provided strong evidence in support of the view that, for certain deep learning architectures, attention can be leveraged to uncover the influence of input tokens on the classifier's decision. Strikingly, regardless of classes and ablation measures, the attention model seems to pick exactly one pivotal target that clearly stands out compared to other tokens in the sentence in terms of attention scores. It would be interesting to explore, whether adversarial attention distributions in the same vein as for Jain and Wallace (2019) (cf. Section 2) can be found and, if so, which properties they would reveal compared to the one presented in this paper. Regardless of the outcome of such experiments, we would maintain that the results presented here are a valid, because plausible, explanation for the model's behaviour, since we do not agree that an attention distribution needs to be *exclusive* to serve as explanation.
Furthermore, the statistical behaviour of the studied attention model can be motivated with specific properties of the classes LIT and FIG, which differ considerably with respect to the syntactic categories that the model assigns MaxAttention to. This is even more apparent when taking sentence length into account, and also supported by an ablation test using pronominalization that we conducted. This work leaves many interesting options for future work, for example, the consideration of further linguistic features and ablation tests, crosslingual comparisons, and last but not least the comparison to other attention models such as BERT's self attention.

Acknowledgements

We thank the three anonymous reviewers for valuable comments.

10. Bibliographical References

Bahdanau, D., Cho, K., and Bengio, Y. (2016). Neural machine translation by jointly learning to align and translate. *arXiv:1409.0473v7.*

Bastings, J. and Filippova, K. (2020). The elephant in the interpretability room: Why use attention as explanation when we have saliency methods? In *Proceedings of the Third BlackboxNLP Workshop on Analyzing and Interpreting Neural Networks for NLP*, pages 149–155, Online. Association for Computational Linguistics.

Bojanowski, P., Grave, E., Joulin, A., and Mikolov, T. (2016). Enriching word vectors with subword information. *arXiv:1607.04606.*

Devlin, J., Chang, M.-W., Lee, K., and Toutanova, K. (2019). BERT: Pre-training of deep bidirectional Transformers for language understanding. In *Proceedings of the 2019 Conference of the North American Chapter of the Association for Computational Linguistics: Human Language Technologies, Volume 1 (Long and Short Papers)*, pages 4171–4186, Minneapolis, Minnesota. Association for Computational Linguistics.

Ehren, R., Lichte, T., Kallmeyer, L., and Waszczuk, J. (2020). Supervised Disambiguation of German Verbal Idioms with a BiLSTM Architecture. In *Proceedings of the Second Workshop on Figurative Language Processing*, pages 211–220.

Ehren, R., Lichte, T., Waszczuk, J., and Kallmeyer, L. (2021). Shared task on the disambiguation of German verbal idioms at KONVENS 2021. In *Proceedings of the Shared Task on the Disambiguation of German Verbal Idioms at KONVENS 2021.*

Fakharian, S. and Cook, P. (2021). Contextualized embeddings encode monolingual and cross-lingual knowledge of idiomaticity. In *Proceedings of the 17th Workshop on Multiword Expressions (MWE 2021)*, pages 23–32, Online. Association for Computational Linguistics.

Garcia, M., Kramer Vieira, T., Scarton, C., Idiart, M., and Villavicencio, A. (2021). Probing for idiomaticity in vector space models. In *Proceedings of the 16th Conference of the European Chapter of the*

Association for Computational Linguistics: Main Volume, pages 3551–3564, Online. Association for Computational Linguistics.

Haagsma, H., Nissim, M., and Bos, J. (2019). Casting a wide net: Robust extraction of potentially idiomatic expressions. *arXiv:1911.08829v1*.

Haagsma, H., Bos, J., and Nissim, M. (2020). MAGPIE: A large corpus of potentially idiomatic expressions. In *Proceedings of the 12th Language Resources and Evaluation Conference*, pages 279–287, Marseille, France. European Language Resources Association.

Jain, S. and Wallace, B. C. (2019). Attention is not Explanation. In *Proceedings of the 2019 Conference of the North American Chapter of the Association for Computational Linguistics: Human Language Technologies, Volume 1 (Long and Short Papers)*, pages 3543–3556, Minneapolis, Minnesota. Association for Computational Linguistics.

Kingma, D. P. and Ba, J. (2014). Adam: A method for stochastic optimization. *arXiv:1412.6980*.

Pannach, F. and Dönicke, T. (2021). Cracking a walnut with a sledgehammer: XLM-RoBERTa for German verbal idiom disambiguation tasks. In *Proceedings of the Shared Task on the Disambiguation of German Verbal Idioms at KONVENS 2021*.

Rogers, A., Kovaleva, O., and Rumshisky, A. (2020). A primer in BERTology: What we know about how BERT works. *Transactions of the Association for Computational Linguistics*, 8:842–866.

Schmid, H. (1999). Improvements in part-of-speech tagging with an application to German. In Susan Armstrong, et al., editors, *Natural Language Processing Using Very Large Corpora*, pages 13–25. Springer, Dordrecht.

Søgaard, A. (2021). *Explainable Natural Language Processing*. Number 51 in Synthesis Lectures on Human Language Technologies. Morgan & Claypool Publishers, San Rafael, CA.

Taslimipoor, S., Bahaadini, S., and Kochmar, E. (2020). MTLB-STRUCT @Parseme 2020: Capturing unseen multiword expressions using multi-task learning and pre-trained masked language models. In *Proceedings of the Joint Workshop on Multiword Expressions and Electronic Lexicons*, pages 142–148, online. Association for Computational Linguistics.

Vaswani, A., Shazeer, N., Parmar, N., Uszkoreit, J., Jones, L., Gomez, A. N., Kaiser, L., and Polosukhin, I. (2017). Attention is all you need. In *Advances in Neural Information Processing Systems 30*, pages 5998–6008. Curran Associates, Inc.

Vig, J. (2019). A multiscale visualization of attention in the transformer model. In *Proceedings of the 57th Annual Meeting of the Association for Computational Linguistics: System Demonstrations*, pages 37–42, Florence, Italy. Association for Computational Linguistics.

Wiegreffe, S. and Pinter, Y. (2019). Attention is not not explanation. In *Proceedings of the 2019 Conference on Empirical Methods in Natural Language Processing and the 9th International Joint Conference on Natural Language Processing (EMNLP-IJCNLP)*, pages 11–20, Hong Kong, China. Association for Computational Linguistics.

Support Verb Constructions across the Ocean Sea

Jorge Baptista[1,2], Nuno Mamede[2,3], Sónia Reis[1,2]
[1]University of Algarve, [2]INESC-ID, Lisbon, [3]Instituto Superior Técnico, University of Lisbon
[1]Campus de Gambelas, 8005-139 Faro, [2]R. Alves Redol 9, 1000-029 Lisboa,
[3]Av. Rovisco Pais 1, 1049-001 Lisboa
jbaptis@ualg.pt, nuno.mamede@tecnico.ulisboa.pt, smreis@ualg.pt

Abstract

This paper analyses the *support* (or *light*) *verb constructions* (SVC) in a publicly available, manually annotated corpus of multiword expressions (MWE) in Brazilian Portuguese. The paper highlights several issues in the linguistic definitions therein adopted for these types of MWE, and reports the results from applying STRING, a rule-based parsing system, originally developed for European Portuguese, to this corpus from Brazilian Portuguese. The goal is two-fold: to improve the linguistic definition of SVC in the annotation task, as well as to gauge the major difficulties found when transposing linguistic resources between these two varieties of the same language.

Keywords: support-verb constructions, light verbs, predicate noun

1. Introduction

Support-verb (or *light verb*) constructions (SVC) (Gross, 1981; Gross, 1996; Gross, 1998). are a fundamental component of the lexicon and grammar of any language (Constant et al., 2017), conveying a large variety of semantic predicates, in as much the same way as full (or distributional) verbs, predicative adjectives and other predicative elements do. In broad traits, a SVC can be defined as a multiword expression (MWE) that consists of an *elementary* (or *base*) sentence (Gross, 1981) where the predicative nucleus is formed by a *predicate noun* (Npred), which conveys the lexical meaning of the expression, and a *support-verb* (Vsup), an auxiliary element that serves basically to "conjugate" the predicative noun (Gross, 1989, p.38), mostly conveying grammatical values – person-number and tense, but also aspect and modality, and eventually, some stylistic values (Gross, 1998), that the morphology of the predicate noun cannot by itself express. (In this paper, we do not distinguish the terms *light* or *support* verbs, following, among others, (Fotopoulou et al., 2021), who consider that the way authors use them is not consistently correlated with differences between the properties of the constructions.)

Clear examples of SVC, in Portuguese, are: *O Pedro tem fome* lit:'Pedro has hunger' 'Pedro is hungry' (Santos, 2015), *O Pedro deu um abraço ao João* 'Pedro gave a hug to João' (Baptista, 1997b; Calcia, 2022), *O Pedro fez/está em greve* 'Pedro is on strike' (Chacoto, 2005; Dias de Barros, 2014), *É do interesse do Pedro que o João faça isso* 'It is in Pedro's interest that João do this' (Baptista, 2005b).

A key aspect of SVC is that the most relevant of their syntactic-semantic properties result from each verb-noun combination and, though some regularities can be found across large subsets of the SVC *lexicon-grammar* (in the sense of (Gross, 1996)), those properties cannot (and, in our view, should not) be generalized over the lexicon, neither of predicate nouns, nor of the verbs that can function as support-verbs. Definitory formal properties have been discovered, particularly since the (Giry-Schneider, 1978), that allow for a clear distinction between SVC and other, formally identical, constructions with full (or distributional) verbs (see (Ranchhod, 1990; Baptista, 2005b) for an overview). For example, since the predicative noun expresses a semantic predicate, it selects at least one other element for its subject argument (Gross, 1981). In the examples above, this is the relation holding between the predicate nouns and the subject of the SVC, which precludes the possibility of inserting a complement *de N* 'of N' (or a possessive pronoun) modifying the predicate noun that is not correferent to the subject: **O Pedro tem a fome do Rui/a tua fome* lit:'Pedro has Rui's/your hunger', **O Pedro deu um abraço do Rui ao João* lit:'Pedro gave João Rui's hug', **O Pedro está em/fez a greve do Rui* 'Pedro is on Rui's strike', **É do teu interesse do Pedro que o João faça isso* 'It is in Pedro's your interest that João do this'. (Some of these sentences can only be interpreted in the comparative sense of 'the same Npred that', or 'in place/instead of' hence, they are not elementary or base sentences.)

This paper analyses *support-verb constructions* represented in a publicly available, manually annotated corpus of verbal idioms in Brazilian Portuguese (PT-BR). The paper highlights several issues in the linguistic definitions therein adopted for the annotation of this type of MWE. It then reports the results from applying STRING (Mamede et al., 2012; Baptista and Mamede, 2020) [1] to this corpus from Brazilian Portuguese. STRING is a statistical and rule-based nat-

[1]`https://string.hlt.inesc-id.pt/`

Proceedings of the 18th Workshop on Multiword Expressions (MWE 2022) n@LREC2022, pages 26–36
Marseille, 25 June 2022.

ural language processing pipeline, specifically developed for European Portuguese (PT-PT).
The goal of the paper therefore is two-fold: (i) to discuss several issues in the linguistic definition of SVC adopted in the annotation of the corpus, helping to contribute to the clarification of several key concepts; and (ii) to gauge the major difficulties found when applying linguistic resources originally built for PT-PT to a text written in PT-BR, shedding some light on the degree of linguistic similarity between the SVC of these two varieties of the same language.
The paper is structured as follows: Next, Section 2 presents related work on SVC, with a special focus on Portuguese, both European (PT-PT) and Brazilian (PT-BR); Section 3 describes the PARSEME corpus, used in this paper; Section 4, briefly presents the processing of the corpus in STRING and the experiments performed; Section 5 presents and discusses the results obtained; and, finally, Section 6 draws the main conclusions and refers to future work.

2. Related work

Though the idea of nouns as predicative elements in language is quite old in grammar and in language studies, a modern thread can be sourced on (Harris, 1955) and subsequent work (Harris, 1964; Harris, 1976; Harris, 1982; Harris, 1991), while the terms *support-verb* (*Vsup*) and *predicative noun* (*Npred*), and the corresponding concepts here adopted, have been coined by (Gross, 1981), and later extended in (Gross, 1998). Extensive/systematic descriptions of SVC have been produced, within the Lexicon-Grammar framework (Gross, 1996), both for romance and non-romance languages, mostly in the early 80s and in the 90s (and for Brazilian Portuguese mostly since the early 2010s); see (Fotopoulou et al., 2021) for a brief, tough non-exhaustive overview.
For European Portuguese (PT-PT), the language variety that is the focus of this paper, landmarks in this descriptive campaign started in the late 80s, with (Vaza, 1988; Ranchhod, 1990; Baptista, 1997b), and continue until the mid-2000s, (Baptista, 2005b; Chacoto, 2005). Specific constructions, such as Converse (i.e. passive-like) SVC, as originally defined by (Gross, 1989) received attention in multiple works (Vaza, 1988; Baptista, 1997a; Baptista, 1997b); the description of specific transformations, such as Fusion (Gross, 1981) and particular classes of predicate nouns, like instrument nouns (Baptista, 2004) and communication predicates (Reis et al., 2021); or in the context of the more general phenomenon of Symmetry (Baptista, 2005a), i.e. intrinsically reciprocal constructions, as originally defined by (Borillo, 1971).
For Brazilian Portuguese (PT-BR), the language variety of the corpus used in this paper, mention should be made to the SVC with support-verb *fazer* 'do/make' (Dias de Barros, 2014), *dar* 'give' (Rassi, 2015) and *ter* 'have' (Santos, 2015); and for specific aspects of SVC, like the Converse constructions involving the support-verb *dar* 'give' (Calcia, 2016; Calcia and Vale, 2019); the aspectual variants of support-verbs, (Picoli et al., 2021), and non-agentive constructions with *fazer* 'do/make' (Dias de Barros et al., 2013).
Few works have been dedicated to the systematic comparison of the lexicon and grammar of the PT-PT and PT-BR variants, exception made to (Rassi et al., 2016), who compared a subset of converse SVC. An annotated corpus of SVC with support-verb *dar* 'give' has also been produced (Rassi et al., 2015b).
Extensive literature exists on SVC across multiple languages, on their place within the description of multiword expressions (Constant et al., 2017), their relation with fixed, verbal idioms and the challenges they pose to Natural Language Processing (NLP) (Sag et al., 2002). A comprehensive set of references and the current trends in MWE processing can be found in (Ramisch et al., 2020, p.222–223) and in (Cook et al., 2021), among others. Processing SVC Portuguese has been the topic of, among others, (Baptista et al., 2015; Rassi et al., 2014; Rassi et al., 2015a), with recent developments in (Mota et al., 2018; Baptista and Mamede, 2020; Barreiro et al., 2022).
In recent years, the study of multiword expressions (MWE) received a significant boost by the collaborative efforts of a multilingual community gathered around the PARSEME project (Savary et al., 2015)[2], developed under the European Union COST framework. The PARSEME project is aimed at "characterizing MWEs in lexicons, grammars and corpora and enabling systems to process them" (Ramisch et al., 2020, p.107). Under this project, several initiatives were taken, including a Shared Task on automatic identification of MWE. For the Shared Task 1.2 (edition) (Ramisch et al., 2020), a (Brazilian) Portuguese corpus, has been manually annotated for verbal MWE. A major contribution of the project, within this Shared Task, was the construction of "unified guidelines for all the participating languages, in order to avoid heterogeneous, hence incomparable, datasets"[3]. These guidelines take the form of *decision trees*, with specific branches for each one of the two main verbal MWE categories addressed by the project: support-verb constructions and verbal idioms. SVC (or light verb constructions *LVC*, in the authors' terminology), are considered "universal, that is, valid for all languages participating in the task" (Ramisch et al., 2020, p. 224), though there are reasons to believe that they may pertain to many types of languages. Within PARSEME, SVC are organized in 2 subsets (Portuguese examples from the PARSEME training corpus; the succinct defini-

[2]`https://typo.uni-konstanz.de/parseme/index.php` [last access: June 13, 2022]. All URL in this paper were last checked on this date.

[3]The full guidelines for Shared Task Edition 1.1 can be found at: `https://parsemefr.lis-lab.fr/parseme-st-guidelines/1.1/`

tions below were also taken from (Ramisch et al., 2020, p. 224)): (a) **LVC.full**, "in which the verb is semantically totally bleached", e.g. *fazer uma palestra* 'make a speech'; (b) **LVC.cause**, "in which the verb adds a causative meaning to the noun", e.g. *dar origem a* (lit. 'give origin to', 'gives rise to'). The project's participant teams produced *corpora* manually annotated for MWE, and for several languages (+18), including (Brazilian) Portuguese (PT-BR). These *corpora* have been updated and extended throughout several editions of the Shared Task, and in this paper Portuguese data from the latest Shared Task 1.2. edition (2020) will be used.

3. SVC in the PARSEME corpus

The PARSEME Portuguese corpus[4] is divided into training (80%), development (10%) and testing (10%) partitions. In this paper, only the testing partition was considered (though the entire corpus has been processed by STRING).

According to the information distributed with the corpus, it consists of 27,904 sentences, 638,002 tokens, where 3,145 SVC (or *light verb* constructions, noted 'LVC.full', in the authors' terminology), and 94 LVC.cause (=causative constructions) have been manually annotated. The testing partition consists of 2,770 sentences, +62.6 thousand tokens, and, according to the documentation, it includes 337 LVC.full and 7 LVC.cause.

According (Ramisch et al., 2020, p.226), "the Portuguese corpus contains sentences from the informal Brazilian newspaper *Diário Gaúcho* and from the training set of the [Universal Dependencies] treebank" (UD_Portuguese-GSD v2.1). We could not find information on the method used to sample the sentences included in the corpus.

A sample of 1,000 sentences (4.54% of the corpus) is reported (idem, p.227) to have been double-annotated, and the following agreement metrics were reported: F_{span} (0.713) is the F-measure between annotators, K_{span} (0.684) is the agreement on the annotation span and K_{cat} (0.837) is the agreement on the VMWE category. These results seem to indicate the sufficiency of the content of the guidelines and the training of the annotators, yielding reasonable consistency of the annotation process, given the complexity of the task.

Lexical variety

Digging deeper into the corpus content, one can note that the distribution of some SVC constructions seems somewhat skewed. A large number come from text on sport (football), and not all support-verb/predicate noun combinations seem natural: 134 instances of *gol* 'goal' (*fazer* 'do' and *marcar* 'score', ?*dar* 'give'); 30 *falta* (*fazer*, *marcar*, *sofrer* 'suffer', ?*cometer* 'comit'); 13 *passe* (*fazer* 'make, do', *receber* 'receive'); 11 *pênalti* 'penalty' (*marcar*, *sofrer*); etc. Because of the lack of information on the sampling strategy, no further comment can be made on the fact that 6.8% of the SVC instances concern vocabulary from this specific domain.

As shown in the examples above, the lexical variety of SVC in the corpus looks sometimes skewed by the occurrence of several instances of the same predicate nouns with the same support-verb, without any obvious relevant change, neither in the meaning nor in the syntactic structure of the SVC, which would add value to their inclusion in the corpus. For example, a certain number of nouns designate measurable quantities, usually accompanied by a quantification phrase, e.g. *área* 'area' (x8), *população* 'population' (x2), where one can find some that are technical terms drawn from Astronomy: *ascenção* (*reta*) 'right ascension', *declinação* 'declination' (x2), *excentricidade* 'excentricity' (x6), *inclinação* 'inclination', e.g.

> *Possui uma excentricidade de 0.03574140 e uma inclinação de 11.03095º.* 'It has an eccentricity of 0.03574140 and a tilt of 11.03095º.'.

The purpose of including these astronomical terms in the corpus is not entirely clear. Still, it is interesting that other senses of these predicate nouns, such as *excentricidade* 'excentricity' *inclinação* 'inclination', as illustrated below, are absent from the data, e.g. *O Pedro é de uma certa excentricidade* 'Pedro is of a certain eccentricity' ('Pedro is eccentric') (Baptista, 2005b). On the other hand, many of these nouns designating measurable quantities can undergo a restructuring transformation (or alternation) (Baptista and Ranchhod, 1998), leaving them superficially as a complement of the measuring unit:

> *O mundo tem 510 bilhões de km2 de área total* 'The world has 510 billion km2 of total area' [5]
> = *O mundo tem uma área total de 510 bilhões de km2* 'The world has a total area of 510 billion km2'

however, none of these restructured forms seems to have been captured by the corpus.

Naturally, the fact that the corpus is produced out of real texts and it was built to be used in the training of machine-learning based systems perfectly justifies this aspect of the lexical distribution of SVC, even if the documentation is scarce on the sampling method used (if any) to select the sentences therein. In our more lexicographic-oriented and rule-based approach to the automatic identification of SVC in texts, lexical and syntactical diversity is a good feature to put the STRING system to the test.

[4] https://gitlab.com/parseme/parseme_corpus_pt

[5] https://www.ufjf.br/

Linking operator verb (*Vop*)

In some cases, and for theoretical reasons, we do not concur with the description of SVC given to some structures found in the corpus. For example, the concept of linking operator-verb (*Vopl*) construction, proposed by (Gross, 1981, p.30) seems to be ignored by the corpus annotators and it is dealt with as an ordinary SVC construction; for example (*Vopl* construction emphasized):

> *A Cátedra Milton Santos* tem como objetivo *a difusão de informações* 'The Milton Santos Chair *has as its aim* (=aims) to disseminate information(id=pt_br-ud-train-s7942);
> *o especial da TV Globo* terá como tema *a vida de Dolores Duran* 'the TV Globo special *will have as theme* the life of Dolores Duran' (id=diario_gaucho_16311).

These nouns (*objetivo* 'objective' and *tema* 'theme') have a clear support-verb (*Vsup*) construction, with a standard syntactic configuration, where the predicative noun is usually the direct complement of the support-verb e.g. (*Vsup* construction emphasized):

> *(A constituição de) a cátedra* tem *um* objetivo *preciso* '(The constitution of) the chair has a precise purpose;
> *O programa* tem *um* tema *interessante* 'The program has an interesting theme'

Furthermore, the predicative nature of the preposition phrase introduced by *como* 'as' (or, alternatively, by *por* lit.: 'by', 'idem') hints at the existence of the corresponding sentences with copula verbs (Paiva Raposo, 2013), e.g.

> *A difusão de informações* era *o objetivo da cátedra* 'Dissemination of information was the goal of the chair';
> *A vida de Dolores Duran* era *o tema do programa* 'Dolors Duran's life was the theme of the program';

A similar situation occurs with operator verb *ter* on adjectival/participial constructions or on SVC with *estar Prep*:

> *Já Federer* ... teve *uma* campanha mais perturbada ... 'Federer [=person] ... had a more troubled/disrupted campaign'
> *Pelo segundo ano consecutivo, o Cruzeiro* teve *uma* campanha abaixo de_as expectativas. 'For the second year in a row, Cruzeiro [football club] has fallen short of expectations' (lit.: had a campaign below expectations')

These can hardly be thought of as elementary SVC sentences, for they yield to a transformational analysis that recovers the underlying elementary sentence under *ter* 'have': *A campanha foi perturbada / esteve abaixo das expectivas* 'The campaign was disrupted / was below expectations' On the other hand, a clear SVC construction of this predicate noun exists and it is patent in the corpus:

> *Os jovens* ... *estão* fazendo a campanha *com a cara e a linguagem deles* 'Young people are making the campaign with their face and their language'

Finally, and again with noun *campanha* 'campaign', there are some cases where the notion of support-verb seems too much stretched:

> ... *o partido foi vítima de uma intensa* campanha promovida *pela oposição de direita e seus aliados* ... 'the party was the victim of an intense campaign promoted by the right-wing opposition and its allies'

In this case, the verb *promover* 'promote' has been analysed as a support-verb, probably because the (semantic) **agent** of *campanha* happens to coincide with the (syntactic) subject of the verb (*a oposição de direita e seus aliados* 'the right-wing opposition and its allies'). However, and in our perspective, the verb can not be considered a support-verb for its subject may not be correferent to the semantic agentive argument of the noun in its direct object position: *O Pedro promoveu a campanha do Rui* 'Pedro promoted Rui's campaign' (Notice, by the way, how the corpus ignored the expression *ser vítima de* 'be the victim of'. On SVC with copula verbs, see below).

Causative operator verb (*Vopc*)

Another case of operator verb, also originally described by (Gross, 1981), is the causative operator verb (Vopc), which has, nevertheless, been integrated into the PARSEME Guidelines [6] and represented by the category LVC.CAUSE. In the STRING system, this structures are lexically associated with the predicate noun construction and, when adequately captured, they are represented by a VOPCAUSE dependency (Baptista and Mamede, 2020). So, a simple matter of different notation might seem to be the case, here. Still, the annotation of this category seems inconsistent in the corpus. For example, the following instances were either marked with `LVC.cause`, or missed, or marked as `LVC.full` (=SVC):

> *A ausência do sexo também* traz *uma forte* angústia (marked with `LVC.cause`) 'The absence of sex also brings a strong anguish'
> *Nós* ... *estamos ansiosos para montar um*

[6] `https://parsemefr.lis-lab.fr/parseme-st-guidelines/1.2/?page=050_Cross-lingual_tests/020_Light-verb_constructions__LB_LVC_RB_`

time competitivo, que seja divertido e traga orgulho *para os fãs* (the *Vopc* was missed) 'We are looking forward to building a competitive team that is fun and brings pride to the fans'
Caro V., a tua postura é sempre admirável, o que faz com que *tua lealdade a esta coluna só me* dê orgulho (marked as `LVC.full`) 'Dear V., your posture is always admirable, which makes me proud of your loyalty to this column'

Some of these *Vopc*, such as *fazer com que* 'make' 'lit.: make with that'), in the last example (missed), had already been mentioned in Portuguese literature (Baptista, 1999).
To conclude this topic, some instances of predicate noun constructions corresponding to the concept of causative operator-verb (*Vopc*) have been found to have been annotated as SVC. This distinction is not always made in the literature. For example, (de Athayde, 2000) largely ignores it and assimilates Vopc constructions to SVC with support-verb *fazer* 'do/make', while (Chacoto, 2005) keeps a clear-cut distinction (as we do). Besides, (Gross, 1998), who originally proposed the concept in (Gross, 1981), revised his initial position and proposed to treat Vopc as a special type of support-verb. In our view of the issue, we concur with the PARSEME classification criteria (see 6). The semantic added-value of **cause** introduced by Vopc is distinct from the function of Vsup (and the merely grammatical or stylistic values Vsup convey). Thus, this specific **cause** semantic value must somehow be captured for an adequate representation of the meaning relations among multiple elements within the sentence.
Secondly, the theoretical construct of linking operator-verb (*Vopl*), also introduced by (Gross, 1981), has been by and large been ignored in the corpus annotation. There is no clear indication in the literature on how to deal with this formal variation, though we posit that it may not be adequate to mix it together with standard SVC. Unlike Vopc, no new lexical element of meaning is introduced in the sentence, since the Vopl recuperates one of the arguments of the underlying predicate noun (and often it also structures this noun syntactical construction). It has been proposed (Ranchhod, 1990, p.183 ff.) that the use of Vopl be seen as a type of saliency-inducing device (in a similar as extraposition or clefting). In the Harrissian framework (Harris, 1991) that we adopted, this is a specific type of operation, in much the same way, but with a different meaning-inducing effect, as Vopc. Hence, in the same way as LVC.cause (within PARSEME) or the VOPCAUSE dependency (within STRING), a distinct notation may be required.

SVC with *ser* and *estar*
Also, it is interesting to notice that concerning SVC involving otherwise copula verbs *ser* and *estar* 'be', while they have been, in general, ignored (and eventually excluded from SVC) as per PARSEME Guidelines), they are still showcased in the corpus, where some (very few) of this SVC expressions can be found, both with support-verb *ser* 'be':

> <Title of a song> *é sucesso!* 'is [a] hit (lit.: success)' ... *um comercial da Tim era sucesso na tevê* 'a Tim commercial was a hit on TV'

and with support-verb *estar Prep* 'be Prep' (Ranchhod, 1990):

> *Você está com saudade do frio?* '' *Ela está com febre, dores no corpo e coriza* 'She has a fever, body aches and a runny nose' (id=diario_gaucho_16030); *Quando não está de licença* (id=pt_br-ud-train-s7822)

Standard/Converse SVC
Finally, even though appropriately signalling them as SVC, PARSEME does not distinguish between *standard* (or active-oriented) SVC, where the subject is the **agent** of the semantic predicate expressed by the predicative noun, from *converse* (or passive-oriented) SVC, where the subject is the **patient** (or the **object**) of that same semantic predicate; e.g. *O Pedro deu um abraço ao João = O João recebeu/levou um abraço do Pedro* 'Peter gave John a hug=John got a hug from Peter' This Conversion transformation (Gross, 1981; Gross, 1989) is very productive in many languages and has already received extensive linguistic descriptions in Portuguese, both in the European (Baptista, 1997a; Baptista, 1997b; Baptista, 2005b), and, moore recently, in the Brazilian variety (Calcia, 2016; Calcia and Vale, 2019; Calcia, 2022). These different types of SVC need to be both described and appropriately annotated in corpora, like STRING does, as they have an impact, among other aspects, on the determination of the semantic roles of the predicate noun's argument slots. We have counted many converse-like SVC structures (34) in the testing partition, which signals that this phenomenon is not rare in the corpus. Because of this lack of distinction, in the evaluation of the STRING's output, the standard/converse opposition was not taken into consideration.

4. Processing SVC in the PARSEME corpus

The test partition of the PARSEME corpus was processed using the STRING natural language processing pipeline (Mamede et al., 2012; Baptista and Mamede, 2020). This system performs all basic text processing tasks, including text segmentation into sentences, tokenization, dictionary-based part-of-speech (PoS) tagging, rule-based and statistical PoS disambiguation, and parsing. The parsing module is a rule-based parser, XIP (Aït-Mokhtar et al., 2002), that, among

other tasks, extracts dependency relations (such as SUBJ[ect], CDIR (direct object), etc.), between the basic constituents (chunks) heads.
Since most SVCs are formally identical to ordinary verbal constructions (the SVC status resulting from the specific verb-noun combination), the overall strategy adopted in STRING consists in, firstly, capturing the syntactic dependencies holding between the predicate noun and the verb, and then extracting a specific dependency SUPPORT_VSUP linking them. The system can be configured to output only the desired dependencies. Fig. 1 shows the result from parsing the sentence *A Ana marcou dois gols* 'Ana has scored two goals', where only some dependencies have been shown.

```
SUPPORT_VSUP-STANDARD(gols,marcou)
SUBJ_PRE(marcou,Ana)
CDIR_POST(marcou,gols)
0>TOP{NP{A Ana} VF{marcou} NP{dois gols}}
```

Figure 1: A sentence parsed by STRING

The -STANDARD suffix in the SUPPORT_VSUP dependency indicates that this is a *standard* (or active-oriented) SVC (in the case of a *converse* construction, a -CONVERSE suffix would be used instead). Fig. 2 shows the dependency rule used to extract the SUPPORT_VSUP dependency shown in the previous Figure.

```
if (( VDOMAIN(#1,#2[lemma:"fazer"]) ||
 VDOMAIN(#1,#2[lemma:"marcar"]) ) &
 (MOD[post,relat](#3[lemma:"golo"],#2) ||
 CDIR(#2[transf-passiva:~],#3[lemma:"golo"]) ||
 SUBJ(#2[transf-passiva],#3[lemma:"golo"]) ||
 (ANTECEDENT[relat](#3[lemma:"golo"],#4[pronrel]) &
 SUBJ(#2[transf-passiva],#4) ) ) &
 ~SUPPORT[vsup-standard](#3,#2) )
 SUPPORT[vsup-standard=+](#3,#2)
```

Figure 2: Parsing rule for predicate noun *golo* 'goal'

Briefly, this rule matches the lemma of the verb *marcar* 'score' and checks whether there is a direct complement whose lemma is *golo* 'goal'. The rule also takes into consideration the situation where the predicate noun is the pivot of a relative clause, or the subject of a passive sentence. All these rules are automatically generated (Baptista and Mamede, 2020) from the database that encodes the linguistic (structural, syntactic, semantic, and transformational) properties of the predicative nouns' lexicon (which is therefore called a *lexicon-grammar*). In its current state, the lexicon-grammar of PT-PT SVC contains 5,800 entries (ambiguous predicate nouns, with multiple word senses, constitute several, separate entries), an ongoing description is being done for another 3,320 nouns. One of the purposes of this paper is to gauge the current lexical coverage of this linguistic resource and the system using it, on a previously unseen corpus of data, and, furthermore, on a corpus from a different variety of the language.

In order to allow for the semi-automatic comparison between the PARSEME SVC annotations and the STRING's output, a program was built in-house that detects the PARSEME SVC.full tag, and retrieves the two related elements, returning for that sentence the SUPPORT_VSUP dependency in the STRING's format. This is, in no way, a trivial task, since per PARSEME conventions, the SVC.full tag can be marked either on the line with the support-verb, or on the line with the predicative noun (for example, in the case of passive sentences). Also, as the text segmentation criteria is not exactly the same, some sentences in the PARSEME corpus were split by the STRING, and had to be manually adjusted to avoid mismatches.
The evaluation of the STRING's performance, thus, consists in the comparison between two parallel files aligned at the sentence level (as it is illustratyed in Fig.3-4). The sentence parsing output is the same in both figures, since it was performed by STRING. In sentence 1, we find the SVC *fazer uma aparição* 'make an appearance', while in sentence 2 *tomar uma providência* 'make a provision', which is in the passive.

```
SUPPORT_VSUP-STANDARD(aparição,fez)
1>TOP{PP{PP{Em 2} PP{de outubro} PP{de 2009}} , PP{
em o 10º aniversário} PP{de a SmackDown} , NP{The
Rock} VF{fez} NP{uma aparição} AP{especial} PP{em
um vídeo} AP{pré-gravado} .}

SUPPORT_VSUP-STANDARD(providência,tomada)
2>TOP{NP{Se} NP{nenhuma providência} VCOP{for} VCPART
{tomada} , NP{a população} VTEMP{vai} VASP{voltar a}
VINF{usar} NP{lamparinas} ADVP{ADV{a a noite}} e NP
{geladeira} PP{a querosene} .}
```

Figure 3: PARSEME corpus (Reference)

```
TP:SUPPORT_VSUP-STANDARD(aparição,fez)
1>TOP{PP{PP{Em 2} PP{de outubro} PP{de 2009}} , PP{
em o 10º aniversário} PP{de a SmackDown} , NP{The
Rock} VF{fez} NP{uma aparição} AP{especial} PP{em
um vídeo} AP{pré-gravado} .}

FN:SUPPORT_VSUP-STANDARD(providência,tomada)
2>TOP{NP{Se} NP{nenhuma providência} VCOP{for} VCPART
{tomada} , NP{a população} VTEMP{vai} VASP{voltar a}
VINF{usar} NP{lamparinas} ADVP{ADV{a a noite}} e NP
{geladeira} PP{a querosene} .}
```

Figure 4: STRING output

In the STRING's output 4, when an identical result was obtained, this was marked as a true-positive (TP). When no output was obtained, the dependency in reference was copied to the STRING's output file and marked as a false-negative (FN). There are also cases of sentences that were not marked as SVC, neither in the corpus annotation nor in the STRING's output. These are also considered FN and could only be detected by manual inspection. The manual analysis of the output also allowed for the correction of some cases as false-positives (FP) or as true-negative (TN). These cases will be presented and discussed in the next section.

5. Results and Discussion

Table 1 shows the results from the processing of the testing partition of the PARSEME corpus by STRING. This partition consists of 2,770 sentences (as segmented by STRING), where 311 instances of LVC.full had been manually annotated in the PARSEME corpus. The TP (true-positive cases) correspond to instances where the STRING adequately marked a SVC; the FP (false-positives) are instances where a SUPPORT dependency was incorrectly extracted; and FN (false-negatives) are instances of SVC ignored by the system.

Table 1: Results from comparing the annotations in the testing partition of PARSEME corpus and the annotation of the same corpus as performed by STRING.

TP	FP	FN
197	20	270
P	**R**	**F**
0.91	0.42	0.58

Considering the 2,770 phases of the corpus, the system's precision was high, though recall is low. From the 311 sentences marked in the PARSEME corpus, the STRING system correctly identified 154 as SVC, missed 149 and incorrectly marked 8. If one strictly considers the annotation in the PARSEME corpus as the reference (golden standard), these partial results from STRING correspond to an accuracy of 49%.

As a first comment on these results, and considering that the construction of the lexicon-grammar of PT-PT SVC is still a work in progress, one could say that these figures are promising, but that there is still much room for improvement. Next, we provide some error analysis and discuss the problematic results.

False-negatives (FN) cases

Four major situations can be distinguished: (i) the predicate nouns are still under description in the lexicon-grammar of STRING; (ii) the predicate nouns have not yet been included in the lexicon-grammar; (iii) the support-verb has not been associated with the predicate noun in the lexicon-grammar; and, (iv) some parsing issue prevented the system from capturing the SVC. We briefly present each one of these situations.

(i) nouns under description

Some of the instances not recognized by STRING concern predicate nouns that are already in the system's lexicon but are still undergoing linguistic description, so they were not used in the parsing. We did not consider these results to be a major problem, rather the natural consequence of a work in progress. These are the following predicate nouns (notice that some are repeated): *baixa*, *convenção*, *convivência*, *dano*, *decisão*, *dever*, *disponibilidade*, *extorsão*, *facilidade*, *grandeza*, *hábito*, *maneira*, *medida*, *obra*, *perda*, *rachadura*, *reclamação*, and *validade*.

(ii) nouns missing in the lexicon-grammar

On the other hand, there is an expressive number of predicative nouns that are not in the STRING's lexicon. Some of these nouns are used in quite usual constructions, hence the urgency in integrating them into the lexicon and to make an adequate description of them: *aniversário*, *antecedentes*, *área*, *autonomia*, *características*, *chefe*, *crime*, *endereço*, *equívoco*, *êxito*, *favoritismo*, *grafitagem*, *homicídios*, *índice*, *lar*, *lembranças*, *matchpoints*, *moleza*, *padrão*, *passado*, *população*, *potencial*, *prazer*, *presença*, *problema*, *procedimento*, *propriedade*, *repertório*, *significado*, *subvenção*, *tempo*, *tratado*, *treinamento*, *turnê* (PT-PT: *turné*, from French: *tournée*), *video-chamada* (ortographic variant of: *videochamada*), *vínculo*.

(iii) support-verb is not associated with the predicate noun in the lexicon-grammar

There is an important number of cases where the SVC has not been identified because the support-verb had not been associated with that particular predicate noun in the lexicon-grammar.

realizar: *ação*, *apresentação*, *audiência*, *concorrência*; ***cometer***: *assalto*; ***assinar***: *acordo*, *contrato*; ***ter***: *cura*, *marcação*, *relação*; ***possuir***: *excentricidade* (Astron.), experiência, *inclinação* (Astron.), *poder*; ***apresentar***: *sinal*.

Several support-verbs, often occurring in converse constructions, have also been missed in the lexicon-grammar: ***sofrer***: *acidente*; ***levar***: *advertências*, *medo* (only in PT-BR), *tombo*; ***passar por*** (=*sofer*): *cirurgia*; ***tomar***: *cuidado*, gols (BR), *precaução*, *providência*; ***chegar a***: *orgasmo*.

(iv) parsing issues

A large number cases correspond to situations where the system failed to recognize the SVC. It would not be possible to go through all those cases in this paper, and a detailed debug of the system's performance is underway.

Some situations, however, can already be reported, for they are clear. For example, in the next sentence, the predicate noun *ajuste* 'adjustment' has been incorrectly PoS-tagged as a verb (*ajustar* 'adjust'), so the SVC was not captured.

> *A prática de fazer* ajuste *no superávit com os dividendos tem sido comum nos últimos anos* 'The practice of adjusting the surplus with dividends has been common in recent years'

In other cases, a particular syntactic construction prevented the parsing from extracting the key dependency required to capture the SVC. This is the case of sentence:

> *Três integrantes de um bando que fez* um dos maiores *ataques a banco dos últimos anos*

no Estado ... 'Three members of a gang that carried out one of the biggest bank attacks in recent years in the State ... ',

where the partitive determiner *um dos Adj ataques* 'one of the Adj attacks' precluded the extraction of the direct object dependency between the support-verb *fazer* and the predicate noun *ataque*.

In some of the cases above, as the SVC detection is carried out at a later stage of the rule-based parsing process, accumulated errors in the previous stages impede the correct identification and extraction of the `SUPPORT _VSUP` dependency. This particularly obvious in the case of PoS-tagging errors. Other situations may involve some development and further refinement of the STRING's underlying rule-based grammar.

True-negatives (TN) cases
Several predicate nouns (such as *checagem* 'checking'), or, else, specific support-verb-noun combinations (e.g. *levar medo* 'be afraid'), are exclusive of the PT-BR variety, so they could not have been previously included the PT-PT lexicon-grammar. This is the case of: ***dar***: *olhada*; ***levar***: *bola*, *medo*, ***realizar***: *checagem*; ***receber***: *premiação*; ***sofrer***: *pane*, ***ter***: *contato* (em PT-PT *contacto*); ***tomar***: *gols*.
In other cases, the PT-BR shows a specific lexical (*registro*) or orthographical variant (*pênalti*, in PT-PT: *penálti*) of the word, that have not been properly lemmatized in the STRING's lexicon.
A few spelling errors also prevented the system from matching. For example, the hesitant use of the hyphen is one of those cases: *video-chamadas*.

False-positives (FP) cases
False-positive (FP) cases, though in a smaller number, correspond to the situation where, for some reason, the system failed the parsing. The following is an interesting example:

Seria uma boa surpresa e uma prova de que amor não tem hora nem dia marcados.

In this case, the system extracts a direct complement dependency between *tem* 'have' and *prova* 'proof', hence triggering the extraction of the SUPPORT dependency: `SUPPORT_-VSUP-STANDARD(prova,tem)`.

6. Conclusions and future work

In this paper, we analyzed the support-verb constructions manually annotated in a publicly available corpus of Brazilian Portuguese (PT-BR) multiword expressions (MWE), which was originally built within the scope of the project PARSEME. We emphasize that one of the reasons for using this corpus is the fact of it being publicly available and having been independently annotated. We parsed this corpus using the natural language processing system STRING, purposefully developed for Portuguese, whose SVC lexicon-grammar has been specifically built for the European variety (PT-PT). The construction of this linguistic resource is still ongoing. Both the system and its rule-based parser, as well as the SVC lexicon-grammar of European Portuguese were briefly described. The goal of this paper was to gauge the performance of the STRING system on this corpus with texts from the Brazilian variety (PT-BR), manually annotated for SVC. We briefly described the PARSEME corpus and the way it was processed by STRING, to retrieve the dependencies corresponding to the syntactic relation between the support-verb and the predicate noun. We compare the corpus SVC annotations with the STRING output. Results are encouraging, as precision is high (91%), but there is still much room for improvement, since recall is relatively low (42%). Many of the predicative nouns in the corpus that were not recognized by STRING were already included in the system's lexical-syntactical database, but had not yet undergone a full linguistic description, so they had been left out of the parsing. Similarly, for many predicate nouns, though they had been already described in the lexicon-grammar and were used by the parser, the full range of the variants of the basic or elementary support-verb had not been yet encoded in the lexicon-grammar. In some cases, this is due to the PT-BR language variety, for example, in cases where *possuir* 'possess' is often used in PT-BR instead of the elementary support-verb *ter* 'have', more common in PT-PT. The same seems to happen with many instances of *realizar* 'perform', a common variant of *fazer* 'do/make'. On the use of these (so-called) *stylistic* variants (Ranchhod, 1990; Baptista, 2005b) and the extension of elementary support-verbs, our approach to SVC is similar to that of the PARSEME Directives, namely, we also:

> take a broader scope than what is usually considered in the literature by taking in cases in which the verb has light semantics *per se* (it only bears morphology, such as the tense and mood, in any case), which hence cannot be described as "bleached" as is usually said of support-verbs.

On the other hand, we adopt the general Lexicon-Grammar approach, as posited by (Fotopoulou et al., 2021) for *aspectual* variants of support-verbs, which, in our view, would improve the granularity of SVC description within the PARSEME framework.
In other cases, the PT-PT lexicon-grammar lacks sufficient coverage in the determination of lexical variants of support-verbs. For example, the variants *passar/passar por* 'pass, pass through' had been entirely left out. Naturally, as a work in progress, the description of the lexicon-grammar is yet to be concluded. In this sense, a non-negligible number of predicate nouns had not yet been even listed in the database, and

some of them are quite usual/commonly used predicates. Their integration in lexicon-grammar and subsequent linguistic description is, therefore, urgent.
A more complex situation arises when the SVC construction, in principle, should have been recognized by STRING, but was not (false-negative). The detailed analysis of these cases is still underway but it may be due to a variety of causes. Paramount among them is the fact that the SVC detection and the extraction of the SUPPORT_VSUP dependency is performed by the STRING rule-based parser at the final steps of processing, hence it suffers from the accumulation of errors in the previous analysis stages. A major factor in this sub-optimal performance comes from the PoS-tagging phase. In other cases, the syntactic context is such that, in the previous stages of parsing, it prevents the key dependencies required for SVC extraction (e.g. a direct object, a subject or even a simple noun modifier dependency) from being adequately extracted, thus hindering the SVC extraction phase. For example, the specific syntactic structure of a noun phrase headed by the predicate noun with the support-verb participle as its modifier (e.g. *ação realizada* 'action performed'), a structure derived from the SVC passive sentence (v.g. *realizar uma ação*), though it had been mentioned in (Baptista and Mamede, 2020; Barreiro et al., 2022), does not seem to be working properly in the parser. Since this is a common structure used in PT-BR news, a relevant part of the missing SVC seems to be due to this case.
The partition of the PARSEME annotated corpus, as well as the reference built for this paper are to be made available in the STRING project site to the NLP (and especially to the MWE/SVC) interested community.
Besides the completion of the PT-PT SVC lexicon-grammar, several venues are open to future work. We envisage the analyse the entire corpus fully parsed with STRING, once the lexicon-grammar has been deemed satisfactorily complete, in order to retrieve: new (missed) instances of SVC, as well as instances of operator verbs. The lexicon-grammar and the new annotation will then be made available to the community.

7. Acknowledgements

Research for this work was supported by national funds through Institution, under grant ref. UIDB/50021/2020.

8. Bibliographical References

Aït-Mokhtar, S., Chanod, J.-P., and Roux, C. (2002). Robustness beyond shallowness: Incremental deep parsing. *Natural Language Engineering, 8*, pages 121–144.

Baptista, J. and Mamede, N. (2020). Syntactic Transformations in Rule-Based Parsing of Support Verb Constructions: Examples from European Portuguese. In Alberto Simões, et al., editors, *9th Symposium on Languages, Applications and Technologies (SLATE 2020)*, volume 83 of *OpenAccess Series in Informatics (OASIcs)*, pages 11:1–11:14, Dagstuhl, Germany. Schloss Dagstuhl–Leibniz-Zentrum für Informatik.

Baptista, J. and Ranchhod, E. (1998). Propriétés des phrases élémentaires associées à l'expression de grandeurs mesurables. exemples du portugais. *Cahiers de l'Institut de Linguistique de Louvain*, 24(3-4):49–61, September 24-27, 1998.

Baptista, J., Rassi, A. P., Santos-Turati, C., de Barros, C. D., Vale, O. A., and Mamede, N. (2015). Integrated processing of support verb constructions in Portuguese, 19-20 March 2015.

Baptista, J. (1997a). Conversão, nomes parte-do-corpo e restruturação dativa. In Ivo Castro, editor, *Actas do XII Encontro da Associação Portuguesa de Linguística*, volume 1, pages 51–59, Lisboa, 30 de Setembro a 2 de Outubro de 1996, Braga-Guimarães, Portugal. Associação Portuguesa de Linguística, APL/Colibri.

Baptista, J. (1997b). *Sermão, tareia* e *facada*: uma classificação das expressões conversas *dar–levar*. *Seminários de Linguística 1*, pages 5–37.

Baptista, J. (1999). *Fazer/Fazer com*: Um verbo-operador do português. *Seminários de Linguística*, 3:163–171.

Baptista, J. (2004). Instrument nouns and fusion. predicative nouns designating violent actions. In Christian; Leclère, et al., editors, *Lexique, Syntaxe et Lexique-Grammaire (Syntax, Lexis and Lexicon-Grammar). Hommage à Maurice Gross.*, Linguisticae Investigationes Supplementa, pages 31–40. John Benjamins Publishing Co., Amsterdam/Philadelphia.

Baptista, J. (2005a). Construções simétricas: argumentos e complementos. In Olga Figueiredo, et al., editors, *Estudos de homenagem a Mário Vilela*, pages 353–367. Faculdade de Letras da Universidade do Porto.

Baptista, J. (2005b). *Sintaxe dos Predicados Nominais com* ser de. Fundação para a Ciência e a Tecnologia & Fundação Calouste Gulbenkian, Lisboa.

Barreiro, A., Mota, C., Baptista, J., Chacoto, L., and Carvalho, P. (2022). Linguistic resources for paraphrase generation in Portuguese: a Lexicon-Grammar approach. *Language Resources and Evaluation*, pages 1–35.

Borillo, A. (1971). Remarques sur les verbes symétriques. *Langue Française*, 11(1):17–31.

Calcia, N. P. and Vale, O. (2019). Construções conversas do português do Brasil. Descrição e classificação iniciais. *Linguamática*, 10(2):13–20, January.

Calcia, N. (2016). Descrição e classificação das construções conversas no português do Brasil. Master's thesis, Universidade Federal de São Carlos, São Carlos-SP, Brasil.

Calcia, N. P. (2022). *Dar e receber um abraço: uma análise da conversão em português brasileiro*. Ph.D.

thesis, Universidade Federal de São Carlos, São Carlos-SP, Brasil, março.

Chacoto, L. (2005). *O Verbo FAZER em Construções Nominais Predicativas*. Ph.D. thesis, Universidade do Algarve, Faro.

Constant, M., Eryigit, G., Monti, J., van der Plas, L., Ramisch, C., Rosner, M., and Todirascu, A. (2017). Multiword expression processing: A survey. *Computational Linguistics*, 43(4):837–892.

Cook, P., Mitrović, J., Escartín, C. P., Vaidya, A., Osenova, P., Taslimipoor, S., and Ramisch, C. (2021). Proceedings of the 17th Workshop on Multiword Expressions (MWE 2021). In *Proceedings of the 17th Workshop on Multiword Expressions (MWE 2021)*.

de Athayde, M. F. M. Q.-P. (2000). *A estrutura semântica das construções com verbo-suporte preposicionadas do português e do alemão*. Ph.D. thesis, Faculdade de Letras da Universidade de Coimbra, Coimbra.

Dias de Barros, C., Vale, O. A., and Baptista, J. (2013). Description and classification of nominal predicates with the support verb fazer (make/do) in Brazilian Portuguese. In Jorge Baptista et al., editors, *Proceedings of the 32nd International Conference on Lexis and Grammar (CLG'2013)*, pages 165–170, Faro, Portugal, September. Universidade do Algarve - FCHS.

Dias de Barros, C. (2014). *Descrição e classificação de predicados nominais com o verbo-suporte* fazer*: especificidades do Português do Brasil*. Ph.D. thesis, Universidade Federal de São Carlos, São Carlos-SP, Brasil.

Fotopoulou, A., Laporte, E., and Nakamura, T. (2021). Where do aspectual variants of light verb constructions belong? In *Proceedings of the 17th Workshop on Multiword Expressions (MWE 2021)*, pages 2–12. Association for Computational Linguistics.

Giry-Schneider, J. (1978). *Les nominalisations en Français: l'opérateur faire dans le lexique*. Librairie Droz, Genova.

Gross, M. (1981). Les bases empiriques de la notion de prédicat sémantique. *Langages*, 15(63):7–52.

Gross, G. (1989). *Les construction converses du français*. Droz, Genève.

Gross, M. (1996). Lexicon-grammar. In Keith Brown et al., editors, *Concise Encyclopedia of Syntactic Theories*, pages 244–259. Pergamon, Cambridge.

Gross, M. (1998). La fonction sémantique des verbes supports. *Travaux de Linguistique: Revue Internationale de Linguistique Française*, 37(1):25–46.

Harris, Z. S., (1955). *Co-occurrence and transformation in linguistic structure*, pages 143–210. D. Reidel Publishing Company.

Harris, Z. (1964). The elementary transformations. In Henry Hiz, editor, *Papers on Syntax*, pages 211–235. D. Reidel Publishing Company.

Harris, Z. (1976). *Notes du Cours de Syntaxe*. Editions du Seuil, Paris.

Harris, Z. S. (1982). *A Grammar of English on Mathematical Principles*. New York: John Wiley & Sons.

Harris, Z. S. (1991). *A Theory of Language and Information. A Mathematical Approach*. Clarendon Press, Oxford.

Mamede, N., Baptista, J., Diniz, C., and Cabarrão, V. (2012). STRING - A Hybrid Statistical and Rule-Based Natural Language Processing Chain for Portuguese. In Alberto Abad, editor, *Int. Conf. on Computational Processing of Portuguese (PROPOR 2012) - Demo Session*. http://www.inesc-id.pt/ficheiros/publicacoes/8578.pdf.

Mota, C., Baptista, J., and Barreiro, A. (2018). The lexicon-grammar of predicate nouns with *ser de* in Port4NooJ. In *International Conference on Automatic Processing of Natural-Language Electronic Texts with NooJ*, pages 124–137. Springer.

Paiva Raposo, E. (2013). Predicações secundárias. In Eduardo et al. Paiva Raposo, editor, *Gramática do Português*, volume 2, pages 1340–1356. Fundação Calouste Gulbenkian.

Picoli, L., Vale, O. A., and Laporte, E. (2021). Aspecto verbal nas construções com verbo-suporte. *Revista do GEL*, 18(1):204–229.

Ramisch, C., Savary, A., Guillaume, B., Waszczuk, J., Candito, M., Vaidya, A., Barbu Mititelu, V., Bhatia, A., Iñurrieta, U., Giouli, V., Güngör, T., Jiang, M., Lichte, T., Liebeskind, C., Monti, J., Ramisch, R., Stymne, S., Walsh, A., and Xu, H. (2020). Edition 1.2 of the PARSEME shared task on semi-supervised identification of verbal multiword expressions. In *Proceedings of the Joint Workshop on Multiword Expressions and Electronic Lexicons*, pages 107–118, online, December. Association for Computational Linguistics.

Ranchhod, E. (1990). *Sintaxe dos predicados nominais com "estar"*. Instituto Nacional de Investigação Científica (INIC).

Rassi, A., Santos-Turati, C., Baptista, J., Mamede, N., and Vale, O. (2014). The fuzzy boundaries of operator verb and support verb constructions with dar "give" and ter "have" in Brazilian Portuguese. In *Proceedings of the Workshop on Lexical and Grammatical Resources for Language Processing (LG-LP 2014), COLING 2014*, Dublin, Ireland, August. Workshop on Lexical and Grammatical Resources for Language Processing (LG-LP 2014), COLING 2014, Dublin, August 24, 2014, COLING 2014.

Rassi, A., Mamede, N., Baptista, J., and I, O. V. (2015a). Integrating support verb constructions into a parser. In *Proceedings of the Symposium in Information and Human Language Technology (STIL'2015)*, pages 57–62.

Rassi, A. P., Baptista, J., and Vale, O. A. (2015b). Um corpus anotado de construções com verbo-suporte em português. *Gragoatá*, 39(1):207–230, Junho, 2015.

Rassi, A., Calcia, N., Vale, O. A., and Baptista, J.

(2016). Estudo contrastivo sobre construções conversas em PB e PE. In O. Nadin, et al., editors, *Léxico e suas interfaces: descrição, reflexão e ensino*, pages 199–218. Cultura Acadêmica.

Rassi, A. P. (2015). *Descrição, classificação e processamento automático das construções com o verbo* dar *em português brasileiro*. Ph.D. thesis, Universidade Federal de São Carlos, São Carlos-SP, Brasil.

Reis, S., Mamede, N., and Baptista, J. (2021). Predicados de comunicação em português europeu: nominalizações e nomes autónomos. *Revista da Associação Portuguesa de Linguística*, (8):237–259, Out.

Sag, I. A., Baldwin, T., Bond, F., Copestake, A., and Flickinger, D. (2002). Multiword Expressions: A Pain in the Neck for NLP. In Alexander Gelbukh, editor, *Proceedings of CICLing*, pages 1–15, Mexico City, Mexico, February.

Santos, C. (2015). *Construções com verbo-suporte* ter *no Português do Brasil*. Ph.D. thesis, Universidade Federal de São Carlos, São Carlos-SP, Brasil.

Savary, A., Sailer, M., Parmentier, Y., Rosner, M., Rosén, V., Przepiórkowski, A., Krstev, C., Vincze, V., Wójtowicz, B., Losnegaard, G. S., Parra Escartín, C., Waszczuk, J., Constant, M., Osenova, P., and Sangati, F. (2015). PARSEME–PARSing and Multiword Expressions within a European multilingual network. In *7th Language & Technology Conference: Human Language Technologies as a Challenge for Computer Science and Linguistics (LTC 2015)*.

Vaza, A. (1988). Estruturas com nomes predicativos e verbo-suporte *DAR*. Master's thesis, Faculdade de Letras da Universidade de Lisboa, Lisboa, Portugal.

A Matrix-Based Heuristic Algorithm for Extracting Multiword Expressions from a Corpus

Orhan Bilgin
Lancaster University, Linguistics and English Language Department
County South, Lancaster University, Lancaster, UK, LA1 4YL
orhan@zargan.com

Abstract

This paper describes an algorithm for automatically extracting multiword expressions (MWEs) from a corpus. The algorithm is node-based, i.e. extracts MWEs that contain the item specified by the user, using a fixed window-size around the node. The main idea is to detect the frequency anomalies that occur at the starting and ending points of an ngram that constitutes a MWE. This is achieved by locally comparing matrices of observed frequencies to matrices of expected frequencies, and determining, for each individual input, one or more sub-sequences that have the highest probability of being a MWE. Top-performing sub-sequences are then combined in a score-aggregation and ranking stage, thus producing a single list of score-ranked MWE candidates, without having to indiscriminately generate all possible sub-sequences of the input strings. The knowledge-poor and computationally efficient algorithm attempts to solve certain recurring problems in MWE extraction, such as the inability to deal with MWEs of arbitrary length, the repetitive counting of nested ngrams, and excessive sensitivity to frequency. Evaluation results show that the best-performing version generates top-50 precision values between 0.71 and 0.88 on Turkish and English data, and performs better than the baseline method even at n=1000.

Keywords: multiword expression, MWE, phraseology, extraction, ngram, observed frequency, expected frequency, Turkish, English

1. Introduction

Multiword expressions (MWEs) are conventionalized word combinations such as *at the expense of ...*, *good morning*, *execute an agreement*, *31 January 2016*, *United Nations Children's Fund*, or *the proverbial elephant*. They are complex structures that contain syntactic, morphological, phonological, semantic, pragmatic, and discourse-functional information (Croft and Cruse, 2004, p. 258) and behave as single units of meaning (Sinclair, 2004, p. 39).

MWEs have been defined in terms of their non-compositionality (Villavicencio et al., 2005), lexical, syntactic and semantic idiosyncrasy (Sag et al., 2002; Baldwin and Kim, 2010; Mel'čuk, 1998), lexicalization (Wray, 2009; Maziarz, Szpakowicz, and Piasecki, 2015) semantic unity (Moon, 1998; Calzolari et al., 2002), syntactic unity (Kjellmer, 1987; Dias, 2003), institutionalization (Pawley and Syder, 1983), pragmatic specialization (Siepmann, 2005) and frequency (Grant and Bauer, 2004; Gries, 2008), among others. This diversity of approaches probably reflects the inherently complex nature of the phenomenon (Wray and Perkins, 2000, p. 3; Schmitt and Carter, 2004, p. 2).

MWEs are numerous; Jackendoff (1997) estimates that they number on about the same order of magnitude as individual words (p. 156). They are frequent; Erman and Warren (2000) report that on average they make up 55% of spoken and written language (p. 37). In view of this pervasiveness, a *MWE lexicon*, i.e. a classified inventory of habitually co-occurring lexical items, is an essential component of the description of any language (Mel'čuk, 2006, p. 3; Moon, 2008, p. 314). It is also important for natural language processing (NLP) and related disciplines, where MWEs still are an unsolved problem (Shwartz and Dagan, 2019; Nivre, 2021, p. 99). Despite the recent success of deep learning models in various NLP tasks, at least some of the performance issues faced by end-to-end pipelines like *Stanza* (Qi et al., 2020) and *UDPipe* (Straka and Straková, 2017) and the systems that use them seem to be caused by the following facts: (a) they use individual words as a unit of analysis, despite convincing evidence that "the normal primary carrier of meaning is the phrase and not the word" (Sinclair, 2008, p. 409), and (b) they rely on a strict separation of the lexical, morphological, syntactic, and semantic levels, ignoring the ubiquity of MWEs, which can be viewed as "data structure[s] that [integrate] all possible kinds of linguistic information in a single representation" (Trijp, 2018). The solution might lie in developing more complex data structures that recognize the existence of a phraseological level that crosses word boundaries and cuts across the traditional levels of analysis. MWE lexicons are essential linguistic resources in this regard.

Because unaided speakers cannot reliably discover significant recurring patterns in their native language through conscious reflection (Church et al., 1991, p. 1; Stubbs, 2002, p. 219), MWE lexicons must be created automatically or semi-automatically, using large amounts of usage data. The task of *MWE extraction*, then, can be defined as "a process that takes as input a text and generates a list of MWE candidates, which can be further filtered by human experts before their integration into lexical resources." (Constant et al., 2017, p. 847)

A large number of methods have been proposed for the automatic extraction of MWEs from corpora during the last fifty years (Section 2). Most of the focus has been on resource-rich Indo-European languages like English, German and French. This paper reports on an effort to develop a MWE extraction algorithm that requires as little linguistic knowledge as possible. Although the algorithm was primarily designed for Turkish, a language whose complex morphology has proven to be challenging for NLP (Oflazer, 2014, p . 639), preliminary results show that it performs equally well on English data (Section 4.3), suggesting that it is to some extent language-independent.

After discussing existing methods in Section 2, I will describe the proposed algorithm in Section 3, present the results of an experiment to evaluate its performance in Section 4, and discuss results and make concluding remarks in Section 5.

Proceedings of the 18th Workshop on Multiword Expressions (MWE 2022) n@LREC2022, pages 37–48

2. Existing Extraction Algorithms

The majority of MWE extraction algorithms are based on the statistical manipulation of *ngrams*, i.e. sequences of *n* (continuous or discontinuous) items, usually words or morphemes, obtained from a corpus. In most applications, the relevance (i.e. 'MWEhood') of a given ngram is determined using some measure of the strength of the attraction between the items (known as an *association measure*; see Pecina (2005) and Hoang, Kim, and Yan, (2009) for reviews). Additional linguistic and/or statistical filters and thresholds can be used to improve results. The output is a score-ranked list of MWE candidates.

Extraction methods can be classified along several axes: Some methods are designed to extract any type of MWE (Choueka, Klein, and Neuwitz, 1983), while others focus on specific types such as verb-particle constructions (Ramisch et al., 2008) or preposition-noun constructions (Keßelmeier et al., 2009). Some extract only MWEs that contain a specific word/lemma (Kilgarriff and Tugwell, 2001; Cheng et al., 2009), while others extract MWEs without regard to their lexical content (Banerjee and Pedersen, 2003). Another basic parameter is whether or not a given method can deal with discontinuity, i.e. the interruption of a MWEs elements by additional material. Most methods only deal with continuous MWEs (Aires, Lopes, and Silva, 2008), but some deal with both continuous and discontinuous ones (da Silva et al., 1999).

Most extraction algorithms combine statistical methods with linguistic knowledge, which can be integrated into the system in one or more pre- or post-processing steps. This can take several forms such as POS-tagging (Justeson and Katz, 1995; Lossio-Ventura et al., 2014), lemmatization (Daille, 1994; Evert and Krenn, 2001), morphological analysis (Al-Haj and Wintner, 2010; Kumova-Metin and Karaoğlan, 2010), syntactic parsing (Smadja, 1993; Uhrig, Evert, and Proisl, 2018), stop lists (Frantzi and Ananiadou, 1999; Banerjee and Pedersen, 2003), synsets (Pearce, 2001), morphosyntactic patterns (Ramisch, Villavicencio, and Boitet, 2010; Passaro and Lenci, 2016), and semantic tags (Piao et al., 2003; Dunn, 2017). Combining statistical methods with linguistic knowledge involves a trade-off: Methods that use linguistic knowledge may perform better (Wermter and Hahn, 2006, p. 791), but are more language-dependent; while methods that do not use linguistic knowledge are more language-independent, but might have more limited performance.

There are at least four persistent challenges MWE extraction systems faced in their more than fifty-year history. The first is that, although MWEs frequently are longer than two words, virtually all association measures used in MWE extraction are designed to only extract bigrams, i.e. sequences of two items (Wahl and Gries, 2020, p. 88). Several techniques have been proposed to generalize association measures to ngrams longer than two (da Silva et al., 1999; van de Cruys, 2011; Dunn, 2018).

A second challenge is that extraction methods do not behave identically at different frequency ranges (Evert and Krenn, 2001, Section 4.3). For example, the association measure *pointwise mutual information* is known to produce extremely high association scores for low-frequency MWEs, while *t-score* does the same for high-frequency MWEs (Gries, 2010, p. 14). This is a problem even if one tries to use the appropriate measure for the appropriate frequency range. First, it is not easy to accurately describe how a given association measure behaves at different frequencies. Second, determining the exact point where one measure stops being useful and another measure would perform better requires experimentation, and is therefore prone to error. Reduced or zero sensitivity to frequency is a desirable property for an extraction method.

A third problem is that most extraction methods require the setting of one or more parameters for optimum performance. This is problematic because setting a parameter accurately requires experimentation, which is prone to error and introduces the risk of data overfitting. Moreover, the correct value of a parameter depends on various factors such as the language and size of the corpus, the association measures used for extraction, and the type(s) of MWE being extracted (da Silva et al., 1999).

The fourth persistent challenge has been variously referred to as *nested terms* (Frantzi, Ananiadou, and Mima, 2000, p. 117), *overlapping chains* (Mason, 2006, p. 155) and *included components* (O'Donnel, 2011, p. 166). Consider the expression *strawberry ice cream*. Any sentence that contains this trigram also contains the two bigrams *strawberry ice* and *ice cream*. A method that extracts *strawberry ice cream* as a valid MWE because its frequency is high enough would tend to extract the two bigrams as well, since their frequencies will, by definition, be at least as high as that of the original trigram. The problem is that one of the bigrams (*ice cream*) is a valid MWE, while the other (*strawberry ice*) is not, and a purely frequency-based extraction method has no mechanisms to make the correct decision. Several methods have been proposed to deal with this problem (Kita et al., 1994, p. 25; Ren et al., 2009, p. 49; Wei and Li, 2013, p. 519).

3. Proposed Algorithm[1]

3.1 General Characteristics

This paper proposes an algorithm for extracting continuous, i.e. uninterrupted MWEs from a corpus. The algorithm relies on the concept of co-selection in line with Sinclair's (1987) *idiom principle*, according to which "speakers and writers co-select the words they speak and write in order to produce units of meaning, even though the words might appear to be analysable into segments" (quoted in Cheng et al., 2009, p. 239). Since co-selection is a cognitive phenomenon that cannot be observed directly, the algorithm uses textual co-occurrence as a proxy. Therefore, as is the case with other statistical extraction techniques, the results are valid only to the extent this approximation is valid.

The main idea behind the algorithm is to detect the *frequency anomalies* that occur at the starting and ending points of a MWE, which, for purposes of this paper, is defined as a *recurring sequence of linguistic units, i.e. words and/or morphemes*. The algorithm detects these

[1] A Python implementation of the proposed algorithm is available at https://github.com/melanuria/mwe_extractor.

anomalies by manipulating several matrices of ngram frequencies.

The proposed algorithm is *node-based*, i.e. extracts MWEs that contain the item specified by the user, using a fixed window-size around the node. It uses a *candidate generation and ranking* approach, where the input is a set of concordances containing the node, and the output is a score-ranked list of MWE candidates. It is *knowledge-poor*, i.e. does not require linguistic knowledge, except as may be necessary for segmenting the raw input into words or morphemes (Section 3.2). According to the experiment in Section 4, the algorithm seems to be *language-independent*, at least to some extent. Finally, it is *computationally efficient*, with a time complexity of $O(n)$.

3.2 From Concordances to Ngrams

The raw input consists of N concordance lines that contain the node specified by the user. Although the node is usually a simplex content word, also bound morphemes, complex word-forms and even multiple word-forms can be used as node. The user also specifies two window sizes, W_L and W_R, for the left and right context of the node, respectively.[2] A pre-processor then converts each of the N concordance lines into a sequence of W_L+1+W_R elements (e.g. a 7-gram with the node in the middle, if window size is three on both sides).

The next step is to identify sentence boundaries and punctuation marks, which are treated as *boundary tokens* that MWEs cannot cross. All boundary tokens and any other tokens that are farther away from the node are replaced by the dummy string ###. Finally, position prefixes are added to all tokens, where *Ln* and *Rn* represent the nth token in the left and right contexts, respectively, and *KW* represents the node. Table 1 shows three raw concordance lines and ngrams for English, for a window size of three on both sides.[3]

Concordance1: *and global warming at the same time provide alternative livelihood for the hill indigenous people.* Ngram1 = {L3_at, L2_the, L1_same, KW_time, R1_provide, R2_alternative, R3_livelihood}
Concordance2: *the vehicles will drive ahead and have our camp set up by the time you arrive.* Ngram2 = {L3_up, L2_by, L1_the, KW_time, R1_you, R2_arrive, R3_###}
Concordance3: *profiles the director and looks at his life and work, including time spent with son noel.* Ngram3 = {L3_###, L2_###, L1_including, KW_time, R1_spent, R2_with, R3_son}

Table 1: Raw data and ngrams for W_L=3 and W_R=3

An important question arises at this point: What is the proper unit of analysis for the MWE extraction task, i.e. what should individual ngram elements consist of? Using word-forms may be appropriate for an analytic language like English, because, compared to a less analytic language, an average English lemma has fewer word-forms grouped under it. Consider the light-verb construction *have a hard time*, which has four variants: *has/had/have/having a hard time*. An obvious solution would be to group these word-forms under the lemma HAVE, which would allow us to abstract away from the syntactically motivated surface variation, and represent the MWE as HAVE *a hard time*.

Although lemmatisation is a viable option, the cost of *not* lemmatising is not prohibitively high in English. In the absence of lemmatisation, the total frequency of the construction is divided among the four versions, resulting in some data sparsity, which makes it somewhat harder to extract the construction, and also causing some fragmentation, which means that the candidate list contains four separate entries for the four versions (assuming the algorithm manages to extract them all).

An agglutinating language like Turkish presents a radically different picture. Consider the N-V collocation *-e zaman ayır*, -DAT time spare, 'to spare time for something'.[4] This construction requires the object to carry a dative marker, which means that, every time the construction is used with a different noun, a different, complex word-form occurs at position L1: *aileme*, family-P1S-DAT, 'to my family'; *ailelerinize*, family-PL-P2P-DAT, 'to your families'; *uykuya*, sleep-DAT, 'to sleep', etc. Moreover, like many other Turkish verbs, *ayır-* has several thousand different realizations[5], depending on the sequence of suffixes attached to it: *ayırdık*, spare-PAST-1P, 'we spared'; *ayıramıyorum*, spare-ABIL-NEG-PRES-1S, 'I cannot spare'; *ayırabilirler*, spare-ABIL-AOR-3P, 'they can spare', etc. This means that, when word-forms are used as units, the total frequency of *-e zaman ayır-* is divided among thousands of different word-form trigrams, resulting in extreme data sparsity, which makes it difficult, if not impossible, to extract the construction. Also the fragmentation problem is exacerbated by several orders of magnitude compared to English, meaning that the candidate list contains a very large number of different entries that instantiate the same construction, once again assuming the algorithm manages to extract them. Similar problems caused by the morphology of Turkish have been discussed by several authors in information extraction contexts (Tür, Hakkani-Tür, and Oflazer (2003); Yeniterzi (2011); Eryiğit et al. (2015, pp. 71-72).

In view of the above, it seems appropriate to use word-forms as ngram elements for English data, and individual

[2] A typical setting would be ±5 (see Smadja, 1993, p. 151; Martin, 1983, quoted in Smadja, 1989, p. 6).

[3] Examples are in Turkish and English since the algorithm has been tested on these two languages (Section 4). All examples are based on data obtained from the *trTenTen12* and *enTenTen20* corpora available at sketchengine.co.uk.

[4] The notation used to describe Turkish morphology cannot be covered here in any depth. The following list of glosses are intended to assist the interpretation of the examples in this paper:
Case markers: **ACC** (accusative), **DAT** (dative), **LOC** (locative), **ABL** (ablative), **GEN** (genitive)
Possessive markers on nouns: **P1S, P2S, P3S, P1P, P2P, P3P**
Plural marker: **PL**
Negation marker: **NEG**
Compound marker: **CM** (identical to **P3S** in form)
Tense/aspect/modality markers: **ABIL** (abilitative), **AOR** (aorist), **CAUS** (causative), **COND** (conditional), **DES** (desiderative), **EVID** (evidential), **FUT** (future), **IMP** (imperative), **NEC** (necessitative), **OPT** (optative), **PAST** (past), **PRES** (present)
Relativizers: **OBJREL** (object), **SUBJREL** (subject)
Person markers on verbs: **1S, 2S, 3S, 1P, 2P, 3P**

[5] Although the exact figure is difficult to calculate, a quick corpus query suggests that the trTenTen12 corpus at sketchengine.co.uk contains more than 2,000 unique word-forms (types) based on this verb.

morphemes for Turkish data.[6] To achieve this, Turkish concordance lines have been processed by the morphological analyser described by Çöltekin (2010), which generates *all* possible analyses for each word-form. And this brings us to the problem of *morphological ambiguity*. Consider the following sentence:

Ürünü istediği zaman alabileceğini bilen müşteri, alımı erteler.
'Knowing that he/she can purchase the product any time he/she wants, the customer postpones the purchase.'

For the node *zaman*, 'time', and a window size of five on both sides, the word-forms *ürünü*, *istediği* and *alabileceğini* are morphologically ambiguous, each having two possible morphological analyses. This results in eight possible morpheme sequences (ambiguities underlined):

ürün-ACC *iste*-OBJREL-ACC *zaman al*-ABIL-FUT-CM-ACC
ürün-CM *iste*-OBJREL-ACC *zaman al*-ABIL-FUT-CM-ACC
ürün-ACC *iste*-OBJREL-CM *zaman al*-ABIL-FUT-CM-ACC
ürün-CM *iste*-OBJREL-CM *zaman al*-ABIL-FUT-CM-ACC
ürün-ACC *iste*-OBJREL-ACC *zaman al*-ABIL-FUT-P2S-ACC
ürün-CM *iste*-OBJREL-ACC *zaman al*-ABIL-FUT-P2S-ACC
ürün-ACC *iste*-OBJREL-CM *zaman al*-ABIL-FUT-P2S-ACC
ürün-CM *iste*-OBJREL-CM *zaman al*-ABIL-FUT-P2S-ACC

To be able to use individual morphemes rather than word-forms as their unit of analysis, several studies on information extraction in Turkish (Küçük and Yazıcı, 2009; Kumova-Metin and Karaoğlan, 2010; Yeniterzi, 2011; Şeker and Eryiğit, 2012; Kazkılınç, 2013, Güngör, Güngör, and Üsküdarlı, 2019) have resorted to *morphological disambiguation* (*i.e.* a mechanism that selects one of the available morphological analyses as the "correct", or at least the most probable, one). But this is dangerous in a MWE extraction setting because morphological disambiguation in agglutinating languages is not a trivial task and its performance relies, among several other factors, on the proper handling of MWEs. In other words, using a morphological disambiguator in a MWE extraction algorithm amounts to using the output of a task to perform another task when the outcome of the former depends on the latter. This is why the proposed algorithm refrains from disambiguating the morphological analyses. Instead, whenever there are more than *n* possible analyses, it randomly chooses *n* of them. This is an obviously more inferior but more cautious approach.

In an experimental step to deal with morphological variability in Turkish, possessive markers on nouns are replaced by the 'super-tag' POSS. To draw a parallel to English, this allows the system to treat, say, *for the first time in my/your/his/her/its/our/their life/lives* as instances of the abstract MWE *for the first time in one's life*.

The last step for both English and Turkish is to pre-calculate the following global frequencies:

- Position-specific frequency of every token (e.g. frequency of *spent* at position R_1); and
- position-specific frequency of each of the $(W_L+1)\times(W_R+1)$ uninterrupted, node-containing sub-sequences of the *N* concordance lines (e.g. frequencies of *same time*, *same time provide*, etc.)

3.3 Observed Frequencies

The co-selection matrix of observed frequencies, *O*, is a W_L+1 by W_R+1 matrix that stores the observed ngram frequencies the algorithm uses to extract MWEs:

$$O = \begin{bmatrix} f(KW) & f(KW \cdots R_1) & f(KW \cdots R_2) & f(KW \cdots R_3) \\ f(L_1 \cdots KW) & f(L_1 \cdots R_1) & f(L_1 \cdots R_2) & f(L_1 \cdots R_3) \\ f(L_2 \cdots KW) & f(L_2 \cdots R_1) & f(L_2 \cdots R_2) & f(L_2 \cdots R_3) \\ f(L_3 \cdots KW) & f(L_3 \cdots R_1) & f(L_3 \cdots R_2) & f(L_3 \cdots R_3) \end{bmatrix}$$

Row and column indices correspond to the left and right context of the node, respectively. Each matrix element stores the observed frequency of an uninterrupted sub-sequence that starts at the token represented by the row-index and terminates at the token represented by the column-index. For instance, matrix element $O_{4,3}$ for Ngram1 in Table 1 stores the observed frequency of the 6-gram that starts at L_3 and ends at R_2 (shorthand notation $L_3 \ldots R_2$), i.e. the sub-sequence *at the same time provide alternative*. In other words, each matrix element shows how many times the corresponding sub-sequence of an individual ngram occurs in the entire input.

The topological organization of the matrix is such that moving from a given matrix element to the element on the right represents adding a new token to the right of the original sequence, and moving to the element below represents adding a new token to its left. The top-left element, $O_{1,1}$, which represents the bare node, is the starting point, and the sub-sequences get incrementally longer as one moves from there to the bottom-right element, which represents the longest sequence determined by W_L and W_R.

Critically, each of the *N* concordance lines included in the analysis has its own co-selection matrix. The co-selection matrix is a *local* artefact that allows the algorithm to select the best-performing sub-sequence(s) of a single ngram, using *global* frequency values obtained from the entire input data.

3.4 Adjusting Observed Frequencies

The next step is to deal with the *nesting problem* discussed in Section 2 by adjusting the co-selection matrix of observed frequencies. In mathematical terms, the problem is that every sub-sequence $L_m \ldots R_n$ contains $((m+1) \times (n+1)) - 1$ shorter sub-sequences, which means that, whenever the frequency of $L_m \ldots R_n$ is incremented, the frequencies of each of those shorter sub-sequences are incremented as well. To prevent this repetitive counting, matrix *O* is processed element-by-element, starting at the bottom-right corner and proceeding diagonally to the shorter sub-sequences, until the top-left corner is reached. At every step, the frequency of the sub-sequence being processed is deducted from the frequencies of all shorter sub-sequences. The end result is *O'*, the *adjusted co-selection matrix of observed frequencies*.

Below is an example for Ngram1 in Table 1:

$$O'_{Ngram1} = \begin{bmatrix} 47880 & 3 & 0 & 0 \\ 42 & 0 & 0 & 0 \\ 195 & 0 & 0 & 0 \\ 1754 & 0 & 0 & 0 \end{bmatrix}$$

[6] This is not a dichotomy but a continuum. It seems safe to assume that the more synthetic a language is, the more it would benefit from a morpheme-based treatment.

3.5 Expected Frequencies and Aggregate Matrix

3.5.1 Definitions

The proposed algorithm works by comparing O' to either the co-selection matrix of expected frequencies (E), or to the aggregate matrix (A). The following definitions are needed to describe these two methods:

Definition 1: The probability of observing a given token at a given position is approximated by dividing the number of times that token occurs at that position by the number of ngrams included in the analysis:

$$p(R2\_arrive) = \frac{f(R2\_arrive)}{N}$$

Definition 2: The probability of *not* observing a given token at a given position is approximated by taking the complement of the probability of observing that token in that position:

$$p(R2\_arrive') = 1 - \frac{f(R2\_arrive)}{N}$$

Definition 3: The expected probability of observing a sequence $L_m \ldots R_n$ is approximated by multiplying the probabilities of observing each token in the sequence, the probability of *not* observing L_{m+1}, and the probability of *not* observing R_{n+1}.[7] For example, in relation to Ngram1 in Table 1:

$$p(L_2 \cdots R_1)_{Ngram1} = p(L2\_the) \times p(L1\_same) \times$$

$$p(R1\_provide) \times p(L3\_at') \times p(R2\_alternative')_8$$

Definition 4: The co-selection matrix of expected frequencies (E) is calculated by applying Definition 3 to each sub-sequence in O', and multiplying the resulting matrix by the scalar N, to convert expected probabilities to expected frequencies:

$$E = N \begin{bmatrix} p(KW) & p(KW \cdots R_1) & p(KW \cdots R_2) & p(KW \cdots R_3) \\ p(L_1 \cdots KW) & p(L_1 \cdots R_1) & p(L_1 \cdots R_2) & p(L_1 \cdots R_3) \\ p(L_2 \cdots KW) & p(L_2 \cdots R_1) & p(L_2 \cdots R_2) & p(L_2 \cdots R_3) \\ p(L_3 \cdots KW) & p(L_3 \cdots R_1) & p(L_3 \cdots R_2) & p(L_3 \cdots R_3) \end{bmatrix}$$

Definition 5: The aggregate matrix A is equal to the matrix-sum of the N adjusted co-selection matrices of observed frequencies:

$$A = \sum_{i=1}^{N} O'_i$$

3.5.2 Using the Co-selection Matrix of Expected Frequencies to Detect Anomalies

The co-selection matrix of expected frequencies of a given ngram (E) contains the expected frequencies of each sub-sequence in O'. Just as every individual ngram has its own O', every individual ngram has its own E. The expected frequencies matrix provides a baseline for detecting anomalies in an O' matrix:

$$E_{Ngram1} = \begin{bmatrix} 49598 & 209 & 0 & 0 \\ 65 & 0 & 0 & 0 \\ 0 & 0 & 0 & 0 \\ 0 & 0 & 0 & 0 \end{bmatrix}$$

According to E_{Ngram1}, the expected frequency of $L_3 \ldots KW_{Ngram1}$ (the sub-sequence *at the same time*) is zero. Since the corresponding frequency in O'_{Ngram1} (f=1754, Section 3.4) is significantly higher than zero, the sequence *at the same time* has a high probability of being a MWE.

3.5.3 Using the Aggregate Matrix to Detect Anomalies

The aggregate matrix A shows how the total probability mass is distributed among matrix elements *in the aggregate*. There is only one aggregate matrix for every node word, and the sum of its elements is always equal to 1.0. Just like E, A provides a baseline for detecting anomalies in individual O matrices.

The aggregate matrix for *time*:[9]

$$A_{time} = \begin{bmatrix} 0.9479130 & 0.0158255 & 0.0003455 & 0.0000100 & 0.0000005 & 0.0000002 \\ 0.0275413 & 0.0008389 & 0.0001221 & 0.0000020 & 0.0000003 & 0.0000008 \\ 0.0048604 & 0.0002991 & 0.0000333 & 0.0000010 & 0.0000002 & 0.0000012 \\ 0.0020924 & 0.0000586 & 0.0000026 & 0.0000003 & 0.0000002 & 0.0000009 \\ 0.0000314 & 0.0000013 & 0.0000002 & 0.0000001 & 0.0000001 & 0.0000009 \\ 0.0000070 & 0.0000009 & 0.0000010 & 0.0000009 & 0.0000008 & 0.0000047 \end{bmatrix}$$

According to this, an average O' matrix for the node *time* is expected to have 2.75% of its total frequency in the matrix element $O'_{2,1}$. If an individual O' matrix has significantly more than 2.75% of its total frequency in $O'_{2,1}$, this would indicate that the sub-sequence represented by that element ($L_1 \ldots KW$) has a higher-than-average probability of being a MWE.

3.6 Calculating Scores

A distinctive feature of the proposed algorithm is that a separate O and a separate E, and consequently a separate score matrix S is generated for each of the N items in the input data. This allows the algorithm to *locally* select only those sub-sequences that have the highest probability of being a MWE, thus preventing the remaining sub-sequences from 'contaminating' the statistics. Considering that most existing methods indiscriminately generate all possible sub-sequences of a given ngram, the proposed method ensures a dramatic[10] reduction in the amount of data that will have to be considered during score-aggregation and ranking.

[7] When $m=W_L$ and/or $n=W_R$ (i.e. along the bottom and right edges of the matrix), the probabilities of not observing L_{m+1} and R_{n+1} are undefined, and are thus assumed to be 1.0.

[8] $p(KW)$ can be omitted because it is by definition equal to 1.0 (all ngrams contain the node KW in the middle).

[9] Unlike the earlier examples, this example uses a window size of five on both sides. For ease of presentation, the matrix has been normalized by dividing it by the sum of its elements.

[10] A (5+1)×(5+1)=36-fold reduction for a typical window-size of 5 on both sides, assuming the algorithm selects a single top-performing candidate from each score matrix.

As mentioned in Section 3.5.1, S is calculated by comparing O' to either A or E. In the former case, S is simply equal to O'/A. In the latter case:

$$S = \frac{\log_2(O' + 1)}{\log_2(E + a)}$$

where a is a constant correction factor to avoid logarithms of zero (and one of the parameters in the experiment in Section 4).

A possible modification to the score matrix is *length adjustment*, where every element of S is divided by the length of the sub-sequence represented by that element. Length adjustment is another parameter in the experiment described in Section 4.

3.7 Selecting Candidates

Having obtained N score matrices for the N concordance lines, the next step is to select the best MWE candidate(s) that each concordance line will forward to the score aggregation and ranking stage. Two parameters relevant at this point are c, the number of candidates to be selected from each score matrix, and t, the minimum score required for being selected. In formal terms, the set of candidates consists of the c ngrams whose score in S is equal to or greater than t. If c=3 and t=1.5, for instance, three sub-sequences with the highest scores will be selected, and those with a score of 1.5 or higher will be forwarded to the score aggregation stage.

3.8 Score Aggregation and Candidate-Ranking

The next step is to aggregate the scores of the candidates selected in the previous step. Three methods will be tested for this purpose. In the first method named '*add-one*', the aggregate score of a MWE candidate is incremented by one every time the score-selection algorithm selects it. In the second one named '*add-score*', aggregate score is incremented by the candidate's score in S every time it is selected. In the third one named '*max*', aggregate score is equal to the highest score a candidate obtains in any of the score matrices that select it.

The result of this final step is a score-ranked list of MWE candidates. Top thirty candidates generated by the algorithm for the English word *time* and the Turkish word *zaman*, 'time', are given in Table 2, for N=50,000, and using *Method A* described in Section 4.3.

Rank	English	Turkish
1	*at the same time*	*son zamanlarda*
2	*from time to time*	*her zamanki gibi*
3	*for the first time*	*o zaman*
4	*at the time*	*uzun zamandır*
5	*this time*	*-dıkları zaman*
6	*for a long time*	*kimi zaman*
7	*over time*	*bu zamana kadar*
8	*at that time*	*o zamana kadar*
9	*at this time*	*bir zamanlar*
10	*for the first time in*	*her zamankinden daha*
11	*all the time*	*işte o zaman*
12	*most of the time*	*ne zaman*
13	*a lot of time*	*hiç bir zaman*
14	*at the time of the*	*-e baktığımız zaman*
15	*at a time*	*zaman*
16	*at any time*	*her zaman olduğu gibi*
17	*for some time*	*istediği zaman*
18	*in time*	*-masının zaman*
19	*in real time*	*gerçek zamanlı*
20	*at the time of*	*olduğu zaman*
21	*it is time to*	*her zaman*
22	*of time*	*kısa zaman*
23	*during this time*	*dediği zaman*
24	*at a time when*	*uzun zamandan beri*
25	*every time*	*ne kadar zaman*
26	*of all time*	*ilerleyen zamanlarda*
27	*the time*	*baktığın zaman*
28	*and at the same time*	*o zamandan beri*
29	*for the time being*	*zaman diliminde*
30	*at the right time*	*-mak için zaman*

Table 2. Top-30 candidates for *time* and *zaman*, 'time'

4. Evaluation

4.1 General

The standard approach to evaluating an information extraction system is to report both precision and recall, but this is not a straightforward task in a MWE extraction context. The main problem is that a gold standard against which to compare the results is difficult to define and obtain. One could use an existing resource like a machine-readable dictionary or a wordnet (Schone and Jurafsky, 2001), or a database specifically designed to evaluate MWE extraction systems (Kumova-Metin and Taze, 2017). But such resources are not available for all languages, and their coverage of MWEs is far from complete. Alternatively, one could use what Constant et al. (2017) refer to as *post hoc human judgment*, where each entry in a score-ranked candidate list is manually marked either as a MWE or a non-MWE by one or more experts (p. 853).

The second question is whether to report both precision and recall, or just precision. Most authors have chosen the former alternative (Smadja, 1993; Evert and Krenn, 2001; Eryiğit et al., 2015; Taşçıoğlu and Kumova-Metin, 2021), although several others report only precision (Shimohata, Sugio, and Nagata, 1997; Zhai, 1997; Frantzi, Ananiadou, and Mima, 2000; Dias, 2003). Reporting recall assumes that the researcher has access to the set of all MWEs in a language (or at least the set of all MWEs in the sample used in the study), while reporting precision involves the more reasonable assumption that it is possible to know whether or not a given sequence is a MWE.

This study will refrain from reporting recall. This is because the number of MWEs one finds in a corpus is closely linked to how broadly one chooses to define phraseology. MWE extraction has a relatively short history, and the true extent of the phraseological tendency in human languages is still not sufficiently explored. In other words, we cannot safely assume that we know "the set of all MWEs", or even what it means to know such a thing. It thus seems to be more appropriate to initially adopt a broad definition of phraseology, and then reduce its scope to the extent required by the data.

The 'broad definition of phraseology' adopted in this paper uses the following settings for the six parameters proposed by Gries (2008, p. 4):

i. a MWE may consist of roots or affixes, but must contain at least one lexically specified element;
ii. a MWE must have at least two elements, and cross at least one word boundary (no upper limit to the number of elements);
iii. the observed frequency of a MWE must be higher than its expected frequency;
iv. the elements of a MWE may not be interrupted by other elements (i.e. continuous MWEs only);
v. MWEs may exhibit lexical, syntactic and morphological variability;
vi. a MWE must constitute a semantic unit but does not have to be semantically non-compositional.

The design of the algorithm and the nodes selected already make sure that MWE candidates comply with (i), (ii) and (iii). So, the expert only has to focus on (iv), according to which *have a good time* is a MWE but *have an unexpectedly and unbelievably good time* is not; on (v), according to which *spend quality time* and *spent quality time* are both valid MWEs; and on (vi), according to which *time limit* is a MWE but *time by* is not (semantic unity required), and both *time and again* and *time and date* are MWEs (semantic non-compositionality allowed but not required).

Using the above criteria, the expert marked 1672, 2132 and 1053 sequences as valid MWEs for the three node words selected in Section 4.2, respectively.[11] Although items marked as valid MWEs involve some redundancy (i.e. several variants of the same MWE marked separately), these numbers are still unexpectedly high, suggesting that the phraseological tendency in both English and Turkish is stronger than generally assumed, at least when a broad definition of phraseology is adopted. Existing MWE repositories for Turkish (Eryiğit, İlbay, and Can, 2011; Adalı et al., 2016; Kumova-Metin and Taze, 2017; Berk, Erden, and Güngör, 2018) contain 4,000-30,000 MWEs for the entire language. Thus, they cannot be used as a gold standard in a study that adopts a broad definition of phraseology, where a single word can have around one thousand MWEs.

The third question is how to calculate precision. One option is to report the number of true positives among the top 100 or 200 items on the ranked candidate list. Evert and Krenn (2001) criticize this approach, stating that evaluation results would then be based on a small and arbitrary subset of the candidates, which means that "results achieved by individual measures may very well be due to chance" (p. 2). Instead, they calculate precision at every point of the candidate list, which allows them to plot it as a curve (also see Zhai, 1997, p. 6). The precision curve has been adopted by several authors, and seems to have become a standard in the field (Schone and Jurafsky, 2001; Pecina, 2005; Kumova-Metin, 2016).

A final point is whether or not to use a baseline against which the algorithm's performance can be compared. The *naïve ngram* method is frequently used for this purpose. This consists of generating every possible sub-sequence of every ngram included in the study. The baseline is then created either by calculating the probability of a randomly selected sub-sequence being a MWE (Pecina, 2005), by sorting the sub-sequences in decreasing order of frequency and calculating one or more precision values for some portion of that sorted list (Wermter and Hahn, 2004), or both (Krenn and Evert, 2001). As noted by several researchers (Frantzi, Ananiadou, and Mima, 2000, p. 117; Krenn and Evert, 2001, Section 10; Wermter and Hahn, 2004, Section 4.1), the naïve ngram method performs surprisingly well despite its simplicity. Section 4.3 confirms this finding.

In light of the above discussion, this paper will evaluate the proposed algorithm by reporting precision only (using precision curves based on *post hoc* human judgment), by using the naïve ngram method as a baseline, and by designing an experiment that covers all possible combinations of the algorithm's parameters.

4.2 Experiment Design

The algorithm's performance will be evaluated in an experiment that uses various parameter settings. Throughout the discussion in Section 3, the following emerged as possible parameters:

- Observation matrix O can be used with or without nesting adjustment (Section 3.4);
- score matrix S can be calculated using either expected frequencies matrices (E) or the aggregate matrix (A) (Section 3.5);
- score matrix S can be used with or without length adjustment (Section 3.6);
- the correction factor a (Section 3.6) can have different values (2, 4 and 8 selected for experiment);
- different values can be used for c (Section 3.7) (1, 2 and 3 selected for experiment);
- different values can be used for t (Section 3.7) (0, 0.5, 1 and 2 selected for experiment);
- three methods are available for score aggregation (*add-one*, *add-score*, *max*) (Section 3.8)

Accordingly, there are 2×2×2×3×3×4×3=864 possible parameter combinations. The experiment will run the algorithm once for each of these combinations, and evaluate results.

Since the algorithm will be run with 864 different settings, the resulting unified lists contain a large number of candidates, which makes it impracticable to evaluate more than a few items. In view of this, only three items have been included in the experiment (see Section 5 for a discussion of this choice). Since the aim is to test Turkish and English, and MWE-rich and MWE-poor items, the selection consists of the words *time* (expected to be MWE-rich), *zaman*, 'time' (expected to be MWE-rich), and *literatür*, 'academic literature' (expected to be MWE-poor).

The MWE candidate lists for these items were manually annotated by the author (6,190 candidates for *time*, 17,236 candidates for *zaman*, and 10,305 candidates for *literatür*). To minimize bias, the 864 candidate lists generated by the algorithm and the candidate list generated by the naïve ngram method were combined, and the lines randomized.

[11] The manually marked gold-standard files for the three node words are available at https://github.com/melanuria/mwe_extractor/tree/main/data.

This ensured that the annotator had no way of knowing if a given candidate was generated by the algorithm or by the naïve ngram method. Even if the annotator somehow guesses that a candidate was generated by the algorithm, he/she cannot know which of the 864 versions generated it.

4.3 Experiment Results

The nodes *time* and *zaman* were included in the experiment because they refer to the same, very basic, concept in English and Turkish, and are thus expected to be a part of a large number of MWEs, while *literatür* was included for its highly-specialized meaning, expected to result in fewer MWEs. As expected, the two cases had two different best-performing parameter combinations (Table 3), and different precision profiles (Figures 1-4).

Parameter	*Method A*	*Method B*
nesting adjustment	yes	no
comparison method	E matrix	A matrix
length adjustment	none	none
correction factor (*a*)	2	2
number of candidates (*c*)	1	2
score threshold (*t*)	0	0
score aggregation method	add-one	add-one

Table 3. Two best-performing parameter combinations

The combination that performed best for *time* and *zaman* will be named *Method A*, and the one that performed best for *literatür Method B*. Figures 1-3 show the precision curves Method A generated for the three nodes, in each case for the top-1000 candidates. Figure 4 shows the precision curves Method B generated for *literatür*, again for the top-1000 candidates. A dashed line shows the precision of the naïve ngram method, a solid line the precision of the best parameter combination, and thin grey lines the precisions of the remaining 863 combinations.

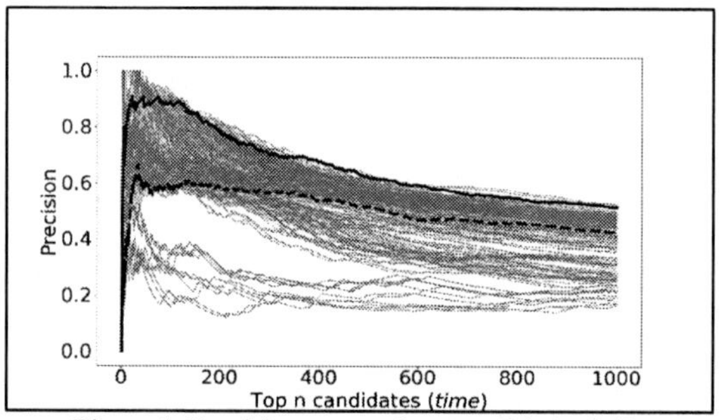

Figure 1. Precision curves for *time* (Method A)

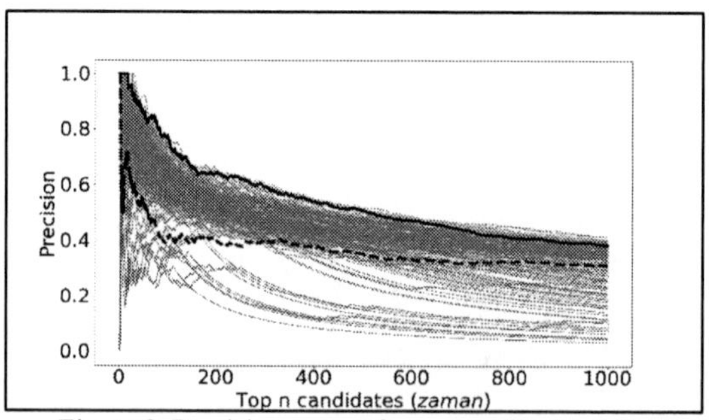

Figure 2. Precision curves for *zaman* (Method A)

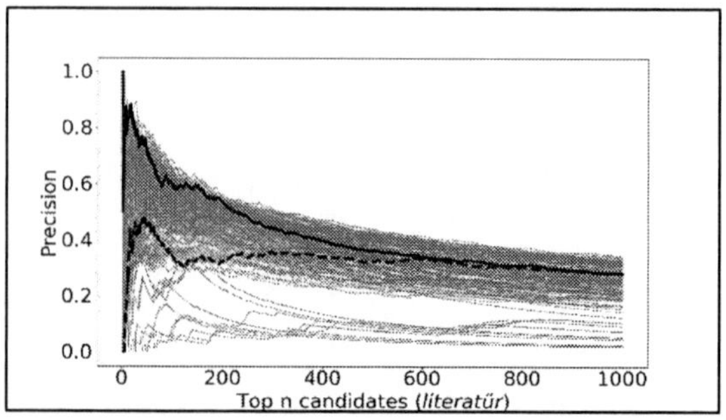

Figure 3. Precision curves for *literatür* (Method A)

The performance of the naïve ngram method confirms findings in the literature. Despite its extreme simplicity, it provides 50-60% precision for the first few hundred items, and 30-40% at n=1000, regardless of the node-word used.

The proposed algorithm gives promising results, especially for the top few hundred items of the candidate lists. For all three nodes, Method A generates top-50 precision values between 0.71 and 0.88, top-100 precision values between 0.60 and 0.88, and top-200 precision values between 0.54 and 0.78. Thus, in applications where a minimum precision of around 0.70 is acceptable and only the most prominent 50 or so MWEs of a word are required, Method A can be used without post-processing. In applications that require larger and more precise MWE lists, the same method can be used to obtain more than 100 MWEs per word, with the manual effort of reviewing the top 150-200 candidates. When the algorithm is used to process, say, the most frequent 20,000 words of a language, the resulting MWE lexicon would probably contain more than one million entries, even after accounting for redundancies.

For the MWE-rich items *time* and *zaman*, Method A consistently performs 20-35 percentage points above the baseline up to n=200, and retains a 10-point lead even at n=1000. For the MWE-poor *literatür*, however, Method A falls towards the baseline more quickly, finally converging with it at around n=600 (Figure 3). In contrast, Method B performs consistently above baseline for this node word, even at n=1000 (Figure 4).

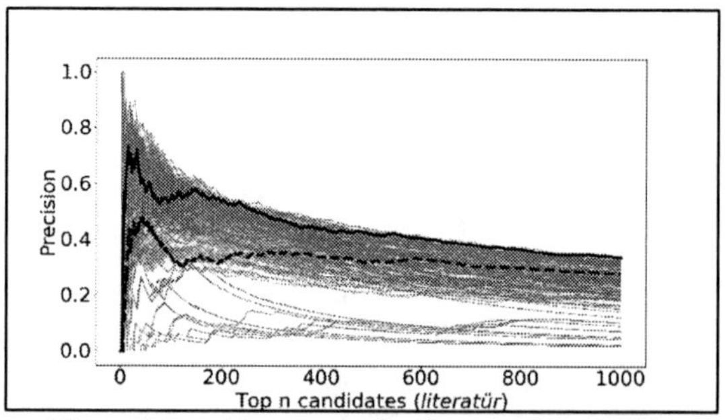

Figure 4. Precision curves for *literatür* (Method B)

Although additional evaluation data is required to reach statistically meaningful conclusions, existing results suggest that Method A provides an efficient method for automatically extracting the phraseology of relatively more frequent and general-purpose words, and/or extracting the most prominent MWEs of each word, while Method B can be used to extract the phraseology of relatively less frequent words with a more specialized meaning, and/or to obtain higher precision at the bottom of the candidate lists.

5. Conclusion

This paper proposed and evaluated an algorithm for automatically extracting MWEs from a corpus. Initial results show that it works equally well for two typologically different languages, English and Turkish.

The algorithm uses a *co-selection matrix* that gradually adds elements to the left and right contexts of a starting element (the node), and works by detecting the frequency anomalies that occur at the starting and ending points of a MWE. It is in this regard conceptually similar to a family of existing algorithms including the *neighbour-selectivity index* algorithm by Choueka et al. (1983), the *Xtract* algorithm by Smadja (1993), and the *LocalMaxs* algorithm by da Silva and Lopes (1999). The most important difference between the proposed algorithm and these earlier algorithms is that the proposed algorithm is node-based, knowledge-poor and computationally efficient. Another important difference is that it can be used to for both *extraction* and *identification*, the latter being "the process of automatically annotating MWE tokens in running text by associating them with known MWE types" (Constant et al., 2017). This is because the algorithm generates matrices for individual input sequences, and can thus determine the top-performing sub-sequences of any sequence entered by the user.

The algorithm has certain properties that address some of the recurring issues in MWE extraction (Section 2). First, it avoids using association measures, which are generally limited to detecting the association between two items. This means that the algorithm can extract sequences of arbitrary length, as long as length does not exceed window size. Second, it solves the frequency sensitivity problem to a certain extent in that the final ranking strictly follows the overall frequency order of the relevant candidates, which means that low-frequency items are not disproportionately pushed to the top of the list, and vice versa. Third, it avoids the nesting problem by applying the adjustment described in Section 3.4, and also by selecting a user-defined number of top-performing sub-sequences from a given ngram and ignoring all remaining sub-sequences. Fourth, it achieves a relatively high precision although it does not require morpho-syntactic patterns or other linguistics filters. In this sense, the algorithm seems to refute Frantzi and Ananiadou (1999), who claim that "the statistical information that is available, without any linguistic filtering, is not enough to produce useful results" (p. 147), and also Wermter and Hahn (2006), who claim that "purely statistics-based measures reveal virtually no difference compared with frequency of occurrence counts, while linguistically more informed metrics do reveal such a marked difference" (p. 785).

The present version of the algorithm also has certain limitations. First, it does not deal with certain types of MWE *variability*, a main challenge in MWE processing (Constant et al., 2017, p. 848). *Morphosyntactic variability* has already been dealt with to some extent (Section 3.2). In contrast, it does not seem easy to generalize the algorithm to deal with *positional variability*, where the order of the elements changes (e.g. *agreement signed by X* vs. *X signed an agreement*).

Second, the algorithm cannot extract discontinuous MWEs, another main challenge in MWE processing (Constant et al., 2017, p. 848). Future work could focus on this limitation as well. One promising avenue is to extend the algorithm to *phrase frames* ("ngrams with one variable slot") and PoS-grams ("a string of part-of-speech categories") (Stubbs, 2007, pp. 90-1). This might be achieved by manipulating the co-selection matrices such that they contain a mixture of lexical items and POS tags, and by treating certain matrix rows and/or columns as *slots* that accept only certain lexical items that have the same part-of-speech or belong to the same semantic class, or only certain affixes that belong to the same paradigm. Another idea would be to combine the method with knowledge-rich pre- or post-processing steps to improve precision.

Third, the algorithm has been evaluated on three words only, and this limits the validity of the results reported in Section 4. The total annotator time available could be allocated to increase (a) the number of experiment parameters tested, (b) the number of words tested, or (c) the number of candidates per word. This being an initial report on the proposed algorithm, it seemed more reasonable to maximize (a) and (c) at the expense of (b), i.e. to test a few candidate lists thoroughly (n=1000) for all possible combinations of the algorithm's parameters. Future work should focus on increasing (b) without compromising (a) or (c), and also increasing the number of reviewers and adding inter-judge agreement to the picture.

The original aim of this study was to design an algorithm to extract Turkish MWEs of arbitrary length. This was partially in response to Biber (2009), who stated that research was required to document sequences that are longer than two words, and asked "how are formulaic expressions realized in other languages; for example, in morphology-rich languages like Finnish or Turkish?" Biber thinks that "different linguistic devices will be required to realize formulaic expressions in these languages" and that "it is not even clear that formulaic language will be equally important in all languages" (p. 301).

The proposed algorithm focuses on three of the more superficial and quantifiable properties of MWEs: (a) A MWE crosses at least one word boundary; (b) a MWE is a sequence of co-selected linguistic elements that function as a single semantic unit; and (c) the elements of a MWE co-occur more frequently than expected. The fact that such a linguistically impoverished algorithm works equally well for English and Turkish suggests that the essential characteristics of the phraseologies of typologically different languages might not be as divergent as Biber thought. Moreover, the fact that 50,000 concordance lines can produce more than one thousand MWE types containing the same word suggests that formulaic language might very well be "equally important in all languages", and probably more important than generally assumed.

6. Bibliographical References

Adalı, K., Dinç, T., Gökırmak, M., and Eryiğit, G. (2016). Comprehensive annotation of multiword expressions for Turkish. *Proceedings of TurCLing*, 60–66.

Aires, J., Lopes, G., and Silva, J. F. (2008). Efficient multi-word expressions extractor using suffix arrays and related structures. *Proceedings of the 2nd ACM Workshop on Improving Non English Web Searching*, 1–8.

Al-Haj, H., and Wintner, S. (2010). Identifying multi-word expressions by leveraging morphological and syntactic idiosyncrasy. *Proceedings of the 23rd International conference on Computational Linguistics*, 10–18.

Baldwin, T., and Kim, S. N. (2010). Multiword Expressions. In N. Indurkhya and F. J. Damerau (Eds.), *Handbook of Natural Language Processing* (Second Edition, pp. 267–292). CRC Press.

Banerjee, S., and Pedersen, T. (2003). The design, implementation, and use of the Ngram statistics package. *Lecture Notes in Computer Science*, 2588, 370–381.

Berk, G., Erden, B., and Güngör, T. (2018). Turkish verbal multiword expressions corpus. *26th Signal Processing and Communications Applications Conference (SIU)*, 1–4.

Biber, D. (2009). A corpus-driven approach to formulaic language in English: Multi-word patterns in speech and writing. *International Journal of Corpus Linguistics*, 14(3), 275–311.

Calzolari, N., Fillmore, C. J., Grishman, R., Ide, N., Lenci, A., MacLeod, C., and Zampolli, A. (2002). Towards Best Practice for Multiword Expressions in Computational Lexicons. *LREC 2002*.

Cheng, W., Greaves, C., Sinclair, J. M., and Warren, M. (2009). Uncovering the extent of the phraseological tendency: Towards a systematic analysis of concgrams. *Applied Linguistics*, 30(2), 236–252.

Choueka, Y., Klein, S. T., and Neuwitz, E. (1983). Automatic retrieval of frequent idiomatic and collocational expressions in a large corpus. *Journal for Literary and Linguistic Computing*, 4(1), 34–38.

Church, K. W., Gale, W. A., Hanks, P., and Hindle, D. (1991). Using Statistics in Lexical Analysis. *Lexical Acquisition: Exploiting On-Line Resources to Build a Lexicon*, January 1991, 115–164.

Constant, M., Eryiğit, G., Monti, J., Plas, L. van der, Ramisch, C., Rosner, M., and Todirascu, A. (2017). Multiword Expression Processing: A Survey. *Computational Linguistics*, 43(4), 837–892.

Croft, W., and Cruse, D. A. (2004). *Cognitive Linguistics*.

Çöltekin, Ç. (2010). A freely available morphological analyzer for Turkish. In *Proceedings of the Seventh International Conference on Language Resources and Evaluation (LREC'10)*.

Da Silva, J. F., and Lopes, G. P. (1999). A local maxima method and a fair dispersion normalization for extracting multi-word units from corpora. *Sixth Meeting on Mathematics of Language*, 369–381.

Da Silva, J. F., Dias, G., Guilloré, S., and Lopes, J. G. P. (1999). Using LocalMaxs algorithm for the extraction of contiguous and non-contiguous multiword lexical units. *Lecture Notes in Computer Science*, 1695, 113–132.

Daille, B. (1994). Study and implementation of combined techniques for automatic extraction of terminology. *The balancing act: Combining symbolic and statistical approaches to language*.

De Cruys, T. (2011). Two multivariate generalizations of pointwise mutual information. *Proceedings of the Workshop on Distributional Semantics and Compositionality*, 16–20.

Dias, G. (2003). Multiword unit hybrid extraction. *Proceedings of the ACL 2003 Workshop on Multiword Expressions: Analysis, Acquisition and Treatment*, 41–48.

Dunn, J. (2017). Computational learning of construction grammars. *Language and Cognition*, 9(2), 254–292.

Dunn, J. (2018). Multi-unit association measures : Moving beyond pairs of words. *International Journal of Corpus Linguistics*, 23(2), 183–215.

Erman, B., and Warren, B. (2000). The idiom principle and the open choice principle. *Text*, 20(1), 29–62.

Eryiğit, G., Adalı, K., Torunoğlu-Selamet, D., Sulubacak, U., and Pamay, T. (2015). Annotation and extraction of multiword expressions in Turkish treebanks. *Proceedings of the 11th Workshop on Multiword Expressions*, 70–76.

Eryiğit, G., İlbay, T., and Can, O. A. (2011). Multiword Expressions in Statistical Dependency Parsing. *Proceedings of the 2nd Workshop on Statistical Parsing of Morphologically-Rich Languages (SPMRL 2011)*, 45–55.

Evert, S., and Krenn, B. (2001). Methods for the qualitative evaluation of lexical association measures. *Proceedings of the 39th Annual Meeting of the Association for Computational Linguistics*, 188–195.

Frantzi, K. T., and Ananiadou, S. (1999). The C-value/NC-value domain-independent method for multi-word term extraction. *Journal of Natural Language Processing*, 6(3), 145–179.

Frantzi, K., Ananiadou, S., and Mima, H. (2000). Automatic recognition of multi-word terms:. the c-value/nc-value method. *International Journal on Digital Libraries*, 3(2), 115–130.

Grant, L., and Bauer, L. (2004). Criteria for Re-defining Idioms: Are We Barking Up the Wrong Tree? *Applied Linguistics*, 25(1), 38–61.

Gries, S. T. (2008). Phraseology and linguistic theory: A brief survey. In *Phraseology: An interdisciplinary perspective* (pp. 3–25).

Gries, S. T. (2010). Corpus linguistics and theoretical linguistics: A love--hate relationship? Not necessarily.... *International Journal of Corpus Linguistics*, 15(3), 327–343.

Güngör, O., Güngör, T., and Üsküdarlı, S. (2019). The effect of morphology in named entity recognition with sequence tagging. *Natural Language Engineering*, 25(1), 147-169.

Hoang, H. H., Kim, S. N., and Kan, M.-Y. (2009). A Re-examination of Lexical Association Measures. *Proceedings of the Workshop on Multiword Expressions: Identification, Interpretation, Disambiguation, Applications*, 31–39.

Jackendoff, R. (1997). *The Architecture of the Language Faculty*. MIT Press.

Justeson, J. S., and Katz, S. M. (1995). Technical terminology: some linguistic properties and an algorithm for identification in text. *Natural Language Engineering*, 1(1), 9–27.

Kazkılınç, S. (2012). *Türkçe Metinlerin Etiketlenmesi* [Master's Thesis, Istanbul Technical University].

Keßelmeier, K., Kiss, T., Müller, A., Roch, C., Stadtfeld, T., and Strunk, J. (2009). Mining for Preposition-Noun Constructions in German. *Workshop on Extracting and Using Constructions in Natural Language Processing*.

Kilgarriff, A., and Tugwell, D. (2001). Word sketch: Extraction and display of significant collocations for lexicography.

Kita, K., Kato, Y., Omoto, T., and Yano, Y. (1994). A comparative study of automatic extraction of collocations from corpora: Mutual information vs. cost criteria. *Journal of Natural Language Processing*, 1(1), 21–33.

Kjellmer, G. (1987). Aspects of English collocations. In *Corpus linguistics and beyond* (pp. 133-140). Brill.

Krenn, B., Evert, S., and others. (2001). Can we do better than frequency? A case study on extracting PP-verb collocations. *Proceedings of the ACL Workshop on Collocations*, 39, 46.

Kumova-Metin, S., and Karaoğlan, B. (2010). Collocation extraction in Turkish texts using statistical methods. *International Conference on Natural Language Processing*, 238–249.

Kumova-Metin, S., and Taze, M. (2017). A procedure to build multiword expression data set. *2nd International Conference on Computer and Communication Systems*, 46–49.

Kumova-Metin, S. (2016). Neighbour unpredictability measure in multiword expression extraction. *Comput. Syst. Sci. Eng.*, 31, 209–221.

Küçük, D., and Yazıcı, A. (2009). Named entity recognition experiments on Turkish texts. In *International Conference on Flexible Query Answering Systems* (pp. 524-535). Springer.

Lossio-Ventura, J. A., Jonquet, C., Roche, M., and Teisseire, M. (2014). Yet another ranking function for automatic multiword term extraction. *International Conference on Natural Language Processing*, 52–64.

Martin, W. J., Al, B. P., and Van Sterkenburg, P. J. (1983). On the processing of a text corpus: From textual data to lexicographical information. *Lexicography: Principles and practice*, 77-87.

Mason, O. J. (2006). *The Automatic Extraction of Linguistic Information from Text Corpora* [PhD Thesis, Birmingham University].

Maziarz, M., Szpakowicz, S., and Piasecki, M. (2015). A Procedural Definition of Multi-word Lexical Units. *Proceedings of the International Conference-Recent Advances in Natural Language Processing*, 427–435.

Mel'čuk, I. (1998). Collocations and lexical functions. *Phraseology: Theory, Analysis, and Applications*, 23–53.

Mel'čuk, I. (2006). Explanatory combinatorial dictionary. *Open Problems in Linguistics and Lexicography*, 225–355.

Moon, R. (1998). *Fixed Expressions and Idioms in English*.

Moon, R. (2008). Dictionaries and collocation. In S. Granger and F. Meunier (Eds.), *Phraseology: An interdisciplinary perspective*.

Nivre, J. (2021). Principles of the UD Annotation Framework. *Dagstuhl Seminar*, 98–99.

O'Donnell, M. B. (2011). The adjusted frequency list: A method to produce cluster-sensitive frequency lists. *ICAME Journal*, 35, 135–170.

Oflazer, K. (2014). Turkish and its challenges for language processing. *Language Resources and Evaluation*, 48(4), 639–653.

Passaro, L. C., and Lenci, A. (2016). Extracting terms with EXTra. *Computerised and Corpus-Based Approaches to Phraseology: Monolingual and Multilingual Perspectives*, 188–196.

Pawley, A., and Syder, F. H. (1983). Two puzzles for linguistic theory: Nativelike selection and nativelike fluency. In *Language and Communication* (pp. 203–239). Routledge.

Pearce, D. (2001). Synonymy in collocation extraction. *Proceedings of the Workshop on WordNet and Other Lexical Resources, Second Meeting of the North American Chapter of the Association for Computational Linguistics*, 41–46.

Pecina, P. (2005). An extensive empirical study of collocation extraction methods. *Proceedings of the ACL Student Research Workshop*, 13–18.

Piao, S. S. L., Rayson, P., Archer, D., Wilson, A., and McEnery, T. (2003). Extracting multiword expressions with a semantic tagger. *Proceedings of the ACL 2003 Workshop on Multiword Expressions: Analysis, Acquisition and Treatment*, Volume 18, 49–56.

Qi, P., Zhang, Y., Zhang, Y., Bolton, J., and Manning, C. D. (2020). Stanza: A Python Natural Language Processing Toolkit for Many Human Languages. *arXiv preprint arXiv:2003.07082*.

Ramisch, C., Villavicencio, A., Moura, L., and Idiart, M. (2008). Picking them up and figuring them out: Verb-particle constructions, noise and idiomaticity. *CoNLL 2008: Proceedings of the Twelfth Conference on Computational Natural Language Learning*, 49–56.

Ramisch, C., Villavicencio, A., and Boitet, C. (2010). Mwetoolkit: A framework for multiword expression identification. *Proceedings of the 7th International Conference on Language Resources and Evaluation, LREC 2010*, 662–669.

Ren, Z., Lü, Y., Cao, J., Liu, Q., and Huang, Y. (2009). Improving Statistical Machine Translation Using Domain Bilingual Multiword Expressions. *Proceedings of the 2009 Workshop on Multiword Expressions, ACL-IJCNLP 2009*, 47–54.

Sag, I. A., Baldwin, T., Bond, F., Copestake, A., and Flickinger, D. (2002). Multiword expressions: A pain in the neck for NLP. *International Conference on Intelligent Text Processing and Computational Linguistics*, 1–15.

Schmitt, N., and Carter, R. (2004). Formulaic sequences in action. *Formulaic Sequences: Acquisition, Processing and Use*, 1–22.

Schone, P., and Jurafsky, D. (2001). Is knowledge-free induction of multiword unit dictionary headwords a solved problem? *Proceedings of the 2001 Conference on Empirical Methods in Natural Language Processing*.

Shimohata, S., Sugio, T., and Nagata, J. (1997, July). Retrieving collocations by co-occurrences and word order constraints. In *35th Annual Meeting of the Association for Computational Linguistics and 8th Conference of the European Chapter of the Association for Computational Linguistics* (pp. 476-481).

Shwartz, V., and Dagan, I. (2019). Still a pain in the neck: Evaluating text representations on lexical composition. *Transactions of the Association for Computational Linguistics*, 7, 403-419.

Siepmann, D. (2005). Collocation, colligation and encoding dictionaries. Part I: Lexicological aspects. *International Journal of Lexicography*, 18(4), 409–443.

Sinclair, J. (2004). The search for units of meaning. In *Trust the Text : Language, Corpus and Discourse*.

Sinclair, J. M. (2008). The phrase, the whole phrase, and nothing but the phrase. In S. Granger and F. Meunier (Eds.), *Phraseology: An interdisciplinary perspective*.

Smadja, F. A. (1989). Lexical co-occurrence: The missing link. *Literary and Linguistic Computing*, 4(3), 163–168.

Smadja, F. (1993). Retrieving Collocations from Text: Xtract. *Computational Linguistics*, 19(1), 143.

Straka, M., and Straková, J. (2017). Tokenizing, POS Tagging, Lemmatizing and Parsing UD 2.0 with UDPipe. *Proceedings of the CoNLL 2017 Shared Task: Multilingual Parsing from Raw Text to Universal Dependencies*, 88–99.

Stubbs, M. (2002). Two quantitative methods of studying phraseology in English. *International Journal of Corpus Linguistics*, 7(2), 215–244.

Stubbs, M. (2007). An example of frequent English phraseology: distributions, structures and functions. In *Corpus linguistics 25 years on* (pp. 87–105). Brill Rodopi.

Şeker, G. A., and Eryiğit, G. (2012). Initial explorations on using CRFs for Turkish named entity recognition. In *Proceedings of COLING 2012* (pp. 2459-2474).

Taşçıoğlu, T., and Kumova-Metin, S. (2021, June). Detection of Multiword Expressions with Word Vector Representations. In *2021 29th Signal Processing and Communications Applications Conference (SIU)* (pp. 1-4). IEEE.

Trijp, Remi van. (2018, September 12). *Fillmore's Dangerous Idea*. http://www.essaysinlinguistics.com /2018/09/12/fillmore/

Tür, G., Hakkani-Tür, D., and Oflazer, K. (2003). A statistical information extraction system for Turkish. *Natural Language Engineering*, 9(2), 181-210.

Uhrig, P., Evert, S., and Proisl, T. (2018). Collocation candidate extraction from dependency-annotated corpora: exploring differences across parsers and dependency annotation schemes. In *Lexical Collocation Analysis* (pp. 111–140). Springer.

Villavicencio, A., Bond, F., Korhonen, A., and McCarthy, D. (2005). Introduction to the special issue on multiword expressions: Having a crack at a hard nut. *Computer Speech and Language*, 19(4), 365–377.

Wahl, A., and Gries, S. T. (2020). Computational extraction of formulaic sequences from corpora. *Computational Phraseology*, 24, 83.

Wei, N., and Li, J. (2013). A new computing method for extracting contiguous phraseological sequences from academic text corpora. *International Journal of Corpus Linguistics*, 18(4), 506–535.

Wermter, J., and Hahn, U. (2004). Collocation extraction based on modifiability statistics. *COLING 2004: Proceedings of the 20th International Conference on Computational Linguistics*, 980–986.

Wermter, J., and Hahn, U. (2006). You can't beat frequency (unless you use linguistic knowledge)--a qualitative evaluation of association measures for collocation and term extraction. *Proceedings of the 21st International Conference on Computational Linguistics and 44th Annual Meeting of the Association for Computational Linguistics*, 785–792.

Wray, A., and Perkins, M. R. (2000). The functions of formulaic language: an integrated model. *Language and Communication*, 20(1), 1–28.

Wray, A. (2009). *Formulaic language and the lexicon*. Cambridge University Press.

Yeniterzi, R. (2011). Exploiting morphology in Turkish named entity recognition system. In *Proceedings of the ACL 2011 Student Session* (pp. 105-110).

Zhai, C. (1997). Exploiting context to identify lexical atoms--A statistical view of linguistic context. *arXiv preprint cmp-lg/9701001*.

Multi-word Lexical Units Recognition in WordNet

Marek Maziarz*, Ewa Rudnicka*, Łukasz Grabowski○

Wroclaw University of Science and Technology*, University of Opole○

Wybrzeże Wyspiańskiego 27, 50-370 Wrocław*, pl. Kopernika 11A, 45-040 Opole○

marek.maziarz@pwr.edu.pl, ewa.rudnicka@pwr.edu.pl, lukasz@uni.opole.pl

Abstract

WordNet is a state-of-the-art lexical resource used in many tasks in Natural Language Processing, also in multi-word expression (MWE) recognition. However, not all MWEs recorded in WordNet could be indisputably called lexicalised. Some of them are semantically compositional and show no signs of idiosyncrasy. This state of affairs affects all evaluation measures that use the list of all WordNet MWEs as a gold standard. We propose a method of distinguishing between lexicalised and non-lexicalised word combinations in WordNet, taking into account lexicality features, such as semantic compositionality, MWE length and translational criterion. Both a rule-based approach and a ridge logistic regression are applied, beating a random baseline in precision of singling out lexicalised MWEs, as well as in recall of ruling out cases of non-lexicalised MWEs.

Keywords: multi-word expressions, Princeton WordNet, lexicality, lexicography, semantic compositionality, sentence embeddings

1. Introduction

The paper takes as its focus the lexicality status of English multi-word expressions (henceforth MWEs) found in Princeton WordNet (PWN, Fellbaum 1998) as well as in its extension enWordNet (enWN), built by a team of bilingual linguists working within the plWordNet group (Rudnicka et al. 2015). Our goal is to devise a method that can be used to distinguish between lexicalized and non-lexicalized multi-word expressions.

The term *multi-word expression* needs clarification. Multi-word expressions are neither ordinary words, nor ordinary syntactic structures, they lie somewhere in-between (Siyanova-Chanturia et al., 2017). Sag et al. (2002) define multi-word expressions as "idiosyncratic interpretations that cross word boundaries (or spaces)". Apart from the frequently mentioned idiosyncrasy or idiomaticity, researchers also emphasise other aspects of MWE nature (Constant et. al., 2017). These include its statistically non-trivial co-occurrence patterns, their status of vocabulary units similar to single words (lexicology, semantics and grammarians' point of view), as well as their particularly baffling behaviour traces, such as syntactic discontiguity, semantic non-compositionality, form variability, and form ambiguity (Calzolari et al., 2002).

MWEs are a real challenge for Natural Language Processing, since their idiosyncratic properties may lead statistical approaches astray (Sag et al., 2002). Constant et al (2017) underline the need for manually validated MWE lexicons, of higher quality than automatically extracted lists. In this paper, we take a closer look at Princeton WordNet, one of the crucial lexical sources of MWEs for English. From a lexicographic perspective, there are a number of fully compositional MWEs in WordNet that can hardly be ascribed the status of a vocabulary unit or found in any existing dictionary. These are exemplified by *rich people* 'people who have possessions and wealth (considered as a group)' or *psychology department* 'the academic department responsible for teaching and research in psychology'. In the newest initiative on the expansion and correction of Princeton WordNet called the Open English WordNet, McCrae et al. (2020: 3) postulate not to add such fully compositional MWEs in the English WordNet. As an example, they give the MWE *French Army* whose meaning can be fully deducted from the meanings of its component words *French* and *army*, both already present in the WordNet.

A different category of synsets with compositional MWEs are the ones exemplified by *biological group* 'a group of plants or animals' or *animal group* 'a group of animals' which are more units of (language) taxonomy than of language itself. They help to organise wordnet structure building top level hierarchy, yet since their lexicality status is very much different from 'ordinary' synsets, they might be tagged as 'artificial synsets', as it is done, for instance, in GermaNet (Hamp & Feldweg, 1997) and plWordNet projects (Piasecki et al., 2009).

Still another group form synsets built of MWEs of the pattern *piece/article of*, such as *piece/article of furniture* (appearing in the same synset as *furniture*) with the gloss 'furnishings that make a room or other area ready for occupancy'. The lexicality status of such MWEs is also varied. Since WordNet is considered the gold standard for NLP-oriented lexicography (MCrae et al., 2019) and the list of WordNet MWEs is used in the MWE recognition task (Riedl & Biemann, 2016; Schneider et al., 2014), as well as for evaluative purposes in the MWE extraction process (Pearce, 2001; Farahmand et al., 2014), assessing the lexicality status of MWEs in WordNet is a task worth researching.

In this paper, we use the term MWE in a broader sense as a cover term for both free and set word combinations (Zgusta, 1971). For word combinations within language vocabulary we reserve the term *multi-word lexical units* (MWLUs). We assume that MWEs that function similarly to single-word lexical units should be called MWLUs and as such recorded in dictionaries or lexical databases. The remaining MWEs should be treated as non-lexicalised ones (non-MWLUs). In other words, we argue that all MWLUs are MWEs, yet the opposite is not always true, the approach taken by Maziarz et al. (in print).

Proceedings of the 18th Workshop on Multiword Expressions (MWE 2022) n@LREC2022, pages 49–54

In short, we compare a sample of PWN and enWN MWEs with several general-purpose English dictionaries. Shedding the burden of proof on dictionary editors, we consider MWLU those MWEs that appear in at least one of the dictionaries. Employing additional linguistic and lexicographic criteria, such as MWE length, its semantic compositionality or translational equivalent criterion (for details, see Sec. 2), we scrutinise their usefulness in the task of automatic recognition of lexicalized MWEs (MWLUs) (Sec. 3 and 4). Since the selected dictionaries contain general usage vocabulary, we believe that such a list of core lexicalised MWEs can be used in NLP for evaluative purposes in the MWE extraction task.[1]

2. Data set

In order to build a data set for our experiments, we applied a rule-based procedure aimed at extracting MWEs from PWN and enWN. For these purposes, MWEs were operationally defined as sequences of graphic words (Sag et al. 2002), separated by at least one space. To extract them, we first drew all PWN and enWN synsets containing such MWE lemmas and next built a dataset of MWE lexical units (LUs, that is lemma, POS, sense number triplets). An inspection of the obtained dataset has shown a number of proper names and specialist terms. We decided to remove them from the MWE dataset, since we focus on common nouns and general-usage vocabulary. Proper names were identified by the internal *Instance* relation and by the inter-lingual I-instance relation to plWordNet synsets. Biological taxonomy and chemistry terms were singled out on the basis of hyponymy relation to the following top synsets: {organism 1}, {biological group 1}, {chemical element 1} and {chemical 1}. After the filtering, we were left with 39,406 MWEs. Their part of speech (POS) statistics are given in Table 1.

	nouns	verbs	adjectives	adverbs
#	33713	4389	540	764
%	86%	11%	2%	1%

Table 1: POS statistics for the MWE dataset

Table 1 shows that most MWEs in the dataset are nouns (86%). Verbs make up for 11%, while adjectives and adverbs are scarce, with (2%) and (1%), respectively.

Now, to verify the lexicality of MWEs in our dataset we decided to consult general-purpose English dictionaries such as Collins[2], Longman[3], Oxford Lexico[4] and Merriam-Webster[5]. For these purposes, we drew a random sample of 200 MWEs from our dataset and looked them up in the reference dictionaries. Crucially, we paid close attention to MWE senses checking if the sense of an MWE in a dictionary matches its sense from PWN or enWN. MWEs that were recorded in at least one dictionary were considered MWLUs. The ones absent from the dictionaries were treated as non-lexicalised multi-word expressions and called non-MWLUs. The results of manual annotation are given in Table 2.

class	nouns	verbs	adject.	adverbs	sum
MWLU	114	9	0	1	124
nonMWLU	68	6	0	1	76
sum	183	15	0	2	200
%	92%	8%	0%	1%	100%

Table 2: POS and lexicality status statistics for a random 200 MWE sample

Table 2 shows that the distribution of POS in the 200 sample mirrors its distribution in the whole MWE dataset (cf. Tab. 1). As for the lexicality status, MWLUs overgrow non-MWLUs by almost a half.

Our ultimate goal was to come up with algorithms which would allow us to recognise MWLUs and non-MWLU in our dataset of 39k MWEs. To this end we applied both a rule-based approach and a statistical one. The 200 MWE sample was used to train a logistic classifier and to evaluate both approaches (Sections 3 and 4). We decided to use several features and automatically annotated with them both the small sample and the whole MWE dataset. The features were as follows:

- the presence of an inter-lingual *I*-synonymy link (Rudnicka et al., 2012) between a pair of Polish (plWordNet) - English (PWN or enWN) synsets (with the English one containing an MWE);
- the presence of an MWE lemma in a Polish-English conglomerate 'cascade' dictionary (Kędzia et al., 2013);
- the length of an MWE in terms of the number of its characters (excluding spaces) and spaces between component words;
- the cosine of an angle between an MPNet (Masked and Permuted Pre-trained Neural Network, Song et al., 2020) sentence embedding 768D vectors calculated separately for an MWE lemma itself and its WordNet gloss;
- the number of an MWE sense.

All of the above *lexicality* features were used in logistic regression, while the I-synonymy and cascade dictionary criteria were solely used in a rule-based approach.

The inter-lingual synonymy relation entails close correspondence in meanings and relation structures (Rudnicka et al., 2012). Our hypothesis is that English MWEs from synsets holding this relation are more likely to be lexicalised. The idea behind using a cascade dictionary is similar. The cascade dictionary is a collection of 12 Polish-English dictionaries and lexical resources arranged in a cascade with the most reliable on the top (Kędzia et al., 2013). It was sufficient to find an MWE in at least one of its 12 sub-dictionaries; we also used each separate dictionary as a predictor for regression (see. Sec. 4 below). Another feature - the length of an MWE is correlated with MWE's frequency in corpora.[6]

[1]Still, corpora do not contain all fixed expressions found in dictionaries and the frequency of such MWEs varies to a great extent (Svensén, 2009: 191).

[2] https://www.collinsdictionary.com/

[3] https://www.ldoceonline.com/

[4] https://www.lexico.com/

[5] https://www.merriam-webster.com/

[6] Indeed, taking SemCor 3.0 corpus (Mihalcea & Moldovan, 2001) and calculating frequency counts *f* for all MWE lexical

We assumed that longer MWEs are much rarer in usage than shorter ones. Semantic similarity between MWE's WordNet definition (gloss) and its lemma approximated semantic compositionality of the MWE (measured in the vector space using word embeddings and cosine similarity).[7] Semantically non-compositional MWEs were supposed to be defined with the use of words semantically more distant from MWE elements. The number of senses is correlated with the relative frequency of a given sense (when compared to other senses; more frequent senses are equipped with higher ranks).[8]

In Figure 1, we present descriptive statistics for five lexicality features (MWE length, MPNet cosine, I-synonymy criterion, cascade dictionary equivalent test and WordNet sense number) across our MWE sample. As shown, MWEs from dictionaries are shorter (Welch's test[9]: $t(123.14) = -4.66$, $p < .001$) and less semantically similar to their definitions (Welch's $t(160.85) = -2.20$, $p = .029$) than MWEs not found in the four reference dictionaries. MWLUs are also more frequently found in the cascade dictionary ("cascDict") than non-lexicalised MWEs (Pearson's chi-squared test: □$^2(1, N = 200) = 10.81$, $p = .001$), while the *I*-synonymy ("synonymy") criterion does not clearly determine class boundaries: 58% of nonMWLUs and 51% of MWLUs had their inter-lingual equivalent in plWN (□$^2 = 0.688$, $p = .407$).[10] Also, higher sense numbers ("senseNo") are characteristic for non-lexicalised MWEs: $t(123) = 2.31$, $p = .023$.

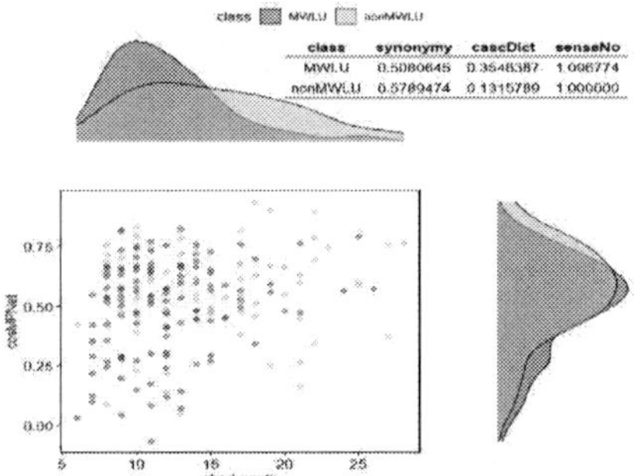

Figure 1: Dictionary-based MWE classes related to lemma length (charLength ~ MWE rarity) and similarity between an MWE definition and its lemma (cosMPNet ~ MWE semantic compositionality). The proportion of *I*-synonymy and cascade dictionary cases per class are shown in the top-right table. Abbreviations: "charLength" - the length of an MWE in characters; "cosMPNet" - cosine similarity of MPNet vectors calculated for MWE lemma and its enWN definition; "synonymy" - *I*-synonymy case; "cascDict" - MWE found in at least one of 12 cascade sub-dictionaries, "senseNo" - sense rank, i.e. the ordinal number of wordnet sense (aka *variant*).

3. Rule-based approach

We attempted to verify the validity of the inter-lingual equivalent criterion in distinguishing between MWLUs and non-MWLUs. We assumed that lexicalised MWEs should have *I*-synonymy and should be found in at least one out of 12 cascade sub-dictionaries. The rule-based procedure allowed to determine the MWLU class with high precision and low recall. In a one-tailed bootstrap percentile test (Tibshirani & Efron, 1993) for greater than zero difference the approach gained higher MWLU class precision than the uniform random baseline ($p = .027$). Also the non-MWLU class was successfully ruled out with 87% recall, clearly above the baseline ($p < .001$). On the other hand, the recall of the MWLU class was lower than the random baseline ($p < .001$). We also could not prove any difference between the rule-based model and the random baseline in terms of the non-MWLU class precision ($p = .17$).

200 MWE sample		real class		efficacy	
		MWLU	Non MWLU	P	R
rule-based	MWLU	32	10	**76%**	26%
	Non MWLU	92	66	42%	**87%**
random baseline		real class		efficacy	
		MWLU	Non MWLU	P	R
random class	MWLU	62	38	62%	**50%**
	Non MWLU	62	38	38%	50%

Table 3: Confusion matrix and efficacy of the rule-based approach. Symbols: P - precision; R - recall. Bolded values are significant at .95 confidence level in bootstrap testing

Figure 2 presents classes established using manual rules with regard to five lexicality features for the 200-MWE sample. In contrast to real classes (Fig. 1), the rules seem not to take into account neither MWEs' length (~ frequency) nor their semantic compositionality. Instead, they rely solely (quite successfully) on translational criteria.

All in all, from the initial sample of 39,406 English MWEs, we obtained 6,390 potential MWLUs with the estimated precision of 76%. To validate the result, we randomly selected 18 MWEs out of the prediction class of MWLUs. Only 2 MWEs were not found in the four reference English dictionaries, which yields a 90%

units we obtained the following values of MWE mean lengths $mL(f)$ (in characters): $mL(f = 1) = 11.1$, $mL(2) = 10.7$, $mL(3) = 10.4$, $mL(4) = 10.0$, $mL(f = 5+) = 9.8$. A similar law for simplex words is known as Zipf's law (Piantadosi et al., 2011).

[7] Pickard (2020), for instance, used the cosine similarity for the comparison between MWE lemma embedding vectors and their constituent word embeddings.

[8] For SemCor 3.0 and all lexical units (not only for MWEs) we obtained following values of mean frequency F per a given sense ordinal number $\#n$: $F(\#1) = 8.0$, $F(\#2) = 7.2$, $F(\#3) = 5.8$, $F(\#4+) = 5.2$. If we take into account only MWEs, we would get something unintuitive: $F_{MWE}(\#1) = 2.7$ and $F_{MWE}(\#2+) = 2.8$ (the difference is significant at 5% significance level in the *U* Mann-Whitney test).

[9] Welch's *t*-test for two samples (Delacre et al., 2017).

[10] This unexpected tendency can be due to the fact that I-synonymy is a synset-level relation and not a lexical unit one. Synsets are built of one, two or even more lexical units and the degree of interlingual correspondence between specific pairs of Polish-English LUs within a pair of Polish-English synsets linked by this relation can differ.

confidence interval for the precision in the 67-97% range.[11]

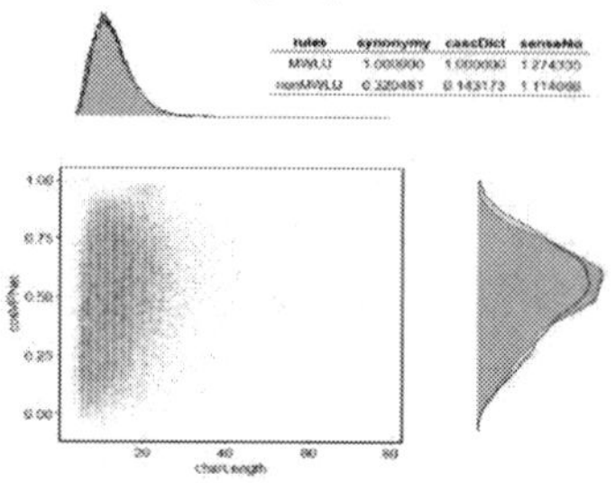

Figure 2: Classes obtained using manual rules with regard to lemma length (charLength ~ MWE rarity) and similarity between an MWE's definition and its lemma (cosMPNet ~ MWE semantic compositionality). Proportion of *I*-synonymy and cascade dictionary cases per class are shown in the top-right table. Abbreviations as in Figure 1.

4. Statistical approach

We used the same 200 MWE sample and took into consideration all calculated lexicality features. Then, ridge logistic regression was applied and precision and recall statistics were calculated in non-parametric .632 bootstrap cross-validation, with 1,000 repetitions (Efron, 1983; Efron & Tibshirani, 1997). Each time the training data set had to be balanced by resampling the smaller class of non-lexicalised MWEs with replacement. Table 4 presents the mean efficacy of the logistic regression approach. The confusion matrix was averaged from probabilities of each cell in 1,000 iterations.[12] The random baseline was obtained by assuming equal probabilities of both classes. In one-tailed test[13] the logistic model turned out to be better than the uniform distribution random baseline with regard to the precision of the MWLU class ($p < .001$), as well as the precision and the recall of the nonMWLU class ($p = .001$ and $p = .002$, respectively). The difference between the logistic model and the random baseline was insignificant, when we compared the recall of the MWLU class ($yp = .702$ in the test). The recall for the MWLU class was approximately twice as high as in the rule-based approach.

200 MWE sample		real class		efficacy	
		MWLU	Non MWLU	P	R
RLR class	MWLU	55.9	12.8	**83%**	45%
	Non MWLU	68.2	63.1	**49%**	**83%**
random baseline		real class		efficacy	
		MWLU	Non MWLU	P	R
rand. class	MWLU	62	38	62%	50%
	Non MWLU	62	38	38%	50%

Table 4: Mean confusion matrix and mean efficacy of the statistical approach. Symbols: P - precision, R - recall, RLR - ridge logistic regression, rand. - random. Bolded values are significant at .95 confidence level in bootstrap testing

We re-taught the model on the whole 200 MWE sample and used it to assess the lexicality of all MWEs in WordNet.[14] The sign of parameters of the regression function for the non-MWLU class is clearly visible in Figure 3. *I*-synonymy ("synonymy"), MWE length ("charLength"), MWE complexity ("noOfSpaces") and MPNet vectors cosine ("cosMPNet") are positively correlated with the confidence level of logistic regression and help increase the probability of ascribing non-lexicality status to an MWE, while sense variant number ("senseNo") and cascade dictionary criterion ("cascDict") decrease the probability (blue bars, "coeff"). MWE length in characters, cascade dictionary criterion and cosine similarity could be treated as the most prominent lexicality features in the regression model (Spearman's rho > 0.3).

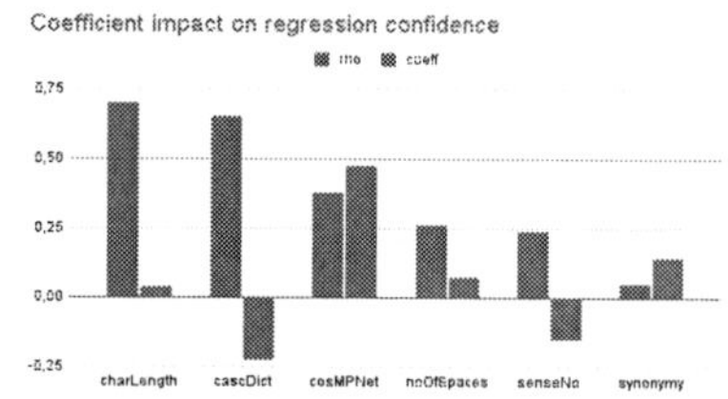

Figure 3: Relative impact of lexicality features on the logistic function for the "non-MWLU" prediction class. With blue bars we mark regression coefficients (both cascDict and senseNo are negatively correlated with the confidence measure). Lexicality features are ordered according to the value of their *absolute* correlation with the regression confidence (red bars).

Finally, 18,971 MWEs were labelled "MWLU" by the logistic model (48% of all 39,406 MWEs). Figure 4 shows descriptive statistics for five lexicality features including MWE length, its semantic compositionality, I-synonymy, cascade dictionary criterion and sense variant. The prediction class "MWLU", as compared to "non-MWLU" class, contained more frequent and less semantically

[11] These include 16 MWEs found in dictionaries: *acid precipitation, alkaline battery, computational linguistics, cross section, dialectical materialism, electronic paper, field-effect transistor, fire ship, knock over, lapis lazuli, melanocyte-stimulating hormone, safe sex, white paper, wind farm, wisdom tooth, yolk sac*; while two MWEs were not included in any of our reference dictionaries, namely *diplomatic mission* and *masonry heater*.

[12] From the equation

$$[1] \quad Pr_i(j) = \sum_{i=1}^{n}[0.632 \cdot Pr_i^{test}(j) + 0.368 \cdot Pr_i^{subst}(j)],$$

where $Pr_i(j)$ signifies the probability of the *j*-th cell in *i*-th repetition, the superscript ^{test} denotes the bootstrap out-of-bag testing sample, while ^{subst} refers to the bootstrap (unbalanced) training set substituted to the model taught on the very same (though balanced) sample (Efron, 1983).

[13] We calculated percentile intervals for differences between 0.632 bootstrap CV logistic regression results and random baseline estimates.

[14] More precisely speaking, those MWEs that were neither proper names, nor chemistry/biology terms.

compositional MWEs, which was intuitively expected. Also, cases of cascade sub-dictionaries were much more frequent in the "MWLU" class than in the class of "non-MWLU". *I*-synonymy, however, was more frequently found in the "non-MWLU" class. Prominent senses (with higher ranks/ lower sense ordinal numbers) occurred more frequently across the non-lexicalised class of MWEs.

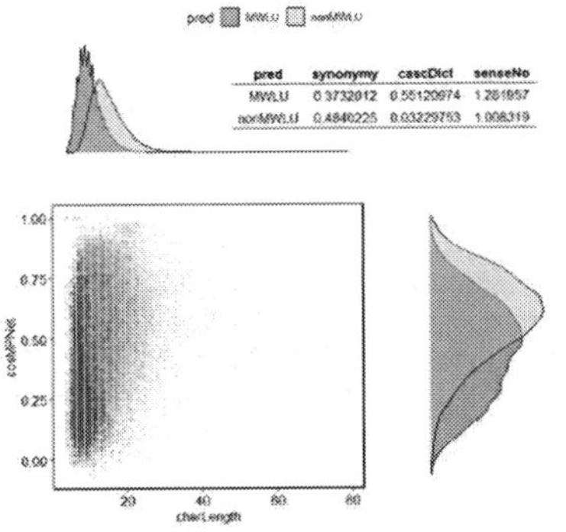

Figure 4: Logistic regression prediction classes with regard to lemma length (charLength ~ MWE rarity) and similarity between an MWE's definition and its lemma (cosMPNet ~ MWE semantic compositionality). Proportion of *I*-synonymy and cascade dictionary cases per class is shown in the top-right table. Abbreviations as in Figure 1

To validate the precision of the "MWLU" class assignments, we randomly drew 50 MWEs from the 19k "MWLU" prediction class. Only 9 word combinations were not found in any of the four reference English dictionaries, which means a 95% confidence interval for the precision in the range of 71-90%.[15] This result is in accordance with the .632 bootstrap CV precision estimate ($P = 83\%$).

We publish datasets used in this research under the CC BY-SA 4.0 licence on GitHub (https://github.com/MarekMaziarz/Multi-word-lexical-units).

[15]These include 41 MWEs found in dictionaries: *acid precipitation, alkaline battery, anonymous ftp, Ashcan school, Babinski sign, bell ringing, blank out, cerebral peduncle, chin wag, cloven foot, come to life, cross section, double up, dust mop, easy chair, electronic paper, field-effect transistor, fire ship, fish cake, food allergy, frig around, go on, Gram stain, ice tongs, knock over, lapis lazuli, light up, on one hand, OTC stock, peel off, post exchange, procrustean bed, rat cheese, safe sex, squad room, tank suit, wet suit, white paper, wind farm, wisdom tooth, yolk sac*; 9 MWEs were not spotted in any of our four dictionaries, i.e. *butt against, chip at, dummy up, iron trap, masonry heater, pack of cards, soaking up, vena pylorica* and *vulvar slit.* Please note that validation samples drawn for both rule-based and statistical approaches partially overlapped (cf. footnote 11).

5. Conclusions

In this study, we undertook an attempt at extracting the subset of multi-word lexical units (MWLUs) from PWN and its extension, enWordNet, by using two different approaches. In a rule-based approach and logistic regression, we were able to filter out many non-lexicalised MWEs with high precision (> 70%). The completeness of both approaches differed though. The rule-based approach yielded approximately 25% of all MWLUs, while the statistical approach captured nearly 50% of the existing MWLUs. In absolute figures, we obtained 6,4k MWLUs and 19k MWLUs from WordNet, respectively. Importantly, both approaches made use of different lexicality features. As regards the rule-based approach, the features such as *I*-synonymy and cascade dictionary equivalent were used, while the statistical approach additionally capitalised on other automatically measured features: MWE length measured in characters, the cosine of the angle between embedding vectors calculated for WordNet glosses and MWE lemmas, MWE sense ordering in WordNet, and also on the existence of equivalents in each constituent cascade dictionary.

The proposed procedures and methods, which were designed to extract multi-word lexical units (MWLUs) from PWN and enWN, can be applied to NLP as a gold standard list of lexicalised MWEs. For example, they can be used to evaluate MWEs extracted from corpora. Moreover, additional research is still required to develop more precise guidelines for the inclusion of MWLUs into lexical databases such as wordnets.

Our approach, though successful, for sure could be improved. The greatest need now is to broaden the recall of the MWLU class. We plan to do this by applying new features to the statistical approach. Also the translational criterion of I-synonymy could be administered more properly on the level of lexical units (not synsets).

6. Acknowledgements

This research has been funded by the Polish National Science Centre under the grant agreement No UMO-2019/33/B/HS2/02814.

7. Bibliographical References

Calzolari, N., Fillmore, C. J., Grishman, R., Ide, N., Lenci, A., MacLeod, C., & Zampolli, A. (2002, May). Towards best practice for multiword expressions in computational lexicons. In *LREC Vol. 2*, pp. 1934-1940.

Constant, M., Eryiğit, G., Monti, J., Van Der Plas, L., Ramisch, C., Rosner, M., & Todirascu, A. (2017). Multiword expression processing: A survey. *Computational Linguistics*, 43(4): 837-892.

Delacre, M., Lakens, D., & Leys, C. (2017). "Why psychologists should by default use Welch's t-test instead of student's t-test." *International Review of Social Psychology,* 30(1): 92-101. https://doi.org/10.5334/irsp.82

Efron, B. (1983). Estimating the error rate of a prediction rule: improvement on cross-validation. *Journal of the American Statistical Association*, 78(382): 316-331.

Efron, B., & Tibshirani, R. (1997). Improvements on cross-validation: the 632+ bootstrap method. *Journal of the American Statistical Association*, 92(438): 548-560.

Farahmand, M., & Martins, R. T. (2014). A supervised model for extraction of multiword expressions, based on statistical context features. In *Proceedings of the 10th workshop on multiword expressions (MWE)* pp. 10-16.

Fellbaum, Ch. (Ed.) (1998). WordNet: An electronic lexical database, Cambridge, MA: MIT Press, 1998.

Hamp, B. and H. Feldweg. 1997. GermaNet - a lexical-semantic net for German. In *Automatic Information Extraction and Building of Lexical Semantic Resources for NLP Applications.*

Kędzia, P., Piasecki, M., Rudnicka, E. and K. Przybycień. (2013). Automatic prompt system in the process of mapping plWordNet on Princeton WordNet." *Cognitive Studies*, 13: 123-141.

Maziarz, M., Grabowski, Ł, Piotrowski, T., Rudnicka, E. & Piasecki, M. (in print). Lexicalisation of Polish and English word combinations: an empirical study. *Poznań Studies in Contemporary Linguistics.*

McCrae, J., Rademaker, A. Bond. F., Rudnicka, E., and Ch. Fellbaum. (2019). English WordNet 2019 – an open-source wordNet for English. *Proceedings of Global Wordnet Conference 2019.* Oficyna Wydawnicza Politechniki Wrocławskiej: Wrocław.

McCrae, J., Rademaker, A., Rudnicka, E., and F. Bond. (2020). English wordNet 2020: improving and extending a wordnet for English using an open-source methodology. *Proceedings of LREC 2020.*

Mihalcea, R., & Moldovan, D. (2001, July). Pattern learning and active feature selection for word sense disambiguation. In *Proceedings of SENSEVAL-2 Second International Workshop on Evaluating Word Sense Disambiguation Systems,* pp. 127-130.

Pearce, D. (2001). Synonymy in collocation extraction. In *Proceedings of the workshop on WordNet and other lexical resources, Second meeting of the North American chapter of the Association for Computational Linguistics,* pp. 41-46.

Piantadosi, S. T., Tily, H., & Gibson, E. (2011). Word lengths are optimised for efficient communication. *Proceedings of the National Academy of Sciences*, 108(9), 3526-3529.

Piasecki M., Szpakowicz S., Broda B. (2009). A Wordnet from the ground up. Wrocław: Oficyna Wydawnicza Politechniki Wrocławskiej.

Pickard, T. (2020). Comparing word2vec and glove for automatic measurement of MWE compositionality. In *Proceedings of the Joint Workshop on Multiword Expressions and Electronic Lexicons,* pp. 95-100.

Riedl, M., & Biemann, Ch. (2016). Impact of MWE resources on multiword recognition. In *Proceedings of the 12th Workshop on Multiword Expressions*, pages 107–111, Berlin, Germany. Association for Computational Linguistics.

Rudnicka, E., Maziarz, M., Piasecki, M. and S. Szpakowicz. (2012). A strategy of mapping Polish WordNet onto Princeton WordNet. In Kay, M. and Boitet, Ch. (eds.), *Proceedings of COLING 2012: Posters.* Mumbai, India, pp. 1039-1048. www.aclweb.org/anthology/C12-2101

Rudnicka, E. Witkowski, W, and M. Kaliński. (2015). Towards the methodology for extending Princeton WordNet. *Cognitive Studies 15.*

Sag, I. A., Baldwin, T., Bond, F., Copestake, A., & Flickinger, D. (2002). Multiword expressions: A pain in the neck for NLP. In *International conference on intelligent text processing and computational linguistics,* pp. 1-15. Springer, Berlin, Heidelberg.

Siyanova-Chanturia, A., Conklin, K., Caffarra, S., Kaan, E., & van Heuven, W. J. (2017). Representation and processing of multi-word expressions in the brain. *Brain and language*, 175: 111-122.

Schneider, N., Danchik, E., Dyer, Ch., & Smith, N. A. (2014). Discriminative lexical semantic segmentation with gaps: running the MWE gamut. *Transactions of the Association for Computational Linguistics*, 2:193–206.

Song, K., Tan, X., Qin, T., Lu, J., & Liu, T. Y. (2020). MPNet: Masked and permuted pre-training for language understanding. *Advances in Neural Information Processing Systems*, 33: 16857-16867.

Svensén, B. (2009). *A handbook of lexicography* (Vol. 1235). Cambridge: Cambridge University Press.

Tibshirani, R. J., & Efron, B. (1993). An introduction to the bootstrap. *Monographs on statistics and applied probability*, 57: 1-436.

Zgusta, L. (1971). *Manual of lexicography.* Academia, Publishing House of Czechoslovak Academy of Sciences, Prague.

Automatic Detection of Difficulty of French Medical Sequences in Context

Anaïs Koptient, Natalia Grabar
CNRS, Univ Lille, UMR 8163 - STL
F-59000 Lille, France
{anais.koptient, natalia.grabar}@univ-lille.fr

Abstract

Medical documents use technical terms (single or multi-word expressions) with very specific semantics. Patients may find it difficult to understand these terms, which may lower their understanding of medical information. Before the simplification step of such terms, it is important to detect difficult to understand syntactic groups in medical documents as they may correspond to or contain technical terms. We address this question through categorization: we have to predict difficult to understand syntactic groups within syntactically analyzed medical documents. We use different models for this task: one built with only internal features (linguistic features), one built with only external features (contextual features), and one built with both sets of features. Our results show an f-measure over 0.8. Use of contextual (external) features and of annotations from all annotators impact the results positively. Ablation tests indicate that frequencies in large corpora and lexicon are relevant for this task.

Keywords: Syntactic Groups, Complexity Detection, Linguistic and Contextual Features, Medical, French

1. Introduction

As any specialized area, medical domain witnesses different types of actors, all involved in the healthcare process and biomedical research, such as medical doctors, patients, nurses, biologists, medical students, or pharmacists. Patients particularly have no particular medical knowledge and may have understanding problems when reading medical information. Indeed, medical domain uses technical terms, such as *cholestatic jaundice* or *mesenteric venous thrombosis*. Such terms have specific and opaque semantics. Yet, the understanding of these notions is crucial for patients as it is intimately linked to their healthcare and wellbeing. It has indeed been shown that a correct understanding of medical notions plays an important role in healthcare process and ensures its success (Hermann et al., 1978; Vander Stichele, 2004; Mcgray, 2005; Eysenbach, 2007). It has also been shown that patients have to face quite frequently technical medical documents, in which the level of technicality is above their understanding:

- information on drug intake, preparation and dosage (Vander Stichele, 1999; Patel et al., 2002);
- clinical documents (Vander Stichele, 1999; Patel et al., 2002) on clinical procedures;
- medical leaflets and consent forms (Williams et al., 1995), specifically created for and typically met by patients during their healthcare process;
- more generally, information for patients found on the Internet (Rudd et al., 1999; Berland et al., 2001; Mcgray, 2005; Oregon Practice Center, 2008; D'Alessandro et al., 2001; Brigo et al., 2015) on different medical topics.

Thus, it is important to detect terms and syntactic groups that can show understanding difficulties for patients. Those terms can then be simplified. In this work, we propose a contribution to this research question: identification of difficult to understand syntactic groups in French medical texts. We first introduce existing works on this question (section 2). We then present the material used (section 3). Next, we describe the method proposed (section 4). Finally, we present the results (section 5) and discuss them (section 6).

2. Related work

Several works have been done throughout the years on the prediction of the difficulty in whole documents (Zheng et al., 2002; Chmielik and Grabar, 2009; Vajjala and Meurers, 2015) and they show good scores, with F-measures higher than 0.9 when different features are used. Indeed, at the text level, several hints are available and give complementary results. Nevertheless, prediction of difficulty of terms and syntactic groups within sentences is a more complex issue.

Works on this issue mainly use supervised learning classifiers with features including linguistic (frequency, length of the word, part-of-speech, number of phonemes, of syllables, phoneme/spelling coherence...) and psycholinguistic (level of abstractness) features (Paetzold and Specia, 2016; Yimam et al., 2018; Gala et al., 2013; Shardlow, 2013; Sheang, 2019; Agarwal and Chatterjee, 2021), as well as word embeddings and contextual features (Yimam et al., 2018; Sheang, 2019). Other works focus on exploitation of frequency. In particular, frequency thresholding is important (Zeng et al., 2005), as the frequency of words is considered to be a good hint to determine their complexity (Leroy et al., 2013; Lindqvist et al., 2013; Rudell, 1993). Another work suggests that the rarity of words may be indicative about their difficulty: the words that are not found in different lexica are considered to be difficult (Borst et al., 2008). (Zaharia et al., 2020) proposed a method using RNN and Transformer-based models. Finally, more recent works use Bert models (Shardlow et al., 2021).

Proceedings of the 18th Workshop on Multiword Expressions (MWE 2022) n@LREC2022, pages 55–66

Le tramadol peut provoquer chez les nouveau-nés des modifications de la fréquence respiratoire, qui sont généralement sans conséquences cliniques préjudiciables.

1	10105	10107	Le	le	DETDMS	Da-ms-d		2	T		1	pouvoir
2	10108	10116	tramadol	tramadol	NCMS	Ncms		2	T		1	pouvoir
3	10117	10121	peut	pouvoir	VINDP3S	Vmip3s		3	V		1	pouvoir
4	10122	10131	provoquer	provoquer	VINF	Vmn--		4	D		2	provoquer
5	10132	10136	chez	chez	PREP	Sp		7	F		2	provoquer
6	10137	10140	les	le	DETDPIG	Da-.p-d		7	F		2	provoquer
7	10141	10152	nouveau-nés	nouveau-né	NCMP	Ncmp		7	F		2	provoquer
8	10153	10156	des	un	DETDPIG	Da-.p-i		9	D		2	provoquer
9	10157	10170	modifications	modification	NCFP	Ncfp		9	D		2	provoquer
10	10171	10173	de	de	PREP	Sp	12|9		D		2	provoquer
11	10174	10176	la	le	DETDFS	Da-fs-d	12|9		D		2	provoquer
12	10177	10186	fréquence	fréquence	NCFS	Ncfs	12|9		D		2	provoquer
13	10187	10199	respiratoire	respiratoire	ADJSIG	Afp.s	12|9		D		2	provoquer
14	10199	10200	,	,	PCTFAIB	Ypw	-		-		2	provoquer
15	10201	10204	qui	qui	PRI	Pr-..n		15	S		3	être
16	10205	10209	sont	être	VINDP3P	Vmip3p		16	V		3	être
17	10210	10222	généralement	généralement	ADV	Rgp	-		-		3	être
18	10223	10227	sans	sans	PREP	Sp		19	H		3	être
19	10228	10240	conséquences	conséquence	NCFP	Ncfp		19	H		3	être
20	10241	10250	cliniques	clinique	ADJPIG	Afp.p		20	B		3	être
21	10251	10265	préjudiciables	préjudiciable	ADJPIG	Afp.p		20	B		3	être
22	10265	10266	.	.	PCTFORT	Yps	-		-	-		-

Figure 1: Syntactic annotation and parsing from Cordial

The main contributions of our work are:

- building annotations of understanding difficulties in French medical documents,
- automatic prediction of understanding difficulties in French medical documents,
- exploitation of internal (linguistic) and external (contextual) features,
- study of the impact when using annotations from several annotators.

3. Material

We use 100 French clinical cases randomly selected from the CAS corpus (Grabar et al., 2018), including a total of 41,384 words. Clinical cases are medical documents similar to clinical reports. They describe the patients medical background, the reason of their consultation, healthcare process and treatments proposed and performed, and the outcome. Such clinical documents can be encountered by patients in their everyday lives. Clinical cases deal with different topics and specialties. They are published and are freely accessible in different sources. They are anonymous.

The corpus with clinical cases is pre-processed. The documents are syntactically analyzed by Cordial parser (Laurent et al., 2009) to divide them into syntactic groups. Figure 1 shows the output from Cordial. We exploit the following syntactic information: the first column with the id of the word within the sentence, and the eighth column with the id of the head of the syntactic group in which the word belongs (words with the same number belong to the same syntactic group). For instance, {*Le tramadol*; *the tramadol*} is a syntactic group where *tramadol* is the head. When a given word belongs to a group within a group, we keep the minimal one, that is, the group within the bigger group. The corpus provides in total 15,053 syntactic groups. The choice to work with syntactic groups instead of words is motivated by the fact that syntactic groups may cover single or multi-word expressions, which convey specific semantics (Baldwin and Kim, 2010) and represent then suitable processing units.

Documents are then annotated manually by nine annotators. The annotators are all native French speakers. They have no medical knowledge or training. Few of them (annotators 5 to 8) are chronically ill with hemophilia, while others have no chronic disorders. The annotators were advised not to use dictionaries or Internet when annotating. They had to do the annotations on the basis of their own knowledge. The annotators are presented with whole documents, where syntactic groups are between brackets, such as indicated on Figure 2. For each syntactic group, the annotators have to indicate if they do not understand it (by annotating it as *not-understood*) or if they are not sure to understand it (by annotating it as *not-sure-to-understand*). In the case they understand a given syntactic group, they do not have to annotate it.

[Her medical background] [shows] [a probable gestational diabetes] [and a HG] [during her first pregnancy]. [The patient] [had then been hospitalized] and [recieved] [an intravenous treatment] [of metoclopramide with] [diphenhydramine followed] [by oral treatment] [with metoclopramide and] [hydroxyzine]. [An extrapyramidal reaction] ([jaw] [stiffness and] [difficulty] [to talk]) [caused] [the cessation] [of metoclopramide]. [Hydroxyzine] [had] [then been replaced] [by the combination] [of doxylamine] [and pyridoxine] (Di-clectinMD).

Figure 2: Translated excerpt from syntactically parsed and annotated clinical case

Further to the annotation process, each document is annotated by at least four annotators, while some documents are annotated by up to six annotators. We computed the kappa of Fleiss (Fleiss, 1971) for four annotators who annotated all the documents. As indicated in Table 1, the kappa for all annotators is 0.175, which is a low value. For some pairs of annotators (1&3, 2&3), kappa shows slightly higher values (0.292 and 0.316).

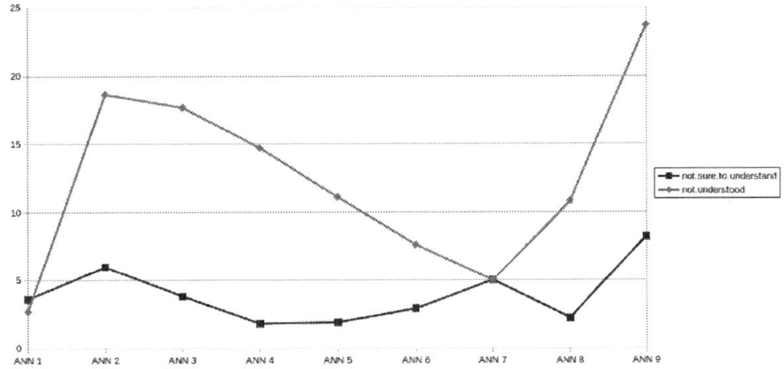

Figure 3: Percentages of *not sure to understand* (blue line) and *not understood* (red line) annotations according to the annotators. Annotators 5 to 8 are chronically ill

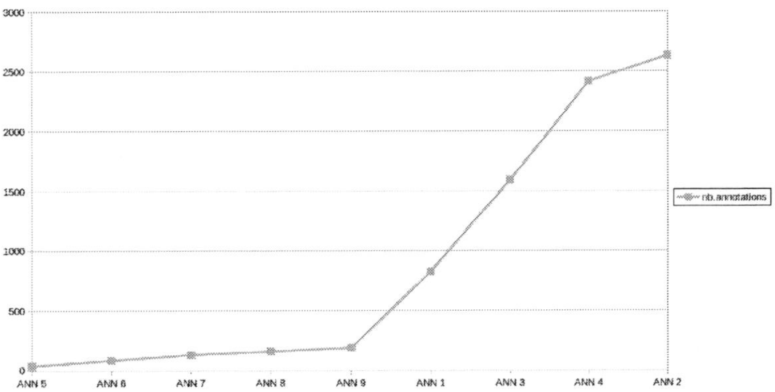

Figure 4: Number of different annotations (*not sure to understand* and *not understood*) from each annotator

We assume this means that the task at hand is very subjective. Besides, it is impossible to do the consensus among the annotators and to convince them that they should understand a given syntactic group. Indeed, this kind of annotations heavily depends on own knowledge and understanding feeling of each person.

Annotators	*Kappa*
all (1-4)	0.175
1 & 2	0.093
1 & 3	0.292
1 & 4	0.1
2 & 3	0.316
2 & 4	0.115
3 & 4	0.048

Table 1: Kappa score for different annotators

Figure 3 shows the percentage, for each annotator, of *not sure to understand* (blue line) and *not understood* (red line) annotations. We can see that annotators who are chronically ill (annotators from 5 to 8) have a lower percentage of *not sure to understand* and *not understood* annotations. For instance, Annotator 7 marked only 5% of syntactic groups as *not understood* and that much syntactic groups as *not sure to understand*. We assume that chronically ill annotators may better understand medical terms than healthy annotators.

Another interesting observation is that the annotations are complementary. Hence, Figure 4 shows the number of new annotations (*not sure to understand* and *not understood*) from each annotator, starting with chronically ill annotators who annotated the lowest number of non-understandable syntactic groups. We can see that the number of different and new annotations is increasing as a new annotator is taken into account. As noticed above, the feeling on understanding difficulty of medical information is a subjective question which depends on the own knowledge and individual experience of annotators. We consider that, in order to obtain a more complete picture on understanding difficulties, it would be necessary to involve a greater number of annotators: they may contribute with more relevant annotations for a given population. In this case, the purpose is not to achieve a better inter-annotator agreement but to obtain the more complete annotations possible.

When the annotations are done, we merge them all together. For this, we keep the strongest annotation for a given syntactic group: if one annotator annotates a given syntactic group as *not understood*, while all the others annotate it as *understood*, we therefore consider this syntactic group as *not understood*. In total, 12,417 syntactic groups belong to the *understood* category, 157 belong to the *not sure to understand* category, and 2,479 belong to the *not understood* category. We decide to merge together *not sure to understand* and *not understood* categories because: the *not sure to understand* category is very small and the difference between these two categories lays in the certainty related to the non-understanding of syntactic groups. This disposition permits also to do a binary classification task.

Figure 2 presents an English translation from annotated clinical case. Syntactic groups are between brackets. Groups in red are annotated as *not understood*, and groups in blue as *not sure to understand*. Hence, we obtain a French dataset with 15,053 syntactic groups annotated according to their difficulty. This dataset is divided into training (75%) and test (25%) sets.

4. Determining the difficulty of syntactic groups in context

We address the prediction of difficulty of syntactic groups as categorization problem: for a given syntactic group, we have to decide if it should be assigned to the category *not understood* or to the category *understood*. We first introduce our approach for determining the difficulty of syntactic groups in context and then describe the experimental setup.

4.1. Approach

We test several supervised learning algorithms implemented in Scikit-Learn (Pedregosa et al., 2011) to determine the difficulty of French medical syntactic groups in context: SVM Linear and RBF (Platt, 1998), Decision Tree (Quinlan, 1993), Multilayer Perceptron (Rosenblatt, 1958), and Random Forest (Breiman, 2001). These classifiers have been used for similar tasks in previous works (Ronzano et al., 2016; Mukherjee et al., 2016; Zampieri et al., 2016; Brooke et al., 2016; Davoodi and Kosseim, 2017; Alfter and Pilán, 2018; Kajiwara and Komachi, 2018) and display accuracies between 0.513 and 0.933.

We exploit internal and external features. Internal features are related to internal and linguistic properties of syntactic groups:

- *Number of letters*. Previous studies have shown that word length correlates with simplicity of text (Keskisärkkä, 2012). Moreover, simplification guidelines (Ruel et al., 2011; OCDE, 2015; UNAPEI, 2019) preconize to use short terms;
- *Number of phonemes*. Number of phonemes is correlated with word length. To determine the number of phonemes, we used the French database Lexique3 (New et al., 2001) and the French adaptation of the Epitran Python module (Mortensen et al., 2018);
- *Number of syllables*, which is, once again, correlated with word length. To determine it, we also use Lexique3 and Epitran;
- *Coherence between spelling and number of phonemes*. This feature corresponds to the ratio between the number of phonemes and the number of letters. Its values are between 0 and 2. If there is no difference then the coherence value is 0, if there is one or two differences the coherence value is 1, and if there are more than two differences the coherence value is 2;
- *Syllable components*. This feature corresponds to three levels of complexity according to the syllable components (coined with consonants C, vowels V and semi-consonants Y) and to their frequency. For instance, syllables like CYV lion (lion), CVC *men*tir (to lie), CV *le*ttre (letter) are very frequent in French, while syllables like CCVC *atten*drir (to soften), VCC ans (years), VC *an*tan (yesteryear), YV ion (ion) are much less frequent in French;
- *Frequency*. Several studies show that the complexity of words can be related to their frequency (Leroy et al., 2013; Lindqvist et al., 2013; Rudell, 1993). We use several sources to compute the frequency:
  - frequency in French lexica: Lexique3 and Manulex (Lété et al., 2004),
  - frequency in a general language corpus (French Wikipedia),
  - frequency in a medical corpus (CLEAR corpus (Grabar and Cardon, 2018)).

  For syntactic groups containing more than one word, we compute the average of frequencies of each word.
- *Presence of words in a list of very basic French vocabulary* built by Catach (Catach, 1984).

Notice that several of these features are inspired by a typology in a related work (Gala et al., 2013).

Among the external features, we count the right and left contexts of the syntactic groups. Hence, for each syntactic group, we extract five words at its left and five at its right, within the sentence.

We build a bi-class model, where each class comes from the manual annotations: *not understood* corresponds to *not understood* and *not sure to understand*; and *understood* corresponds to *understood*.

4.2. Baseline

For the baseline approach, we exploit the UMLS (Unified Medical Language System) (Lindberg et al., 1993):

- if a given syntactic group is present in the UMLS this group is considered as *not understood*. Indeed, in this case, the syntactic group is part of the specialized terminology and may be considered to convey technical meaning,
- if a given syntactic group is not present in the UMLS it is considered as *understood*. In this case, the syntactic group may be considered to convey more general meaning.

4.3. Experimentations

We use supervised learning algorithms with: only internal features, only external features, both internal and external features. We also perform ablation tests: (1) only one feature is used and the remaining features are removed, (2) one feature is removed.

Each experimentation is evaluated within the training dataset through 10-fold cross-validation using recall, precision and f-mesure. Since the classes are unbalanced in the training set (1,978 instances in the *not-understood* class and 10,294 instances in the *understood* class), we train other models on a balanced training set (1,978 instances in *not-understood* and *understood* classes). The 1,978 *understood* instances are selected randomly within the 10,294 *understood* instances from the full train set. In addition, the models built on both training sets (full set and the one with balanced classes) are tested on the test set, and recall, precision and f-mesure are also computed. All results are compared to the baseline.

Besides, all features are exploited with annotations from each annotator used incrementally. The purpose is to observe a possible impact on categorization results when using more annotators.

5. Results

Among the classifiers tested, Random Forest provides the best results in several settings. Also, contrary to other classifiers, it tries to recognize the two categories (*not understood* and *understood*) and not only the largest category (*understood*). Hence, we present the results obtained with this classifier. We first present the classification results obtained with ten-fold cross-validation and on the test set (Section 5.1), we then describe the results of the ablation tests (Section 5.2).

5.1. Classification of syntactic groups

Table 2 shows the results of the ten-fold cross-validation on balanced training set depending on the features used (internal, external, or both) and compared to the baseline. The baseline scores are very low, and this can be explained by the fact that any word linked to medical domain is present in the UMLS, even those that can be understood by non-medical experts. For instance, {*anestésie*; *anesthesia*} is annotated as *understood* in the reference data but is considered as *not-understood* by the baseline method because this term is part of the UMLS. All feature sets outperform the baseline. More specifically, the combination of both sets of features provides the highest scores (0.931 precision, 0.847 recall and 0.877 f-measure) in this setting. With the three sets of features, the values of precision and recall are close to each other.

Model	*Precision*	*Recall*	*F-measure*
Internal	0.805	0.769	0.783
External	0.893	0.798	0.830
Both	0.931	0.847	0.877
Baseline	0.570	0.579	0.573

Table 2: Results of the ten-fold cross-validation with different feature sets and Random Forest obtained on the full training set

Table 3 shows the results obtained on the test set with different models trained on the full training set: internal and external features, both of them, and the baseline. The combination of both external and internal features gives once again the higher scores. Yet, for all models, the scores become lower, and the baseline outperforms other models.

Model	*Precision*	*Recall*	*F-measure*
Internal	0.384	0.500	0.434
External	0.598	0.524	0.248
Both	0.601	0.551	0.310
Baseline	0.567	0,570	0.567

Table 3: Evaluation on the test dataset with different feature sets and Random Forest on the full training set

Table 4 shows the results of the ten-fold cross-validation obtained on the balanced training set with different features used (internal, external, or both) and compared to the baseline. The scores are lower than those obtained on the full training set (see Table 2). The combination of internal and external features outperforms other feature sets. All models outperform the baseline.

Model	*Precision*	*Recall*	*F-measure*
Internal	0.734	0.734	0.734
External	0.730	0.703	0.707
Both	0.798	0.799	0.798
Baseline	0.570	0.579	0.573

Table 4: Results of the ten-fold cross-validation with different feature sets and Random Forest on the balanced training set (both classes are equivalent)

Table 5 shows the results obtained on the test set with different models trained on the balanced training set with different feature sets (internal and external features, both of them), and the baseline. The scores are lower than those obtained on the full training set (see Table 3). The baseline outperforms other models.

Model	*Precision*	*Recall*	*F-measure*
Internal	0.602	0.505	0.101
External	0.384	0.500	0.434
Both	0.407	0.470	0.428
Baseline	0.567	0,570	0.567

Table 5: Evaluation on the test dataset with different feature sets and Random Forest on the balanced training set (both classes are equivalent)

5.2. Ablation tests

We performed two ablation tests: (1) only one feature is exploited and the remaining features are removed, and (2) one feature is removed at a time from the whole feature set. These ablation tests are done with internal features and are evaluated by a ten-fold cross-validation. We compare these results with the baseline and exploitation of all internal features.

Figure 5 shows f-measure when only one feature is used (burgundy line). The features indicated on the horizontal axis are the features which are kept. We compare these results to the exploitation of all internal features (green line) and baseline (yellow line). As already observed, the baseline outperforms the use of internal features only. We can also see that combination of all internal features (green line) is more efficient than each feature taken alone. We observe that the scores become lower with several features used individually: cohesion feature, number of letters and number of syllables, the Catach list, and syllable components. We can provide an explanation on these observations:

- the length of words and syntactic groups is not always correlated with their complexity in medical documents, contrary to long words from the general language texts. Indeed, short medical words, like abbreviations or some medical terms, can correspond to complex notions, while long words do not necessarily correspond to complex terms;
- the Catach list is very short and covers only a small portion of words occurring within medical documents, contrary to lists from Lexique3 and from Wikipedia which are more exhaustive;
- information on syllables (their structure and cohesion) has been first proposed for the classification of scholar manuals from elementary school, in which this information is important and reflects the scholar levels. We assume, these features are less efficient when used on specialized contents: the overall structure of words and syllables becomes more complex when addressing adult population and is no more a salient feature.

Several features related to the frequency of words provide high scores when used individually: frequency in Lexique3, Manulex, in a general language (French Wikipedia) and medical (CLEAR) corpora. This may be due to the fact that (1) these corpora provide a better coverage for words occurring in medical documents, and (2) the words that have higher frequency in these corpora are also more frequent in the language. Hence, they are better understood by the annotators.

Figure 6 shows f-measure obtained when one feature is removed (burgundy line). The features on the horizontal axis are those features which are removed in a given ablation test. We also present the f-measure when all internal features are used (green line) and the baseline (yellow line). Overall, we can see that the scores become lower when one feature is removed, which indicates that each feature is contributing to the results and that their combination is important. Among the features which removal decreases the scores we can find: the frequency in Lexique3, the number of letters, the frequency on Wikipedia and CLEAR corpora, the syllable components. The impact of the frequency from large corpora (Wikipedia, CLEAR, Lexique3) has already been observed and remains coherent with our observations above. The impact of the number of letters and syllable structure is not observed when these features are exploited individually. Yet, they may find their importance in combination with other features.

Figure 7 shows precision, recall and f-measure from ten-fold cross-validation with incremental addition of annotations from each annotators. Globally, with more annotators the scores progressively become better despite the low inter-annotator agreement. We assume that this group of annotators provides annotations which are complementary and which remain coherent.

6. Discussion

We present an error analysis, and discuss the ablation tests performed. We also compare our work with previously published results.

6.1. Error analysis

We randomly selected eight terms, single words (*furosémide* (furosemide), *sevrage* (withdrawal), *hospitalisée* (hospitalized), *ascite* (ascites)) and multi-word expressions (*chlorure chlorobutanol* (chlorobutanol chloride), *oppression thoracique* (chest tightness), *méga-uretère* (mega-ureter), *pré-opératoire* (preoperative)), to analyze the predictions for these terms. Hence, Table 6 shows the reference annotations, and the predictions provided by the baseline and the models based on internal, external and all the features.

- With internal features, either on full or balanced train set, the syntactic groups are classified as *not understood*, which is the minority category. The model trained on the full training set puts 3,424 out of 3,739 syntactic groups in the *not understood* class. The model trained on the balanced training set puts 3,707 out of 3,739 syntactic groups in the *not understood* class. Therefore, the model trained on the full training set seems to

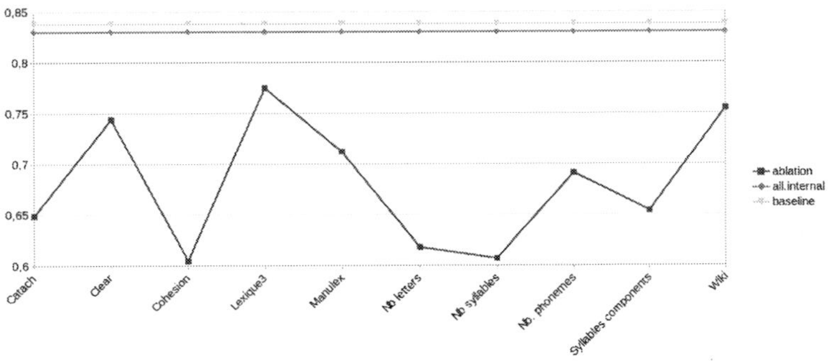

Figure 5: F-measure when only one features is exploited at a time

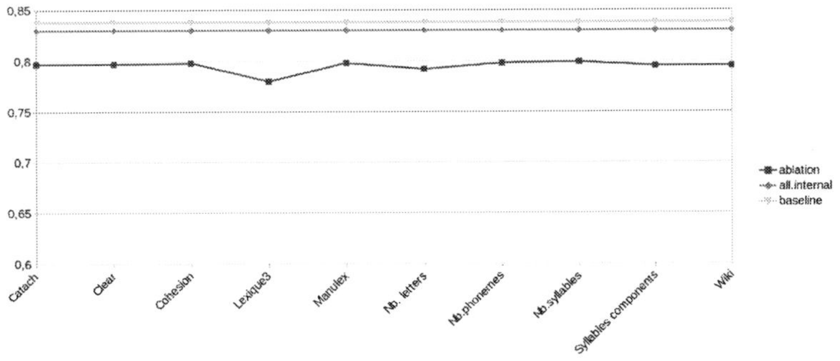

Figure 6: F-measure when one feature is removed

perform better.

- The model based on external features trained on full training set provides wrong predictions for *chlorure chlorobutanol* (chlorobutanol chloride) surprisingly classified as *understood*, and *pré-opératoire* (preoperative) classified as *not understood* certainly because of its length. But overall, this model shows a good performance. The model trained on balanced set classified every syntactic group as *understood*, a non-majority class.
- The model which exploits all the features and is trained on full training set classifies all single-word syntactic groups correctly excepting *hospitalisée* (hospitalized) classified as *not understood* probably because of its length. However, multi-word expressions are all classified as *not understood*. This classification error may also be due to their length. The model trained on balanced training set classified the majority of the syntactic groups as *not-understood* (3,579 out of 3,740).

We assume that low scores obtained when using balanced training set is due to the fact that it contains lower number of instances. However, we believe that the scores can be higher with a larger balanced training set. The baseline only depends on the presence of terms within the UMLS and their recognition. Per se, this is not a very reliable clue because the UMLS is very inclusive. For instance, *sevrage* (withdrawal), which is part of the UMLS, is wrongly predicted as *not understood*. Besides, we also observed that multi-word expressions present a greater challenge for the classification models. Typically, their length may become a confusing feature.

6.2. Ablation tests

According to the ablation tests, frequencies in large corpora (Wikipedia and CLEAR corpora) and lexica (Lexique3) appear to be important features: when removed f-measure decreases while their individual exploitation provides competitive results. As we observed, the size of corpora and lexica may be important as this guarantees that a higher number of words is represented. Besides, their contents may also be important. For instance, the frequencies in Lexique3 are compiled from movie and tv-show subtitles as well as from a book corpus (New et al., 2001), while the frequencies in Manulex are compiled from French scholar books from different levels in primary school. Since Manulex aims to describe children literacy and reading capacity, its exploitation for the analysis of documents written for adults is less useful. The importance of the frequency for the recognition of difficult to understand words has been noticed by several existing works. Indeed, existing work stresses on importance of this feature (Zeng et al., 2005), while several other works ex-

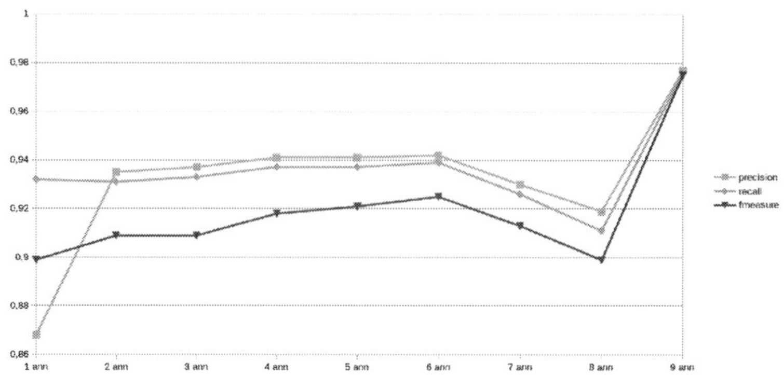

Figure 7: Evaluation measures with incremental addition of annotators, ten-fold cross-validation

syntactic group	*Ref.*	*BL*	*Int. full*	*Ext. full*	*Both full*	*Int. balanced*	*Ext. balanced*	*Both balanced*
furosémide (furosemide)	NU	NU	NU	NU	NU	NU	U	NU
sevrage (withdrawal)	U	NU	NU	U	U	NU	U	NU
hospitalisée (hospitalized)	U	U	NU	U	NU	NU	U	NU
ascite (ascites)	NU	NU	NU	NU	NU	NU	U	NU
chlorure chlorobutanol (chlorobutanol chloride)	NU	NU	NU	U	NU	NU	U	NU
oppression thoracique (chest tightness)	U	NU	NU	U	NU	NU	U	NU
méga-uretère (mega-ureter)	NU	U	NU	NU	NU	NU	U	NU
pré-opératoire (preoperative)	U	U	NU	NU	NU	NU	U	NU

Table 6: Predictions for some syntactic groups (NU: not understood, U: understood)

Previous work	*Feature(s) in common*	*Evaluation*	*F-measure*
(Zampieri et al., 2016)	number of letters	test corpus	0.270
(Ronzano et al., 2016)	number of letters, frequencies	cross-validation	0.735-0.824
(Alfter and Pilán, 2018)	number of letters, number of syllables, frequencies	cross-validation	0.726-0.862
(Alfter and Pilán, 2018)	number of letters, number of syllables and frequencies	test corpus	0.627-0.833
(Kajiwara and Komachi, 2018)	number of letters and frequencies	test corpus	0.745-0.863
(Brooke et al., 2016)	frequencies	test corpus	0.335
(Mukherjee et al., 2016)	number of syllables and presence in basic vocabulary list	test corpus	0.250
(Mukherjee et al., 2016)	number of syllables and presence in basic vocabulary list	cross-validation	0.530
Our work	internal features	test corpus	0.434
	external features	test corpus	0.248
	both	test corpus	0.310
on full training set	internal features	cross-validation	0.783
	external features	cross-validation	0.830
	both	cross-validation	0.877
	internal features	test corpus	0.101
	external features	test corpus	0.434
	both	test corpus	0.428
on balanced training set	internal features	cross-validation	0.734
	external features	cross-validation	0.707
	both	cross-validation	0.798
Baseline	UMLS	test corpus	0.567

Table 7: Comparison with previous works

ploited the frequency for the categorization task (Bingel and Bjerva, 2018; Bingel et al., 2016; Malmasi et al., 2016; Alfter and Pilán, 2018; Kajiwara and Komachi, 2018; Brooke et al., 2016). Besides, one work in French also exploits the frequency from Lexique3, and notices that this feature is important for the task (Gala et al., 2013).

Another observation from the ablation tests is that the number of letters and syllables is less important, although previous works indicate their importance (Gala et al., 2013; Wani et al., 2018). We observe that, even if some features seem to be less important than others individually, both ablation tests indicate that the combination of features improves the results.

6.3. Comparison with previous works

Table 7 shows a comparison with previous similar works, all done with data in English. We consider here the works that have at least one feature in common with our approach. We indicate whether the evaluation is done on a testset or by cross-validation. The comparison is done in terms of the f-measure values. Our results obtained with cross-validation on the full training set are competitive: they are usually higher than those from other works. Results obtained with cross-validation on the balanced training set are closer to those from other works. Finaly, our predictions on test corpus are less competitive yet they overpass several existing works.

7. Conclusion

We proposed to detect difficult syntactic groups in French medical texts thanks to their context (external features) and to their lexical properties (internal features). We use supervised learning algorithms, among which Random Forest appeared to be the best classifier for the task. The models are trained on clinical cases manually annotated according to the difficulty to understand syntactic groups. The dataset is divided in two datasets: training (75%) and test (25%) datasets. We perform several experiments on both full and balanced training sets: exploitation of only internal features (number of letters, number of phonemes, frequencies in corpora and lexica, etc.), exploitation of only external features (five word context on left and right), and of both sets of features. Our baseline is based on the UMLS: if a given syntactic group is part of the UMLS then it is considered as not understood, otherwise it is considered as understood. Two evaluations are performed: ten-fold cross-validation and evaluation on the test dataset. These two evaluations are compared to the baseline. Cross-validation tests indicate that the models built with two sets of features are the most efficient for the task. They shows up to 0.903 f-measure when trained on the full training set and 0.798 f-measure when trained on the balanced training set. However, when all features are exploited on the test dataset, they give relatively low results (0.310 f-measure for the model built on the full training set and 0.428 f-measure on the model built on the balanced training set). We also notice that the reference annotations show low inter-annotator agreement, instead they are complementary: the use of annotations from all annotators progressively improves classification results.

We performed two ablation tests, one where only one feature is kept, and one where one feature is removed at a time. Results of these tests show that the frequency in large corpora and lexica is important, and that word length and number of syllables are less important. We assume that these features require to be combined with other features to show their positive impact on the results. The ablation tests also showed that all features are important, because the best f-measure is obtained when all features are present. We also observed that multi-word expressions present a greater challenge for the classification models. Typically, their length may become a confusing classification feature.

In future work, we plan to enrich the reference dataset with more annotations. As observed, additional annotators enrich the annotated syntactic groups, which improves the classification results. A larger set with the reference data will permit to use approaches involving the Transformers. Besides, as similar datasets are available in other languages (Shardlow et al., 2021; Yimam et al., 2018), we may test our approach on these datasets. Another possible improvement is related to a better consideration of multi-word expressions.

8. Acknowledgements

This work was funded by the French National Agency for Research (ANR) as part of the CLEAR project (Communication, Literacy, Education, Accessibility, Readability), ANR-17-CE19-0016-01.

9. Bibliographical References

Agarwal, R. and Chatterjee, N. (2021). Gradient boosted trees for identification of complex words in context. 09.

Alfter, D. and Pilán, I. (2018). SB@GU at the complex word identification 2018 shared task. In *Proceedings of the Thirteenth Workshop on Innovative Use of NLP for Building Educational Applications*, pages 315–321, New Orleans, Louisiana, June. Association for Computational Linguistics.

Baldwin, T. and Kim, S. N. (2010). Multiword expressions. *Handbook of natural language processing*, 2:267–292.

Berland, G., Elliott, M., Morales, L., Algazy, J., Kravitz, R., Broder, M., Kanouse, D., Munoz, J., Puyol, J., and et al, M. L. (2001). Health information on the Internet. Accessibility, quality, and readability in English ans Spanish. *JAMA*, 285(20):2612–2621.

Bingel, J. and Bjerva, J. (2018). Cross-lingual complex word identification with multitask learning. In

Proceedings of the Thirteenth Workshop on Innovative Use of NLP for Building Educational Applications, pages 166–174, New Orleans, Louisiana, June. Association for Computational Linguistics.

Bingel, J., Schluter, N., and Martínez Alonso, H. (2016). CoastalCPH at SemEval-2016 task 11: The importance of designing your neural networks right. In *Proceedings of the 10th International Workshop on Semantic Evaluation (SemEval-2016)*, pages 1028–1033, San Diego, California, June. Association for Computational Linguistics.

Borst, A., Gaudinat, A., Boyer, C., and Grabar, N. (2008). Lexically based distinction of readability levels of health documents. In *MIE 2008*. Poster.

Breiman, L. (2001). Random forests. *Machine Learning*, 45(1):5–32.

Brigo, F., Otte, M., Igwe, S., Tezzon, F., and Nardone, R. (2015). Clearly written, easily comprehended ? The readability of websites providing information on epilepsy. *Epilepsy & Behavior*, 44:35–39.

Brooke, J., Uitdenbogerd, A., and Baldwin, T. (2016). Melbourne at SemEval 2016 task 11: Classifying type-level word complexity using random forests with corpus and word list features. In *Proceedings of the 10th International Workshop on Semantic Evaluation (SemEval-2016)*, pages 975–981, San Diego, California, June. Association for Computational Linguistics.

Catach, N. (1984). *Liste Orthographique de Base*. Éditions Nathan, Paris.

Chmielik, J. and Grabar, N. (2009). Comparative study between expert and non-expert biomedical writings: their morphology and semantics. *Stud Health Technol Inform.*, 150:359–63.

D'Alessandro, D., Kingsley, P., and Johnson-West, J. (2001). The readability of pediatric patient education materials on the world wide web. *Arch Pediatr Adolesc Med.*, 155(7):807–12.

Davoodi, E. and Kosseim, L. (2017). Clac at semeval-2016 task 11: Exploring linguistic and psycholinguistic features for complex word identification. *CoRR*, abs/1709.02843.

Eysenbach, G. (2007). Poverty, human development, and the role of eHealth. *J Med Internet Res*, 9(4):34–4.

Fleiss, J. L. (1971). Measuring nominal scale agreement among many raters. *Psychological Bulletin*, 76(5):378–382.

Gala, N., François, T., and Fairon, C. (2013). Towards a French lexicon with difficulty measures: NLP helping to bridge the gap between traditional dictionaries and specialized lexicons. In *eLEX-2013*.

Grabar, N. and Cardon, R. (2018). Clear – simple corpus for medical French. In *Workshop on Automatic Text Adaption (ATA)*, pages 1–11.

Grabar, N., Claveau, V., and Dalloux, C. (2018). Cas: French corpus with clinical cases. In *LOUHI 2018*, pages 1–12, Bruxelles, Belgique.

Hermann, F., Herxheimer, A., and Lionel, N. (1978). Package inserts for prescribed medicines: what minimum information do patients need? *Br Med J*, 2(6145):1132–1135.

Kajiwara, T. and Komachi, M. (2018). Complex word identification based on frequency in a learner corpus. In *Proceedings of the Thirteenth Workshop on Innovative Use of NLP for Building Educational Applications*, pages 195–199, New Orleans, Louisiana, June. Association for Computational Linguistics.

Keskisärkkä, R. (2012). *Automatic Text Simplification via Synonym Replacement*. Master thesis, Linköping University, Linköping, Sweden.

Laurent, D., Nègre, S., and Séguéla, P. (2009). L'analyseur syntaxique Cordial dans Passage. In *Traitement Automatique des Langues Naturelles (TALN)*.

Leroy, G., Kauchak, D., and Mouradi, O. (2013). A user-study measuring the effects of lexical simplification and coherence enhancement on perceived and actual text difficulty. *Int J Med Inform*, 82(8):717–730.

Lété, B., Sprenger-Charolles, L., and Colé, P. (2004). Manulex: A grade-level lexical database from French elementary-school readers. *Behavior Research Methods, Instruments and Computers*, 36:156–166.

Lindberg, D., Humphreys, B., and McCray, A. (1993). The Unified Medical Language System. *Methods Inf Med*, 32(4):281–291.

Lindqvist, C., Gudmundson, A., and Bardel, C. (2013). A new approach to measuring lexical sophistication in l2 oral production. *L2 vocabulary acquisition, knowledge and use: New perspectives on assessment and corpus analysis*, pages 109–126, 01.

Malmasi, S., Dras, M., and Zampieri, M. (2016). LTG at SemEval-2016 task 11: Complex word identification with classifier ensembles. In *Proceedings of the 10th International Workshop on Semantic Evaluation (SemEval-2016)*, pages 996–1000, San Diego, California, June. Association for Computational Linguistics.

Mcgray, A. (2005). Promoting health literacy. *J of Am Med Infor Ass*, 12:152–163.

Mortensen, D. R., Dalmia, S., and Littell, P. (2018). Epitran: Precision G2P for many languages. In Nicoletta Calzolari (Conference chair), et al., editors, *Proceedings of the Eleventh International Conference on Language Resources and Evaluation (LREC 2018)*, Paris, France, May. European Language Resources Association (ELRA).

Mukherjee, N., Patra, B. G., Das, D., and Bandyopadhyay, S. (2016). JU_NLP at SemEval-2016 task 11: Identifying complex words in a sentence. In *Proceedings of the 10th International Workshop on Semantic Evaluation (SemEval-2016)*, pages 986–990, San Diego, California, June. Association for Computational Linguistics.

New, B., Pallier, C., Ferrand, L., and Matos, R. (2001). Une base de données lexicales du français contemporain sur internet : Lexique//a lexical database for contemporary french : Lexique. *Annee Psychologique - ANNEE PSYCHOL*, 101:447–462, 01.

OCDE. (2015). *Guide de style de l'OCDE Troisième édition: Troisième édition*. OECD Publishing.

Oregon Practice Center. (2008). Barriers and drivers of health information technology use for the elderly, chronically ill, and underserved. Technical report, Agency for healthcare research and quality. Oregon Evidence-based Practice Center.

Paetzold, G. and Specia, L. (2016). SemEval 2016 task 11: Complex word identification. In *Proceedings of the 10th International Workshop on Semantic Evaluation (SemEval-2016)*, pages 560–569, San Diego, California, June. Association for Computational Linguistics.

Patel, V., Branch, T., and Arocha, J. (2002). Errors in interpreting quantities as procedures : The case of pharmaceutical labels. *Int Journ Med Inform*, 65(3):193–211.

Pedregosa, F., Varoquaux, G., Gramfort, A., Michel, V., Thirion, B., Grisel, O., Blondel, M., Prettenhofer, P., Weiss, R., Dubourg, V., Vanderplas, J., Passos, A., Cournapeau, D., Brucher, M., Perrot, M., and Duchesnay, E. (2011). Scikit-learn: Machine learning in Python. *Journal of Machine Learning Research*, 12:2825–2830.

Platt, J. C. (1998). Fast training of support vector machines using sequential minimal optimization. In *Advances in Kernel Methods - Support Vector Learning*. MIT Press.

Quinlan, J. (1993). *C4.5 Programs for Machine Learning*. Morgan Kaufmann, San Mateo, CA.

Ronzano, F., Abura'ed, A., Espinosa-Anke, L., and Saggion, H. (2016). TALN at SemEval-2016 task 11: Modelling complex words by contextual, lexical and semantic features. In *Proceedings of the 10th International Workshop on Semantic Evaluation (SemEval-2016)*, pages 1011–1016, San Diego, California, June. Association for Computational Linguistics.

Rosenblatt, F. (1958). The perceptron: a probabilistic model for information storage and organization in the brain. *Psychological Review*, 65(6):386–408.

Rudd, R., Moeykens, B., and Colton, T., (1999). *Annual Review of Adult Learning and Literacy*, page ch 5. NCSALL.

Rudell, A. P. (1993). Frequency of word usage and perceived word difficulty: Ratings of kuvera and francis words. *Behavior Research Methods, Instruments, & Computers*, 25:455–463.

Ruel, J., Kassi, B., Moreau, A., and Mbida-Mballa, S. (2011). *Guide de rédaction pour une information accessible*. Pavillon du Parc, Gatineau.

Shardlow, M., Evans, R., Paetzold, G. H., and Zampieri, M. (2021). SemEval-2021 task 1: Lexical complexity prediction. In *Proceedings of the 15th International Workshop on Semantic Evaluation (SemEval-2021)*, pages 1–16, Online, August. Association for Computational Linguistics.

Shardlow, M. (2013). A comparison of techniques to automatically identify complex words. In *ACL Student Research Workshop*, pages 103–109.

Sheang, K. C. (2019). Multilingual complex word identification: Convolutional neural networks with morphological and linguistic features. In *Proceedings of the Student Research Workshop Associated with RANLP 2019*, pages 83–89, Varna, Bulgaria, September. INCOMA Ltd.

UNAPEI. (2019). *L'information pour tous*. UNAPEI.

Vajjala, S. and Meurers, D. (2015). Readability-based sentence ranking for evaluating text simplification. Technical report, Iowa State University.

Vander Stichele, R. (1999). Promises for a measurement breakthrough. In John Wiley & Sons, editor, *Drug regimen compliance. Issues in clinical trials and patient management*, pages 71–83. JM Metry and UA Meyer.

Vander Stichele, R. (2004). *Impact of written drug information in patient package inserts. Acceptance and benefit/risk perception*. Phd thesis, Ghent University, Ghent, Belgium.

Wani, N., Mathias, S., Gajjam, J. A., and Bhattacharyya, P. (2018). The whole is greater than the sum of its parts: Towards the effectiveness of voting ensemble classifiers for complex word identification. In *Proceedings of the Thirteenth Workshop on Innovative Use of NLP for Building Educational Applications*, pages 200–205, New Orleans, Louisiana, June. Association for Computational Linguistics.

Williams, M., Parker, R., Baker, D., Parikh, N., Pitkin, K., Coates, W., and Nurss, J. (1995). Inadequate functional health literacy among patients at two public hospitals. *JAMA*, 274(21):1677–1682.

Yimam, S. M., Biemann, C., Malmasi, S., Paetzold, G., Specia, L., Štajner, S., Tack, A., and Zampieri, M. (2018). A report on the complex word identification shared task 2018. In *Proceedings of the Thirteenth Workshop on Innovative Use of NLP for Building Educational Applications*, pages 66–78, New Orleans, Louisiana, June. Association for Computational Linguistics.

Zaharia, G.-E., Cercel, D.-C., and Dascalu, M. (2020). Cross-lingual transfer learning for complex word identification. *32nd International Conference on Tools with Artificial Intelligence (ICTAI), IEEE*, 10.

Zampieri, M., Tan, L., and Genabith, J. (2016). Macsaar at semeval-2016 task 11: Zipfian and character features for complex word identification. 01.

Zeng, Q. T., Kim, E., Crowell, J., and Tse, T. (2005). A text corpora-based estimation of the familiarity of health terminology. In *ISBMDA 2006*, pages 184–92.

Zheng, W., Milios, E., and Watters, C. (2002). Filtering for medical news items using a machine learning approach. In *Ann Symp Am Med Inform Assoc (AMIA)*, pages 949–53.

Annotating “Particles” in Multiword Expressions in te reo Māori for a Part-of-Speech Tagger

Aoife Finn, Peter-Lucas Jones, Keoni Mahelona, Suzanne Duncan, Gianna Leoni
Te Hiku Media
1 Melba Street, Kaitaia, Aotearoa - New Zealand
aoife@tehiku.co.nz, peterlucas@tehiku.co.nz, keoni@tehiku.co.nz, suzanne@tehiku.co.nz, gianna@tehiku.co.nz

Abstract

This paper discusses the development of a Part-of-Speech tagger for te reo Māori, which is the Indigenous language of Aotearoa, also known as New Zealand. Te reo Māori is a particularly analytical and polysemic language. A word class called “particles” is introduced, they are small multi-functional words with many meanings, for example *ē, ai, noa, rawa, mai, anō* and *koa*. These “particles” are reflective of the analytical and polysemous nature of te reo Māori. They frequently occur both singularly and also in multiword expressions, including time adverbial phrases. The paper illustrates the challenges that they presented to part-of-speech tagging. It also discusses how we overcome these challenges in a way that is appropriate for te reo Māori, given its status an Indigenous language and history of colonisation. This includes a discussion of the importance of accurately reflecting the conceptualization of te reo Māori. And how this involved making no linguistic presumptions, and of eliciting faithful judgements from speakers, in a way that is uninfluenced by linguistic terminology.

Keywords: Māori, te reo Māori, Part-of-Speech Tagging, Indigenous languages, annotation

1. Introduction

This paper discusses a selection of the multiword expressions that occur in the data used to train a Part-of-Speech tagger for Māori.

Hereinafter, multiword expressions will be referred to as MWEs throughout and Part-of-Speech will be called POS. Whilst Māori will be referred to as te reo Māori or alternatively just Māori. Universal Dependencies will be abbreviated to UD. Unless otherwise stated, in this paper “word” means “orthographic word”, i.e. in the written form of the language, a word is separated by white space from other words. By MWE we mean more than two orthographic words that commonly occur and are used today together as a phrase.

We wanted to annotate te reo Māori data and to use it to train a model and achieve our goal of building a POS tagger for te reo Māori. Crucially, while doing so our further goal was to use a tagset that authentically captured te reo Māori. The POS tagger itself, was to be eventually expanded to include a features layer, hereafter FEAT layer, which would add more precise information to the POS labels, for example adding the number and gender of a pronoun. The POS tagger was also to be used as a building block for other natural language processing tools, for example Named Entity Recognition and sentiment analysis etc.

Before proceeding further, it is worth noting that the vision statement of Te Hiku Media is *He reo tuku iho, he reo ora* meaning *A living language transmitted intergenerationally*. This foregrounds the importance of capturing te reo Māori as it truly is, as the language that has passed down through Māori *whānau* (family) from generation to generation. Our mission statement is *Whakatōkia, poipoia kia matomato te reo Māori o ngā haukāinga o Te Hiku o Te Ika* which means *Instil, nurture and proliferate the Māori Language unique to haukāinga of Te Hiku o Te Ika.* This stresses our commitment to the revitalization of te reo Māori to capturing, nurturing and facilitating its growth.

2. A Brief Introduction to te reo Māori

Te reo Māori is the Indigenous language of Aotearoa, which is also known as New Zealand, (Morrison, 2011). It is a member of the Austronesian language family which has approximately 1200 members, (Harlow, 2007). Māori belongs to the Eastern Polynesian branch of Austronesian along with Rapanui, Rarotongan, Tahitian, Tuamotuan, Marquesan, Hawai'ian and Mangarevan, (Du Feu, 1996). According to the Statistics New Zealand government website, there are approximately 185,955 people who registered as speaking Māori in the 2018 census, (see References section below). Māori is a VSO, head-first, dependent-marking language.

Like many of its Polynesian counterparts, Māori is an analytical language, which means that it has many many small words or the aforementioned “particles” that indicate the grammatical roles of words. Some examples of particles include *kē, ai, noa, rawa, mai, anō* and *koa*. This paper will particularly focus on MWEs that consist of these so-called “particles”.

Furthermore, Māori makes great use of polysemy. This means that a single word can have many meanings and many uses. To somewhat illustrate the extent of polysemy in te reo Māori, we look at the sentence *i whara tāku waewae i a Mere i te hōpua heoi i tino riri au i a ia* (1), in which *i* appears four times. In this single sentence, the *i* shows both past tense and also location, which would both receive the POS label AUX. It also marks the agent of the neuter verb *whara* and a direct object, which would both receive the POS label ADP. See the POS labels in the third line of gloss.

1.	I	whara	tāku	waewae
	PST	injure	my	leg
	AUX	VERB	ADPRON	NOUN

Proceedings of the 18th Workshop on Multiword Expressions (MWE 2022) n@LREC2022, pages 67–74

i	a	Mere	i	te
AGT	ART	Mere	LOC	DET
ADP	PART	PROPN	AUX	DET

heoi	tino	riri	au	
so	PST	tino	annoy	1SG
CCONJ	AUX	MOD	VERB	PRON

i	a	ia
DO	ART	3SG
ADP	PART	PRON

"Mere hurt my leg in the pool, so I was very annoyed at her"

If expanding the POS labelling to include a more fine-grained FEAT layer, then the difference between these labels needed for *i* are more striking. The *i* in (1) would receive four different FEAT labels, AUX-pst, AUX-loc, ADP-agt and ADP-do. Outside of this, the word *i* is also used in sentences of comparison. This demonstrates the grammatical variation that a single word can show in a single sentence.

It is also worth emphasising further that neither adjacency nor ordering consistently predict grammatical roles nor how labels should be distributed between words. This can be demonstrated with the identical sentences in (2) and (3). In (2) *kei te* is considered a single word and would receive AUX which is a single POS label, see third line of gloss. It would receive a FEAT label of AUX-pres.

2.

Kei te	mahi	ia
PRES	work	3SG
AUX	VERB	PRON

"She is working"

3.

Kei	te	mahi	ia
LOC	DET	NOUN	3SG
AUX	DET	NOUN	PRON

"She is at work"

On the other hand, in (3), *kei te* is two separate words, *kei* would receive AUX and *te* would receive the DET POS label, see third line of gloss. If including a FEAT layer, *kei* would be labelled AUX-loc and *te* would be labelled with DET-sg.

Therefore, thanks to its particularly analytical and polysemous nature, it can be said that the grammatical role of a word is not always clear or easily ascertained in te reo Māori. Moreover, it is often the case that neither adjacency nor ordering are helpful in this same regard. This complexity of correct labelling of words in te reo Māori presents an obvious challenge to POS tagging, both when annotating and training a model to tag correctly.

Furthermore, as attested by our vision and mission statements mentioned above, our organisation is committed to faithfully and accurately capturing and representing te reo Māori. We do not want to colonise the language with terminology where it is neither applicable nor appropriate, and often founded in European theories of language. In that same vein, our concerns lie with faithfulness to the language, rather than metrics. That is to say that we would rather accurately tag te reo Māori with tags that represent Māori conceptualization, and have initially lower metrics that we can improve on, rather than tagging with an unsuitable tagset and inaccurately representing the language. We view such inaccurate tagging as linguistic colonialism. This is especially pertinent because of the effects of colonisation on the Māori language. So while we did want our annotation guidelines to be compatible with industry standards when possible, it was equally, if not more, important that they had to be appropriate for te reo Māori. Therefore we needed to find a "sweet spot" that best fulfilled both of these criteria.

To begin, the UD guidelines are "based on a lexicalist view of syntax", see References section below. As such, the UD guidelines strongly encourage what we call a one-word-one-POS-label approach. However, that straight-forward lexicalist approach encouraged by the UD guidelines presents problems for te reo Māori. This is problematic because, as shown above in examples (1) through (3), a single word in te reo Māori can have more than one meaning, and crucially more than one use in the grammar of te reo Māori.

It follows that some of the traditional UD grammatical categories for POS tagging were not suitable for use in te reo Māori. At the time of development of the POS tagger, the UD guidelines had never been used to tag an Eastern Polynesian language such as Māori. In that sense, the word classes of Māori are unprecedented from the point of view of UD guidelines. Therefore, we needed to review the existing UD tagging protocols, assess where they were suitable for te reo and if not, then devise tagging new tagging protocols.

From this careful review and considered pre-examination of the UD tagset, our te reo Māori speaking linguists were able to ascertain that parts of the UD tagset would not be suitable for te reo Māori. Having done so, we did not need to use value time or resources tagging te reo Māori with the existing UD tagset. We are a small Māori Indigenous organisation, and given what that would involve, such as training of annotators etc etc, it would not be a worthwhile use of our resources.

ADJ	adjective	PART	particle
ADP	adposition	PRON	pronoun
ADV	adverb	PROPN	proper noun
AUX	auxiliary	PUNCT	punctuation
CCONJ	coordinating conjunction	SCONJ	subordinating conjunction
DET	determiner	SYM	symbol
INTJ	interjection	VERB	verb
NOUN	noun	X	other
NUM	numeral		

Table 1: Universal Dependencies POS labels

On account of this, our annotation guidelines for the POS tagger for Māori were somewhat based on, although non-identical to, the UD guidelines. The 17 labels of the UD guidelines are shown in Table 1. For more information about their requirements see UD guidelines, (link in References section below).

Of interest in this paper, is that during the development of the POS tagger for Māori and these tagging protocols, the issue of MWEs arose and more specifically, the issue of how they should be annotated.

To reiterate, because it cannot be overstated, keeping in mind the unique grammar and history of te reo Māori, it was paramount that we captured the Māori language as accurately as possible and not impose European ideas on the language where they are neither applicable nor appropriate.. We applied this way of thinking throughout our approach to the grammar of te reo Māori. However, in this paper we will limit ourselves to the examination of the word category from te reo Māori called "particles" and specifically when they occur in MWEs.

3. Single Particles in te reo Māori

Before looking at the "particle" MWEs in te reo Māori, we need to familiarise ourselves with their discrete parts, that is the "particles" themselves.

Te reo Māori has a word category called "punga", they are also known as particles, (Harlow 2007). Again, they are small words like *anō, iho, noa, pū, tonu*. A single particle can perform many different functions in Māori. Our investigation of ninety particles found that some particles can accompany and modify up to five different word categories amongst the categories of verbs, nouns, pronouns, adjectives, numerals and negatives. Because the particles do not fit the traditional definitions, or indeed UD definitions, such as adjectives and adverbs we cannot say that the grammatical role is known, at least not in a way that falls under "traditional" grammatical roles. Furthermore and perhaps most importantly, Māori linguists themselves, such as (Harlow, 2007) and (Biggs, 1969), do not use traditional labels to refer to this word class. Therefore, we have a word class that is lacking an appropropriate POS label.

Given that the meanings of the particles are so varied and nuanced, we will simply gloss them as their orthographic word form in the examples in this paper.

For example, the particle *tonu* can modify verbs, nouns, adjectives and negatives. This effectively places it in the categories of adverb and adjective at the same time, as well being a modifier of numerals and negatives. In example (4) it modifies the passivised verb *waiatatia*, we can be sure of this because *tonu* has the added suffix *-tia* to match that of the passive verb. That would typically place *tonu* in the grammatical category of adverbs.

4\. Kei te waiata-tia tonu-tia tēnei waiata

Kei te	waiata-tia	tonu-tia
PRES	sing-PASS	tonu-PASS
tēnei	waiata	
DET	song	

"The song is still being sung"

It is worth mentioning that while te reo Māori does make use of some suffixes, such as the passive suffix here, it is not a language that makes use of inflection and so these are rare throughout the grammar and their use is very limited. In example (5) *tonu* modifies the locative noun *roto*, which leaves it behaving more like a typical adjective.

5\.

Kei	roto	tonu	koe
LOC	inside	tonu	2SG
i	te	whare?	
ADP	DET	house	

"Are you still inside the house?

For the avoidance of doubt, we know that *tonu* is modifying the words that it succeeds because te reo Māori is head initial, and as such modifiers follow the modified. In (6) *tonu* modifies the number *toru*. Example (7) shows us *tonu* modifying the adjective *whero*. Whilst finally in (8), *tonu* modifies the negative *kāore*.

6\.

E	toru	tonu
PRED	three	tonu
ngā	āpōrō	
DET	apple	

"There are still three apples"

7\.

He	whero	tonu
AUX	red	tonu
te	putiputi	
DET	flower	

"The flower is still red"

8\.

Kāore	tonu	te	rangatira
NEG	tonu	DET	chief
i	haina		
PST	sign		

"The chief did not sign"

These examples serve to illustrate the breadth and variety of grammatical uses of particles, and how even when considered singularly they cannot and should not be categorised under traditional grammatical categories.

Be that as it may, central to our interest here is that particles can combine with other particles to create MWEs. What's more, particles can also combine with other words that are not particles, and these combinations create entirely new MWEs. In summation, as regards annotation for the POS tagger, we encountered three challenges. Namely;

How should:

- single word particles, such as *tonu* above, be annotated.
- particles when combined with other particles, be annotated.
- particles when combined with other non-particles, be annotated.

4. Particles Combined with Other Particles

We have seen an example of a single word particle above with *tonu*. Yet, as stated previously, particles can combine with other particles. Furthermore, the combined meaning is not always a direct combination of the single particle meaning.

To give an example, *noa* is a single particle that has many subtle and distinct meanings. The meanings of *noa* are often connected to ideas that have been variously translated *as being without restraint, casually, by accident, spontaneously, randomly, without restriction, merely, solely* and *only*.

Similarly to *tonu* and other particles, it is multifunctional in its grammatical uses and can modify verbs, nouns, adjectives, question words and numbers, and negatives. In example (9), *noa* is modifying the verb *pakipaki*. In (10) the noun *meneti* is modified by *noa,* whereas in (11) *noa* modifies the adjective *māmā*.

9. E pakipaki noa
   PROG clap noa
   ana au
   PROG 1SG
   "I am clapping wildly"

10. E rima meneti noa
    PRED five minute noa
    hei wehe māku
    SCONJ leave for_me
    "I have only 5 minutes to leave"

11. He māmā noa
    AUX simple noa
    te whai whakaaetanga
    DET have agreement
    i a rātou
    ADP ART 3PL
    "An agreement can be gained relatively easily for them"

In (12) *noa* modifies the question word *aha*. And finally in (13), the number *kotahi* is modified by *noa*, whereas in (14) the negative *kīhai* is modified by *noa*.

12. He aha noa te paku?
    AUX what noa DET little
    Lit: "What is merely the smallness?"
    "Why all the fuss?"

13. Kotahi noa te
    one noa DET
    teina o Te Pairi
    Brother ADP Te_Pairi
    "Te Pairi had only one brother"

14. Kīhai noa kia tae te
    NEG noa PREF arrive DET
    pukapuka a Hōne-Heke
    Letter ADP Hōne-Heke
    "Hone-Heke's letter had not arrived"

Yet, when *noa* combines with other particles in which case the meanings can shift again. When *noa* is combined with another particle *iho*, the combination usually gives the sense of *just, only, that and nothing better, s*ee Harlow (2015: 93). Example (15) gives this sense of *noa iho* meaning *just*. By itself, the particle *iho* has many meanings and uses but is most often a directional particle meaning *downwards* like in (16).

15. He whakaaro noa iho
    AUX idea noa iho
    "It's just an idea"

16. Heke iho
    Get_off iho
    "Come down"

Noa can also combine with the particle *atu*. The primary function of *atu*, although it is one of many, is that of a directional particle indicating direction away from the speaker. This is the case in (17) wherein it specifies the direction of the verb *haere*.

17. Haere atu
    go atu
    "Go away"

18. He reka noa atu
    AUX tasty noa atu
    ngā tītipi i ngā rare
    DET chip ADP DET candy
    "Chips are much more tasty than candies"

When *noa* joins with *atu* to become *noa atu,* it is used to intensify comparative senses, as in (18) where it intensifies the adjective *reka*. *Noa atu* can also indicate that something happened *a long time ago*, thus it becomes a kind of time adverbial MWE, see (19).

19. Kua haere noa atu
    PERF go noa atu
    au ki Itāria
    1SG ADP Italy
    "I went to Italy a long time ago"

This leads onto another particle combination, that is *noa* with the particle *ake*. By itself, *ake* is primarily another directional particle indicating upward motion, see example (20) in which it specifies the direction of the verb *piki*. Yet, when in combination with *noa,* it has a similar meaning to *noa atu*, i.e. *a long time ago,* see (21) where it is a time adverbial MWE.

20. E piki ake
    PROG climb ake
    ana au i te maunga
    PROG 1SG ADP DET mountain
    "I'm climbing up the mountain"

21. I wehe ia noa ake
    PSTleave 3SG noa ake
    "He left a long time ago"

Concluding this section with particle MWEs, and specifically the final two which can serve as time adverbials, we now move to look at particles with non-particles in time adverbials MWEs.

5. Particles in Time Adverbs

Sometimes, adverbs in Māori are single word expressions such as *inanahi* in example (22). However many adverbs, specifically adverbial phrases of time, consist of many orthographic words and as such are time adverbial MWEs. As seen previously, the particles themselves have many varied uses and meanings and a particular combination can mean a variation in the meaning of the time adverbial MWE.

22. I haere ia inanahi
    AUX go 3SG yesterday
    "She went yesterday"

By way of illustration, *muri* is usually a locative noun meaning *back, rear* or *behind*. It is shown used in this way in (23). However, it also provides a base for many time adverbial MWEs. In these time adverbial MWEs, it is accompanied by an adposition, and a combination of particles, of which the number can vary.

23. I muri te ngeru
PST behind DET cat
i te rākau
ADP DET tree"
"The cat was behind the tree"

Basic types of time adverbial MWEs can be seen in (24) and (25). In (24) the particle *i* marks past tense and it is followed by *muri* and the particle *iho,* previously seen in examples (15) and (16). The combined overall meaning of this MWE in (24) means *after*. However, it can be seen that the substitution of *iho* with *mai* in (25) extends the overall meaning to include *later* and *afterwards*.

24. I muri iho
PST back iho
"After"

25. I muri mai
PST back mai
"After, later, afterwards"

The particle *mai* also has many many meanings and uses but, like *iho,* is very often used as a directional particle indicating motion towards the speaker as in (26).

26. Whakarongo mai
Listen mai
"Listen to me"

The addition of more particles can again change the meaning. If *tonu* is added to the sentence *i muri tonu iho,* seen in (24), to become *i muri tonu iho*, then the meaning shifts to *straight after*, see (27). But if *tonu* is replaced with *tata* the meaning again changes, but this time it changes to *soon after* as in (28). *Tata* is another particle with various meanings but it often means something akin to *near, almost, slightly* or *just*. This is how it is used in (29).

27. I muri tonu iho
PST back tonu iho
"Straight after"

28. I muri tata iho
PST back tata iho
"Soon after"

29. Kua tata maoa te kai
PERF tata cook DET food
"The food is almost cooked"

Tata can also be added to *i muri mai* which again alters the meaning to *shortly after* as in (30). And when *tonu, iho* and *tata* are combined, the meaning transforms again into immediately after as in (31). In addition, if the particle *i* is changed to *ā*, the entire tense shifts from past to future as in (32).

30. I muri tata mai
PST back tata mai
"Shortly after"

31. I muri tata tonu iho
PST back tata tonu iho
"Immediately after"

32. Ā muri atu
FUT back atu
"In the future"

It could be said that these examples really bring into focus that in every language, there can be a discrepancy between an idea and the number of orthographic words.

This can be seen using both te reo Māori and English time adverbial MWEs as examples. In (33), both languages express the idea of "the day after today" with the single words, *āpōpō* and *tomorrow*. In (34), the idea of "the day after the day after today" is expressed in te reo Māori with a single word *ātahirā*, whereas in English it has many words. By contrast, as shown in (35), the idea of "today" is represented with a single word in English, whereas it is a four-word time adverbial MWE *i te rā nei* in te reo Māori.

33. Āpōpō
"tomorrow"

34. Ātahirā
"the day after tomorrow"

35. I te rā nei
ADP DET day DET
"Today"

The dilemma that faced us was how should these time adverbial MWEs be tagged? Should each orthographic word receive a POS label, and if so with which labels? Or should the phrase be tagged as a single unit, and if so with which POS label?

6. Solution

The previous sections looked at a selection of the various ways in which particles can occur in MWEs in the grammar of te reo Māori.

The question arose as to how we decided to tag them, and how we reached those tagging decisions. Repeating earlier sentiments, we strove to both reflect and to capture the conceptualization of te reo Māori that has been handed down from generation to generation. And importantly, to not presume or impose grammatical characteristics where they are neither applicable nor accurate. And as the UD guidelines had not been developed for, nor used with, a POS tagger for an Eastern Polynesian language such as te reo Māori, we needed to devise a way to capture how speakers conceptualised their language. This was mainly achieved by two methods.

We simply set out to work with te reo Māori speakers, in order to establish their conceptualization of their language. Our group of speakers consisted of highly proficient, specially selected te reo Māori speakers and also te reo Māori-speaking linguists. They have been termed our *rangatira reo*, which roughly translates as "esteemed Māori language leaders". *Rangatira reo* is both the singular and plural term..

We were cognizant of the fact that many speakers' terminology for grammar might have been influenced by their past education, i.e. any pedagogical methods used during their language learning, or any academic theories of the language. These often come with their own terminology. The terminologies, whilst they might be useful for their purpose, are not always the best suited to te reo Māori. A well-known example of this is the verbal category in te reo Māori that are very often known as "stative verbs" in linguistic literature and in learners theory and exercise books. An example of such a verb is shown in (36). Unsurprisingly, in casual conversation many speakers refer to these verbs as "stative verbs", although upon examination they have proven not to be stative in nature.

36. I pau te kai
PST consume DET food
i te ngeru
ADP DET cat
"The cat ate up the food"

Knowing that this could have had an influence on any feedback we received, we strove to mitigate any influences from the past experiences of our *rangatira reo.* Whatsmore, we ourselves did not want to suggest or mention these terms and to unduly influence their answers to our questions. Bearing this in mind, we set out to elicit responses about te reo, but we did this using non-leading questions free of terminology.

37. In these two sentences: "*kei te haere au ki Te Awamutu i tēnei rā*" and "*kei te haere au ki Te Awamutu āpōpō*", are "*i tēnei rā*" and "*āpōpō*" doing the same thing?
    a) Yes, "*i tēnei rā*" and "*āpōpō*" are doing the same thing in the two sentences
    b) No, "*i tēnei rā*" and "*āpōpō*" are not doing the same thing in the two sentences
    c) Other, please elaborate
    d) Please feel free to add any comments, thoughts or insights about the question above or your answer to it.

We wanted to begin by making no presumptions in our examination of te reo Māori with the *rangatira reo.* To that end, we began by checking the most basic premisses. We believed, but strived to confirm, that the time adverbial MWEs such as *i tēnei rā* and the single word adverbs such as *āpōpo* are in fact doing the same job in a sentence. However, we did not want to use the word *adverb*, lest any preconceived ideas of what an adverb should be influence the answer. So we used a simple question such as that in (37) wherein no grammatical terminology was mentioned.

If the *rangatira reo* answered a) then we could then presume that the purpose of both phrases is adverbial. It turns out that this was the most popular answer and is indeed the case.

Having established the basics, we also took this approach with the particles that combined with other particles. For these simple particle combinations, if the *rangatira reo* had answered with a) in (38), we could reasonably infer that *noa iho* should receive a single POS label. If answer b) had been predominant then it could be deduced *noa* and *iho* should receive separate tags. Should c) have been chosen then we could ascertain that yet again *noa* and *iho* should receive separate tags but in the UD syntactic relations layer, the words would be linked together as a flat MWE. Finally, answer d) serves to provide the *rangatira reo* with the opportunity to share their own thoughts or feedback.

38. Ignoring white space between written words, in a phrase such as "*he whakaaro noa iho*", in your mind, is "*noa iho*"...
    a) Made up of one word "*noa iho*"
    b) Made up of two separate words, in this case "*noa*" and "*iho*"
    c) Made up of two separate words, but they are acting together as one, in this case "*noa*" and "*iho*"
    d) Other, please elaborate

To offer a further example, if phrased in a particular way some questions might prompt a particular response, such as the question in (39). First of all, the question names certain grammatical categories i.e. *verb, noun, adjective* and *adverb* and therefore could implicitly suggest them as the answer to our question. Secondly, naming certain grammatical categories it presumes that those "traditional" grammatical categories are appropriate for te reo Māori. This is unsatisfactory because it allows the possibility that the true conceptualization of te reo Māori is overlooked, and a POS label that is neither accurate nor appropriate is applied.

39. Is the "*ake*" in "*ā muri ake nei*"...
    a) a verb
    b) a noun
    c) an adjective
    d) an adverb
    e) other
    If other, please specify_____

Therefore, we opted to use questions phrased like those in (40). These non-leading questions do not suggest nor do they presume the appropriateness of grammatical categories. Again, we were very clear in what we were asking and how each answer was to be interpreted.

40. Ignoring white space between written words, is a phrase such as "*Ā muri ake nei*"...
    a) A single word, made up of one phrase "*ā muri ake nei*"
    b) Made up of many separate words, in this case "*ā*", "*muri*", "*ake*" and "*nei*"
    c) Made up of a primary word "*muri*" which is described by other words like "*ake*" and "*nei*"
    d) Other, please elaborate

To illustrate, in (40), if the *rangatira reo* had answered with a), that would mean that the four words *ā muri ake nei* would receive one single POS label. If the *rangatira reo* had answered with b), each word would receive one POS label. However, in the case that the *rangatira reo* has answered with c) then each word would still receive one POS label, but in the UD syntactic relations layer, each word would also be shown as a dependent of the noun *muri.* This option was influenced by and included due to linguistic knowledge that *muri* is typically a noun, and that it is likely that the other words modify it. Its inclusion could be said to be based on a "hunch" from linguists who speak te reo Māori. However, it is important to mention that the inclusion of c) is just that, and if *rangatira reo* had given negative feedback about it, then it would have been immediately discounted. Finally, there is d) to allow for any unanticipated feedback that the *rangatira reo* may have to contribute. Indeed, if they felt it was appropriate, a *rangatira reo* could have used this opportunity to advocate for the use of traditional grammatical categories, or alternative labelling.

As it happens, c) was markedly the most popular answer, followed by b). This affirmed our "hunch" that either way, each word should receive a separate POS label. No *rangatira reo* identified the time adverbial MWE as a), thereupon ruling out a single POS label for the MWEs.

Whilst the questions in (38) and (40) established that the particles in the MWEs should be tagged with separate POS labels. It still needed to be made clear exactly what labels the particles should receive, and if those labels ought to be from the traditional grammatical categories suggested by the UD guidelines. To that end, we used many questions like that in (41). Again, shying away from explicitly using terms like adjective and adverb etc, we tried to use very neutral language, and we were clear about what we were asking and how the answers should be interpreted.

41. In these two sentences: "*i mahi pai koe?*" and "*he kaitaraiwa pai koe*", is "pai" doing the same thing?
    a) Yes, "*pai*" does the same thing in the two sentences
    b) No, "*pai*" does not do the same thing in the two sentences
    c) Other, please elaborate

In (41), two sentences were given, the first sentence *i mahi pai koe* is translated as *you worked well*, with *pai* describing the verb *mahi*, thus behaving like an adverb, see (42). The second sentence is *you are a good driver* with *pai* describing the noun *kaitaraiwa* therefore behaving like an adjective, see (43).

If a *rangatira reo* answered a), it signified that *pai* is performing the same grammatical role in both sentences and so is capable of behaving like both an adjective and an adverb. Therefore it falls outside of any traditional grammatical roles and requires a new POS label. If a a *rangatira reo* answered b), it signified that *pai* is not not behaving in the same way in the sentences and they should receive different POS labels, such as the traditional UD adjective and adverb labels. However, for these types of questions the *rangatira reo* answered a) indicating that there is a single grammatical category in te reo Māori that does not behave like either an adjective or adverb. Rather, it is more fluid and can modify nouns, verbs and many other grammatical categories as seen in the earlier sections of this paper.

42. I mahi pai koe
    PST work pai 2SG
    "You worked well"

43. He kaitaraiwa pai koe
    AUX driver pai 2SG
    "You are a good driver"

Therefore, bearing in mind our most important goal to accurately and faithfully capture te reo Māori as it is conceptualised in the minds of speakers, we created a new label for these types of words. This label was for particles, and for now it is called modifier or MOD. To illustrate the labelling protocols drawn from our rangatira reo, a time adverbial MWE like *ā muri ake nei* would be annotated for our datasets with the POS labels shown in the third line of the gloss (44), and eventually our POS tagger would tag it in the same way.

44. Ā muri ake nei
    FUT back ake nei
    ADP NOUN MOD MOD
    "In a little while"

All in all, we asked 151 specially designed questions covering 10 different areas of interest. The UD guidelines have 17 labels. We use all of them, but we have an additional 4 labels, including modifier/MOD, that are for te reo Māori. It is important to spotlight that we did not create labels for the sake of it, rather we created them when they were expressly needed.

Coupled with asking our *rangatira reo* our specially designed questions. We have an ever-changing set of guidelines for our annotators. These guidelines were and are under constant review from the *rangatira reo*, meaning that the guidelines are evergreen. By evergreen we mean that, when required, they can always be changed. The guidelines are not static, so when we receive feedback from our *rangatira reo* that our annotation protocols are no longer appropriate, we alter the guidelines immediately. In essence, this means that while the decolonial and re-indigenizing processes are ongoing, the guidelines are being adapted to reflect the latest and most appropriate POS labels for te reo Māori. Of course, that begs the question that if our guidelines are updated, how can the annotated data also remain up-to-date. The answer is a simple one, we have an automatic tagging system in place, that means any words can be retagged as needed, and the POS tagger can be retrained.

7. Conclusions and Future Work

This paper has discussed the challenges encountered when tagging the MWEs of te reo Māori. Ultimately, our annotated datasets included a total of 21 POS labels. Where appropriate MWEs were annotated with te reo Māori appropriate labels, and they were annotated with the correct number of labels suitable for the conceptualization of that particular MWE.

At the time of writing, our datasets have over 40,000 tokens, with text taken from informal text, formal text and from social media. Most importantly, our datasets have successfully trained a model. As such we have successfully built a POS tagger for te reo Māori, called *Whakairo Kupu* meaning *carver of words*. Our current precision and recall are both at 93%.

In terms of access to both the data and the POS tagger, Te Hiku Media operates under its Kaitiakitanga Licence, see an abridged version in (45). More information about the Kaitiakitanga Licence can be found on our Papa Reo website, see references.

1. Data is not owned but as cared for under the principle of kaitiakitanga and any benefit derived from data flows to the source of the data… Te Hiku Media are merely caretakers of the data and seek to ensure that all decisions made about the use of that data respect it's mana and that of the people from whom it descends… Māori data will not be openly released, but requests for access to the data, or for the use of the tools developed under the platform, will be managed using tikanga Māori. Te Hiku Media have been invited to speak on their kaitiakitanga licence and it has been adopted by a government department and a social enterprise.

The POS tagger *Whakairo Kupu* has already been used as a base on which to build a grammar checker for te reo Māori. A FEAT layer is almost complete and it is currently being used to produce a Named Entity Recognition tagger.

8. Abbreviations

1	first person	NOUN	noun
2	second person	PART	particle
3	third person	PASS	passive
ADP	adposition	PERF	perfect
ADPRON	adpositional-pronoun	PL	plural
AGT	agent	PRED	predicative
ART	personal article	PRES	present
AUX	auxiliary	PROG	progressive
CCONJ	coordinating conjunction	PRON	pronoun
DET	determiner	PROPN	proper noun
DO	direct object	PST	past
LOC	location	SCONJ	subordinating conjunction
MOD	modifier	SG	singular

Table 2: Abbreviations

9. References

Biggs, Bruce. 1969. Let's Learn Māori: A Guide to the Study of the Māori Language. Auckland: Reed.

Du Feu, Veronica. 1996. Rapanui. London: Routledge.

Harlow, Ray. 2007. Māori: a linguistic introduction. Cambridge: Cambridge University Press.

Harlow, Ray. 2015. A Māori Reference Grammar. Wellington: Huia Publishers.

Morrison, Scotty. 2011. The Raupō Phrasebook of Modern Māori. Auckland: Penguin Group NZ.

Te Hiku Media - PapaReo, Kaitiakitanga License https://papareo.nz/#kaitiakitanga

Universal Dependencies - Tokenization and Word Segmentation https://universaldependencies.org/u/overview/tokenization.html

2018 Census totals by topic – national highlights https://www.stats.govt.nz/information-releases/2018-census-totals-by-topic-national-highlights-updated

Metaphor Detection for Low Resource Languages: From Zero-Shot to Few-Shot Learning in Middle High German

Felix Schneider[1], Sven Sickert[1], Phillip Brandes[2], Sophie Marshall[2], Joachim Denzler[1]
[1] Computer Vision Group, [2] Institut für Germanistische Literaturwissenschaft
Friedrich Schiller University Jena
Jena, Germany
firstname.lastname@uni-jena.de

Abstract

In this work, we present a novel unsupervised method for adjective-noun metaphor detection on low resource languages. We propose two new approaches: First, a way of artificially generating metaphor training examples and second, a novel way to find metaphors relying only on word embeddings. The latter enables application for low resource languages. Our method is based on a transformation of word embedding vectors into another vector space, in which the distance between the adjective word vector and the noun word vector represents the metaphoricity of the word pair. We train this method in a zero-shot pseudo-supervised manner by generating artificial metaphor examples and show that our approach can be used to generate a metaphor dataset with low annotation cost. It can then be used to finetune the system in a few-shot manner. In our experiments we show the capabilities of the method in its unsupervised and in its supervised version. Additionally, we test it against a comparable unsupervised baseline method and a supervised variation of it.

Keywords: metaphor detection, low resource language, middle high german, zero-shot learning, few-shot learning

1. Introduction

The automatic detection of metaphors is a useful tool for literary studies. While many recent supervised approaches for common languages like English exist, those methods rely on large pretrained models like BERT (Devlin et al., 2019) transformers and on labeled metaphor datasets, as can be seen in the shared task by Leong et al. (2020). Both can not be obtained for low resource languages like Middle High German, which is an older form of German spoken between around 1050 AD and 1350 AD. To enable metaphor detection in such cases we propose a novel unsupervised zero-shot approach based only on simple word embeddings. In our approach, a feedforward neural network transforms the word embeddings of adjective-noun metaphor word pairs into another vector space. This space has the property that common literal word pairs are located near each other while metaphoric word pairs have a large cosine distance between them. This distance can serve as a measure of metaphoricity. We are especially interested in *intentional* metaphors, which are actively used by the authors, and not in so-called *dead* metaphors, wich have experienced a shift in meaning to also include their metaphorical meaning in their base meaning (e.g. leg of a chair), while also recognizing that there exist combinations which may not unambiguously belong to one of those classes.

A metaphor, as a semantic figure of speech, is a way of referring to one concept by mentioning another (Zymner, 2007). An example for this would be the phrase *the car drinks gasoline* (Wilks, 1978), where the word *drinks* from the domain of food consumption is applied to word *car* from the domains of transportation and machines. It carries over its base meaning of consumption of liquids, so that the reader understands that the car consumes fuel. Another example would be the phrase *a sweet thought*. Here the word *sweet* from the domain of taste is applied to the word *thought*. While in its base meaning only physical objects can be sweet, the reader understands by their context knowledge and world knowledge that a sweet taste is considered pleasant and thus the aforementioned phrase means a pleasant thought.

In this work, we concentrate on adjective-noun pairs like *sweet thought*, *raw emotion*, or *clear answer*. With the knowledge of syntactical dependencies also more complex forms can be analyzed. However, we want to limit our approach to methods also applicable to low resource languages like Middle High German, where no syntax parsing is available. Thus, we assume that only part-of-speech tags and token-based word embeddings like word2vec (Mikolov et al., 2013) or fastText (Bojanowski et al., 2017) are obtainable. We do not rely on methods requiring large amounts of training data like transformer models or syntax parsers.

There are different ways to define adjective-noun metaphors to operationalize the search for them. An overview of approaches can be seen in the work of Shutova (2010). One possibility is to define metaphors as a violation of the selectional preference of a word (Wilks, 1975; Wilks, 1978). The approach we focus on defines the adjective that commonly occur together with a noun as their selection preference. When an adjective that does not typically appear together with the noun emerges, this anomaly is called a selection preference violation. This implies that an adjective from another source domain is used to describe something from the target domain of the noun. It fits our definition of a metaphor. Since our approach

Proceedings of the 18th Workshop on Multiword Expressions (MWE 2022) n@LREC2022, pages 75–80
Marseille, 25 June 2022.

should also be applicable to new languages without an existing labeled metaphor dataset in that language, we need to develop an *unsupervised* approach. In Section 3. we explain how to derive such a method from a supervised method.

2. Related Work

The most recent approaches for metaphor detection are based on supervised learning and transformer models such as MIss RoBERTa WiLDe (Babieno et al., 2022), MelBERT (Choi et al., 2021), and DeepMet (Su et al., 2020) . Those models require to be pretrained on a very large corpus with billions of tokens. However, there do not exist corpora of sufficient size to pretrain large language models on for every language. If we want to search for metaphors in low resource languages like Middle High German, using such a large pretrained language model is not possible. Additionally, there may be no training dataset for supervised training available to finetune the model on.

Other approaches like (Reinig and Rehbein, 2019) use supersense taxonomies like GermaNet (Hamp and Feldweg, 1997; Henrich and Hinrichs, 2010) comparable to the English WordNet (Fellbaum, 1998). They deliver information about the domain that certain words belong to. However, those external sources of information are not present for low resource languages like Middle High German. In an earlier unsupervised approach, the authors of (Shutova and Sun, 2013) used grammatical relations between words as the basis for a clustering approach based on hierarchical graph factorization. For this approach syntax parsing is necessary, as well. The authors of (Navarro-Colorado, 2015) propose an unsupervised metaphor detection system based on topic modeling. In comparison, they do not search for adjective-noun pairs but instead for single words with metaphorical meaning inside a sentence.

However, there are also unsupervised approaches that do not rely on big pretrained transformer models. Our *baseline* (Pramanick and Mitra, 2018) clusters adjective-noun pairs using the kmeans algorithm. To cluster the data, six different features are used: (1) abstractness rating of the adjective; (2) abstractness rating of the noun; (3) difference between the abstractness ratings; (4) cosine similarity of the word embeddings of the noun; (5) edit distance from the adjective to the noun, normalized by the number of characters in the adjective; (6) edit distance from the noun to the adjective, normalized by the number of characters in the noun. Clusters are then interpreted as metaphors or non-metaphors. This approach uses information that may not be present in low resource languages (the abstractness rating). However, we consider this a comparable baseline approach to our work. Due to its unsupervised nature, it can also be used on languages without an existing metaphor dataset.

3. Method

Our contribution consists of two parts: First, we propose a feedforward neural network that maximizes the cosine distance between the word vectors of an adjective-noun word pair for metaphors and minimizes the distance otherwise. Second, a way to train this model in a zero-shot setting without any metaphor examples. It also covers a step to finetune the system on human annotated metaphors previously proposed by the unsupervised system.

3.1. Metaphor Ranking

The basic idea of our novel approach is to transform the word embeddings of the adjective and the noun into another vector space, where the distance between words is based on their metaphoricity instead of their co-occurence. The cosine distance between the transformed vectors is small if the word pair is meant literally and large if the word pair has a metaphorical function. We assume, that words which occur often next to each other should have a low distance by the nature of the word embeddings. At the same time, unusual combinations like metaphors should have a higher distance. However, this is not guaranteed, especially with low resource data. As an extreme example, if the whole available corpus consists of poetry, words may be used in a metaphorical context more often than with their literal meaning. Additionally, while hapax legomena in large corpora normally comprise niche expressions, in a low resource language corpus also central words may be hapax legomena.
Our approach thus transforms the word embeddings into a space, where this higher distance between metaphorical words is explicitly encouraged. To transform the word embeddings into the metaphoricity vector space, we use a simple feedforward network N. The network for the transformation of the word embedding e_a of the adjective is the same as for the word embedding e_n of the noun, resulting in their transformed vectors t_a and t_n. This reduces the number of parameters that need to be learned. We then determine the metaphoricity m of the word pair by computing the cosine distance Δ_{cos} of the transformed vectors, as seen in Equation 1.

$$m = \Delta_{cos}(t_a, t_n), t_a = N(e_a), t_n = N(e_n) \quad (1)$$

The cosine embedding function (Payer et al., 2018) is used as a training loss. It maximizes the cosine distance between the transformed vectors if the word pair has a metaphorical meaning and minimizes the distance if the word pair has a literal meaning. Hence, the cosine distance of the transformed vectors then represents the metaphoricity of a word pair and can be used to rank all possible metaphor candidates.

3.2. Unsupervised Zero-Shot Training

As a goal, we also want to apply this method to low resource languages like Middle High German where we do not have a labeled metaphor dataset. This renders supervised training impossible. To mitigate this, we assume the number of metaphorical adjectives in a text to be low enough to make a high amount of adjective-noun pairs in a text good examples for non-metaphors. Based on this assumption, we generate artificial metaphor examples by using the idea of selectional preference violation. We create artificial metaphors by generating random adjective-noun pairs and label those as metaphor examples. While this may not result in semantically useful metaphors, it still satisfies the idea of selectional preference violation to initially train the neural nework. It enables the classifier to distinguish between normal and anomalous word pairs. Afterwards, the trained model can be used to extract real metaphors from the corpus, annotate those and finetune the model.

3.3. Few-Shot Finetuning

With the above mentioned idea, we get a classifier to rank the metaphoricity of adjective-noun pairs using no labeled training data. While the created classifier is not yet specifically tuned for real metaphors, we use it to evaluate how uncommon a word combination is. In contrast to using probability tables of word combinations or similar approaches, our word embedding based approach can also rank word pairs which have not been seen in the training data based on their semantic similarity encoded in the embeddings. Especially in low resource languages with small and non-representative corpora, the infrequent co-occurrence of words may not be sufficient to deduce their metaphoricity.

Our model can thus be refined with a human-in-the-loop bootstrapping approach. Using the zero-shot classifier, we can rank all the adjective-noun pairs in the training corpus by their estimated metaphoricity. An expert can then annotate metaphor candidates based on the ranking to generate a metaphor dataset without the need to annotate the whole text. As our strategy we choose to annotate the top 100 ranked word pairs, the bottom 50 ranked pairs and 50 random examples in every step. We repeat this in an iterative manner, generating metaphor examples of increasing quality with every annotation step. Thus, we create both a metaphor detection model and a dataset without the need to annotate whole corpora.

4. Experiments

To evaluate our embedding approach as well as our unsupervised labeling approach, we conducted several experiments. For reproducability, we make our code publicly available [1]. Since we want to emulate the search for metaphors in low resource languages, we do not use all features that are possible in the German language. Syntax trees, external knowledge bases like GermaNet and large pretrained models like BERT are excluded.

4.1. Data and setup

As a corpus for the German case study to extract non-metaphors in an unsupervised manner, we used the GerDraCor (Fischer et al., 2019) corpus. For the case study on the low resource language Middle High German, we used the Referenzkorpus Mittelhochdeutsch (Klein et al., 2016) to train fastText (Bojanowski et al., 2017) word embeddings. This corpus contains about 2,000,000 words. The model was trained using the *skipgram* approach with 1000 epochs and a learning rate of 0.01 on 8 threads with an embedding vector size of 100. A word vector for every word in the corpus was generated, resulting in 56060 vectors. We took 22 texts from the Mittelhochdeutsche Begriffsdatenbank (Zeppezauer-Wachauer, 2022) to analyze our approach on this language. The CLTK (Johnson et al., 2021) package was used to normalize the character representation of the Middle High German texts and to generate PoS tags. We extracted PoS tags, tokens, and word embeddings for the German data using the spaCy (Honnibal et al., 2020) package.

As annotated metaphor dataset we used the German version (Reinig and Rehbein, 2019) of the TSV metaphor dataset. Additionally, we used their annotated metaphor dataset from German poetry. However, their approach used features based on GermaNet, a supersense taxonomy which can not be assumed to exist for low resource languages. Hence, we did not compare our method to theirs. For the TSV dataset the training set comprised 546 metaphors and 603 non-metaphors, the test set comprised 65 metaphors and 77 non-metaphors, while for the poems dataset the training set comprised 100 metaphors and 487 non-metaphors, the test set comprised 98 metaphors and 280 non-metaphors. Our neural network had an input size of 300 for German and 100 for Middle High German, two hidden layers of size 300 and an output layer of size 100. ReLU was used as an activation function for the hidden layers.

4.2. Baseline

The main advantage of our appraoch is that it uses only POS tags as additional information, while the word embeddings can be learned from a corpus. Since even most very simple methods for metaphor detection use additional information like syntax trees, it is not easy to find a suitable baseline to compare to our approach. As baseline we used the methods explained in Section 2. Since the abstractness features are not present in low resource languages, we also conducted an experiment without these features. The remaining features are the cosine similarity of the word embeddings of the noun, the edit distance from the adjective to the noun, normalized by the number of characters in the adjective, and the edit distance from the noun to the adjective, normalized by the number of characters in the noun. While our baseline method is primarily an unsupervised approach, our approach can also be used in a supervised

[1] https://github.com/cvjena/metaphor-detector

method	TSV	poems
supervised (ours)	0.90	0.82
SVM baseline features (+abst)	0.92	0.77
SVM baseline features	0.67	0.75
zero-shot GerDraCor (ours)	0.70	0.74
zero-shot (ours)	0.57	0.77
baseline (+abst)	0.86	0.76
baseline	0.57	0.79

Table 1: Results of two different experiments: numbers are the average precision, which is the area under the precision-recall-curve. Methods marked with +abst use features that are not present in low resource languages.

	GDC	Schiller	TSV	poems	MHG
base	0.26	0.32	0.70	0.74	0.22
iter 1	0.60	0.44	0.84	0.77	0.61
iter 2	0.71	0.53	0.67	0.74	0.25
iter 3	0.46	0.55	0.72	0.78	0.60
iter 4	0.73	0.62	0.70	0.77	0.40
iter 5	0.95	0.70	0.59	0.78	0.60
iter 6	0.60	0.77	0.70	0.82	0.66

Table 2: Results of the iteratively trained model on the GerDraCor (GDC) and Schiller test sets (precision at top 100) and on the TSV and poetry test sets (average precision); The MHG column shows the results on the Middle High German test set (precision at top 100).

manner. For a fair comparison with our supervised approach, we also used the baseline features with a kernel SVM in a supervised manner.

4.3. Supervised metaphor retrieval

In the most simple case we have a dataset consisting of word pairs which are either labeled as a metaphor or as non-metaphor. Given these labels, our approach can be used without any modification. For our baseline, we trained a kernel SVM with radial basis function (RBF) kernel (Schölkopf and Smola, 2001) with the features of the otherwise unsupervised baseline by (Pramanick and Mitra, 2018). As hyperparameters for the SVM we set the regularization term C to 1.0 and $gamma$ to $auto$. We normalized the features by substracting the mean and dividing by their variance. The baseline features contain an abstractness feature which may not be present in low resource languages. To enable a fair comparison, we used these features both with and without the abstractness feature present and trained SVMs for each approach. Table 1 shows that our supervised approach achieves similar results to the supervised baseline features together with the abstractness. Without abstractness, our approach achieves a higher average precision by 0.13 percent points on the TSV set, while staying in a similar range on the poems set. The baseline results without the abstractness feature on the poems set is interesting, since it even surpasses the baseline with all features present. Our results show that our approach can utilize the information contained in the word embeddings more efficient than the baseline, while we do not need to use the abstractness feature.

4.4. Unsupervised metaphor retrieval

In this experiment, we again used the annotated TSV metaphor dataset and the poems dataset. However, we did not use any examples annotated as metaphors for our zero-shot approach. As explained in Section 3, we used randomly connected adjectives and nouns from the GerDraCor training set as metaphor training examples in one approach. In another approach we used random combinations of the TSV and poems training sets as training. Results in Table 1 (marked as *zero-shot*) show that we get slightly lower average precision than the baseline approach with the abstractness features when using unsupervised GerDraCor pretraining. However, we get far better avarage precision numbers than the baseline approach without the abstractness features when using this pretraining. When the abstractness features are used – which are not available in low resource languages – our approach reaches a lower or similar average precision to the baseline. This shows that our method is especially useful in a low resource language context when no additional features are present, while still remaining in a similar range for languages with more resources.

4.5. Case studies

Our main goal is a method to generate a metaphor dataset and create a metaphor retrieval system for a low resource language with no previously annotated metaphor dataset. To analyze whether our approach is suitable for this, we conducted two case studies: One on German and one on Middle High German.

Setup For the German texts we extracted adjective-noun pairs from one half of the GerDraCor corpus and used them to train the unsupervised zero-shot system. Two sets of random combinations of adjectives and nouns were used as pseudo metaphor examples. Additionally we separated the 11 texts by Friedrich Schiller contained in the GerDraCor corpus to analyze the metaphor detection rates on the works of a single author. For the Middle High German data we used eleven texts from the Mittelhochdeutsche Begriffsdatenbank to extract word pairs. In every iteration we then annotated the top 100 rated unannotated examples in the training corpus, the bottom 50 unannotated examples and another random 50 unannotated examples. This strategy allows to build a metaphor training dataset for both of these languages while finetuning the classifier on the new data. We discarded multiple occurrence of the same word pairs as well as ambiguous examples and detections based on errors like wrong PoS tagging. For German, the final training dataset contained 390 metaphors and 449 non-metaphors, for Middle High German it was 287 metaphors and 365 non-metaphors, respectively. To test our approach, we used our trained models to rank the candidates in the remaining corpora by their metaphoricity. We annotated the top 100 results on the other half of the GerDraCor corpus for German and the top 100 results on eleven other texts from the Mittelhochdeutsche Begriffsdatenbank for Middle High German. Additionally we tested our approach for German on an extra held out dataset from GerDraCor, comprising only the works by Friedrich Schiller, to evaluate our model on a single author from a more recent period.

Results The results in Table 2 show that the zero-shot classifier found 26 metaphors in the general top 100 results for German, 32 metaphors for the works of Schiller, and 22 metaphors in the top 100 results for Middle High German. After only one round of annotation, this already increased to 60 metaphors for German, 44 for Schiller and 61 metaphors for Middle High German. This shows that even with minimal annotation effort, the unsupervised pretraining together with our candidate mining strategy provide a useful model for metaphor detection. However, it can also be seen that for the heterogenous corpora and further iterations this process is still not completely stable. While a tendency towards improvement can be seen, further investigations are necessary. For the single author study on the works of Friedrich Schiller, we see that the results improve with every iteration of finetuning, reaching 77% from an inital 32%.
Below you can find examples of found metaphors in German (DE) and Middle High German (MHG):

grenzenloses Mitleid (DE)
borderless sympathy

ein **aufrichtiges Herz** (DE)
an **upright heart**

Behutsam schreite her auf **leisen Sohlen** (DE)
Gentle shall he tread on **silent soles**

schoenen gewin (MHG)
radiant victory

der vogele **süezer dôz** (MHG)
the birds' **sweet sound**

mit vil **getriuwer huote** (MHG)
with much **faithful loyalty**

5. Limitations

While our approach uses only minimal additional information, POS tags are still needed to find the metaphor candidates. The approach also relies on word embeddings, which have to be trained on the available low resource data. Since the available corpora may not always represent the use of language completely, especially for low resource languages, there is always the danger that the word embeddings do not correctly encode the semantic information of the words, e.g. due to common words in a language occuring only infrequently in the corpus used for training. This may be mitigated to some point by our model, which transforms the word vectors into another space, instead of directly using the word embeddings.

6. Conclusion

In this work, we presented a novel unsupervised method to enable metaphor detection. We demonstrated that our approach improves over comparable baseline approaches. The design of our method allows us to apply it to low resource languages without changes. It produces excellent results when used in a supervised manner. While the results are worse when the method is used without labeled data, the method can still be used to enable a bootstrapping approach. Metaphor candidates are extracted from a text in an unsupervised manner, labeled, and then used to train the supervised method. Thus, our approach on the one hand enables metaphor detection in uninvestigated low resource languages, and on the other hand serves as a powerful supervised tool once the first metaphors have been discovered. An interesting next step would be to combine our approach with other unsupervised approaches mentioned in the related work section that are applicable for low resource languages.

7. Bibliographical References

Babieno, M., Takeshita, M., Radisavljevic, D., Rzepka, R., and Araki, K. (2022). Miss roberta wilde: Metaphor identification using masked language model with wiktionary lexical definitions. *Applied Sciences*, 12(4).

Bojanowski, P., Grave, E., Joulin, A., and Mikolov, T. (2017). Enriching word vectors with subword information. *Transactions of the Association for Computational Linguistics*, 5:135–146.

Choi, M., Lee, S., Choi, E., Park, H., Lee, J., Lee, D., and Lee, J. (2021). MelBERT: Metaphor detection via contextualized late interaction using metaphorical identification theories. In *Proceedings of the 2021 Conference of the North American Chapter of the Association for Computational Linguistics: Human Language Technologies*, pages 1763–1773, Online, June. Association for Computational Linguistics.

Devlin, J., Chang, M.-W., Lee, K., and Toutanova, K. (2019). BERT: Pre-training of deep bidirectional transformers for language understanding. In *Proceedings of the 2019 Conference of the North American Chapter of the Association for Computational Linguistics: Human Language Technologies, Volume 1 (Long and Short Papers)*, pages 4171–4186, Minneapolis, Minnesota, June. Association for Computational Linguistics.

Fellbaum, C. (1998). *WordNet: An Electronic Lexical Database*. Bradford Books.

Hamp, B. and Feldweg, H. (1997). GermaNet - a lexical-semantic net for German. In *Automatic In-*

formation Extraction and Building of Lexical Semantic Resources for NLP Applications.

Henrich, V. and Hinrichs, E. (2010). GernEdiT - the GermaNet editing tool. In *Proceedings of the Seventh International Conference on Language Resources and Evaluation (LREC'10)*, Valletta, Malta, May. European Language Resources Association (ELRA).

Honnibal, M., Montani, I., Van Landeghem, S., and Boyd, A. (2020). spaCy: Industrial-strength Natural Language Processing in Python.

Johnson, K. P., Burns, P. J., Stewart, J., Cook, T., Besnier, C., and Mattingly, W. J. B. (2021). The Classical Language Toolkit: An NLP framework for pre-modern languages. In *Proceedings of the 59th Annual Meeting of the Association for Computational Linguistics and the 11th International Joint Conference on Natural Language Processing: System Demonstrations*, pages 20–29, Online, August. Association for Computational Linguistics.

Leong, C. W. B., Beigman Klebanov, B., Hamill, C., Stemle, E., Ubale, R., and Chen, X. (2020). A report on the 2020 VUA and TOEFL metaphor detection shared task. In *Proceedings of the Second Workshop on Figurative Language Processing*, pages 18–29, Online, July. Association for Computational Linguistics.

Mikolov, T., Chen, K., Corrado, G., and Dean, J. (2013). Efficient estimation of word representations in vector space. In Yoshua Bengio et al., editors, *1st International Conference on Learning Representations, ICLR 2013, Scottsdale, Arizona, USA, May 2-4, 2013, Workshop Track Proceedings.*

Navarro-Colorado, B. (2015). A fully unsupervised topic modeling approach to metaphor identification - una aproximacion no supervisada a la deteccion de metaforas basada en topic modeling.

Payer, C., Štern, D., Neff, T., Bischof, H., and Urschler, M. (2018). Instance segmentation and tracking with cosine embeddings and recurrent hourglass networks. In *Proceedings of Medical Image Computing and Computer Assisted Intervention – MICCAI 2018 - 21st International Conference*, Lecture Notes in Computer Science, pages 3–11. Springer Verlag Heidelberg, September.

Pramanick, M. and Mitra, P. (2018). Unsupervised detection of metaphorical adjective-noun pairs. In *Proceedings of the Workshop on Figurative Language Processing*, pages 76–80, New Orleans, Louisiana, June. Association for Computational Linguistics.

Reinig, I. and Rehbein, I. (2019). Metaphor detection for german poetry. In *Proceedings of the 15th Conference on Natural Language Processing (KONVENS 2019): Long Papers*, pages 149–160, Erlangen, Germany. German Society for Computational Linguistics & Language Technology.

Schölkopf, B. and Smola, A. J. (2001). *Learning with Kernels: Support Vector Machines, Regularization, Optimization, and Beyond.* MIT Press, Cambridge, MA, USA.

Shutova, E. and Sun, L. (2013). Unsupervised metaphor identification using hierarchical graph factorization clustering. In *Proceedings of the 2013 Conference of the North American Chapter of the Association for Computational Linguistics: Human Language Technologies*, pages 978–988, Atlanta, Georgia, June. Association for Computational Linguistics.

Shutova, E. (2010). Models of metaphor in NLP. In *Proceedings of the 48th Annual Meeting of the Association for Computational Linguistics*, pages 688–697, Uppsala, Sweden, July. Association for Computational Linguistics.

Su, C., Fukumoto, F., Huang, X., Li, J., Wang, R., and Chen, Z. (2020). DeepMet: A reading comprehension paradigm for token-level metaphor detection. In *Proceedings of the Second Workshop on Figurative Language Processing*, pages 30–39, Online, July. Association for Computational Linguistics.

Wilks, Y. (1975). A preferential, pattern-seeking, semantics for natural language inference. *Artificial Intelligence*, 6(1):53–74.

Wilks, Y. (1978). Making preferences more active. *Artificial Intelligence.*

Zymner, R. (2007). Metapher. In *Metzler Lexikon Literatur 3. Aufl. Stuttgart/Weimar*, pages 494–495.

8. Language Resource References

Fischer, Frank and Börner, Ingo and Göbel, Mathias and Hechtl, Angelika and Kittel, Christopher and Milling, Carsten and Trilcke, Peer. (2019). *Programmable Corpora: Introducing DraCor, an Infrastructure for the Research on European Drama.* Zenodo.

Klein, Thomas and Wegera, Klaus-Peter and Dipper, Stefanie and Wich-Reif, Claudia. (2016). *Referenzkorpus Mittelhochdeutsch (1050-1350), Version 1.0).*

Zeppezauer-Wachauer, K. (2022). Mittelhochdeutsche begriffsdatenbank (mhdbdb). Universität Salzburg. Interdisziplinäres Zentrum für Mittelalter und Frühneuzeit (IZMF). Koordination: Katharina Zeppezauer-Wachauer. 1972-2022 (laufend). URL: http://www.mhdbdb.sbg.ac.at/ (12.04.2022).

Automatic Bilingual Phrase Dictionary Construction from GIZA++ Output

Albina Khusainova, Vitaly Romanov, Adil Khan
Innopolis University
Innopolis, Tatarstan, Russia
{a.khusainova, v.romanov, a.khan}@innopolis.ru

Abstract

Modern encoder-decoder based neural machine translation (NMT) models are normally trained on parallel sentences. Hence, they give best results when translating full sentences rather than sentence parts. Thereby, the task of translating commonly used phrases, which often arises for language learners, is not addressed by NMT models. While for high-resourced language pairs human-built phrase dictionaries exist, less-resourced pairs do not have them. We suggest an approach for building such dictionary automatically based on the GIZA++ output and show that it works significantly better than translating phrases with a sentences-trained NMT system.

Keywords: phrase translation, machine translation, automatic bilingual dictionary construction, phrase dictionary, language resources

1. Introduction

Second language learners and users typically utilize their first language to find translations to the words, phrases, and sentences in a second language. People translate sentences when there is a ready text in a source language, whether it is copied or composed by a user. However, when a user forms a sentence right away in a second language, s/he often needs to consult a dictionary for the correct translation of a word or a phrase, and this is especially true for writing in the second language (Jun, 2008).

Learning the vocabulary of words in the second language is a basic step. However, it is not enough to know individual words, since most of the time it is phrases that play the role of semantic units, not words, so studying collocations is essential (Vasiljevic, 2014). For this reason, good language learning tools always teach words and phrases together, so that the user is able to understand and form coherent sentences based on them. Thus, for creating language learning tools it is necessary to have not only word dictionaries but also high-quality phrase dictionaries.

For second language users, on the other hand, the need for phrase dictionaries also arises in many contexts. For instance, when reading texts that contain unfamiliar words or phrases—a good example is e-books that have tooltips with dictionary items. Users might be interested in a phrase translation directly or, if they come across a new word, they might want to know the common collocations of that word together with their translations, which also leads to phrase dictionaries.

Another common use case is writing in a second language. When the idea is being verbalized, a user either immediately recalls the needed words and collocations or, otherwise, has to first translate them from the first language. In the latter case, it is very important to provide the user with a list of possible translations such that s/he can choose the one that carries the intended meaning and best matches the context. Providing such lists is only possible if corresponding language resources (dictionaries) exist.

Word-level translations can usually be found in human-built dictionaries, and sentence translations can typically be obtained using online NMT tools. However, when it comes to phrases, the situation is different. Usually, only rich-resourced language pairs do have good manually constructed bilingual common phrase dictionaries. Still, they are often incomplete, or too narrow, for example, limited to noun phrases. As for the neural translation, models trained on whole sentences often do not provide high-quality output for phrases—it can be simply erroneous or there can be a single translation while actually there exist many equally good alternatives. This is frequently alleviated by incorporating data from existing dictionaries—when a user searches for a common phrase translation, the system switches from neural translation to simple dictionary lookup. However, as already mentioned, such dictionaries often do not exist for many language pairs.

In this work, we suggest a way to construct a bilingual phrase dictionary automatically based on a corpus of parallel texts. We retrieve candidate translations from a phrase table which is the output of the statistical tool GIZA++ (Brown et al., 1993; Och and Ney, 2003) and then filter and sort them using heuristics. As a result, we get a phrase dictionary that can be used as-is or can serve as a basis for a manually constructed dictionary. We examine the resulting dictionary and measure its quality against the golden standard and NMT translation. Finally, we make the constructed Russian-English phrase dictionary available online as a linguistic resource.

Proceedings of the 18th Workshop on Multiword Expressions (MWE 2022) n@LREC2022, pages 81–88

2. Related work

Phrase translation as a separate task is not presented in the literature. However, there are some, mostly older, works on *collocation translation*. Since the term *collocation* is very related to the term *phrase* as we understand it, we consider the literature on collocation translation to be relevant. The most recent work (Garcia et al., 2019) suggests using word embeddings to find bilingual collocations—first mapping collocation *bases* and then their possible collocates. The limitation of such approach is that it restricts collocation translations to very exact correspondences only, whereas quite often phrases can be more idiomatic. Also, according to their approach, the number of words in a collocation should correspond to the number of words in its translation, which is also often not the case. For example, English phrase 'bring about' can be translated as a single word 'вызывать' (vyzyvat') in Russian.

As for earlier works, Smadja et al. (1996) translate collocations word by word by maximizing Dice coefficient scores between source and target collocations in a parallel corpus. They make an assumption that any source collocation has a unique translation in the target language, which is not very realistic. In a similar manner, Kupiec (1993) separately extracts noun phrases in two languages and maximizes their co-occurrence using a bilingual corpus.

Rivera et al. (2013) assume that collocations in both languages have the same part of speech (POS) structure. Using dictionaries, they find a translation for a *base* word and then search for co-occurring target language collocations with the same POS-structure in the sentences of a parallel corpus. Seretan and Wehrli (2007) employ a similar approach where bilingual dictionaries are used to find *base* translations and syntactic parsing is applied to find corresponding collocations.

In our case, phrases are not in general expected to have the same syntactic or POS-structure. Also, since we do not focus on collocations only, choosing the *base* word might be ambiguous. Hence, we do not consider approaches that match *base* words and rely on syntactic/POS correspondences.

Instead, we are inclined towards methods that find phrase translations using word alignment. One of the strongest statistical tools for aligning words in parallel sentences is GIZA++ (Brown et al., 1993; Och and Ney, 2003). Although the underlying IBM word alignment models were developed decades ago, GIZA++ still cannot be fully outperformed by modern neural methods. Only recently some works (Zenkel et al., 2020; Chen et al., 2020b) which employ neural architectures were able to show some improvements over GIZA++. However, the analysis shows that these improvements are due to better recall but not precision. In our case, precision is more important, since when constructing a dictionary, it is better to have fewer but more accurate results.

When the words are aligned in both source-to-target and target-to-source directions, the resulting alignments are combined using the 'grow-diag' method (Koehn et al., 2005). The phrases are then extracted and aligned based on the *consistency* criteria: "The words in the phrase pair have to be aligned to each other and not to any words outside" (Koehn et al., 2005). As a result, there is a list of phrases with their possible translations, scored by their probabilities. It is called a *phrase table* and it was originally intended to be a part of the statistical machine translation system. Nowadays, statistical machine translation is replaced by neural machine translation, however, this by-product, a phrase table, still proves to be useful.

Works similar to ours which use phrase tables to build/extend bilingual dictionaries include Richardson et al. (2014), Daiga Deksne (2018), and Chen et al. (2020a). The next section describes our approach in full detail.

3. Methodology

We aim at constructing a phrase dictionary, and we need to define what we mean by *phrase*. We understand phrase as an n-gram of words that carry some clear meaning, co-occur more often than simply by chance (as collocations), and whose overall meaning may not necessarily be understood from the individual words (as idioms). We need to note that due to the chosen alignment method's restriction, we only consider contiguous phrases.

Usually, when constructing a bilingual dictionary, the first step is to identify the collocations/phrases in the source language. In this work, we do not have this task because we use a ready human-built monolingual specialized dictionary as a source of phrases. Thus, our main interest is to develop a procedure that would provide the highest possible translation quality.

To build a phrase table, we used the Russian-English sub-corpus of CCMatrix dataset (v1) (Schwenk et al., 2021) downloaded from OPUS (Tiedemann, 2012). The size of the sub-corpus is approximately 140 million sentences. We aligned the words in the parallel corpus using GIZA++ with the 'grow-diag-final-and' heuristic. The default configuration of the Moses pipeline[1] (Koehn et al., 2007) was used to produce a phrase table. The excerpt of the resulting phrase table is given in Figure 1. For any source phrase there is a number of translation candidates along with scores, word alignments, and counts. Let us denote English phrase as e, and foreign (Russian in our case) phrase as f. Then three counts are given:

$count(e)$, number of times e was identified as a phrase in a parallel corpus;

$count(f)$, number of times f was identified as a phrase in a parallel corpus;

[1] https://www.statmt.org/moses/

$count(e, f)$, number of times phrase e was translated as phrase f.

Based on these counts the probability scores are calculated as:

$p(f|e) = count(e, f) \ / \ count(e)$, inverse phrase translation probability;

$p(e|f) = count(e, f) \ / \ count(f)$, direct phrase translation probability.

We are interested in $count(e, f)$ and probabilities $p(f|e), p(e|f)$.

3.1. Selecting Translations

The process of selecting translations is as follows. We first sort all the candidates by their $count(e, f)$, which is the number of times two phrases appear to be translations of each other, and take the top 10 candidates. This is equivalent to sorting by $p(e|f)$, since $count(f)$ is the same number for a given source phrase. We then filter these candidates using thresholds. First, we filter by direct phrase translation probability $p(e|f)$, then by inverse phrase translation probability $p(f|e)$, and finally by $count(e, f)$.

We found out empirically that setting $p(e|f)$ threshold based on counts leads to better results compared to using a single universal threshold. The threshold for direct phrase translation probability $p(e|f)$ should be inversely related to $count(f)$: the more times a phrase appears in a corpus, the more appropriate translations will be identified and thus their individual probabilities will be lower. With this in mind, we set gradual thresholds for $p(e|f)$: from 0.2 for $count(f) < 50$ down to 0.04 for $count(f) > 1000$.

We also set a threshold for $p(f|e)$ to 0.04 because this helps to filter out the common type of wrong translations: when a phrase is translated as some irrelevant but highly frequent phrase or, more often, word as 'the', 'to', etc. In this case, the probability $p(e|f)$ can be very high, since the alignment error is systematic, but $p(f|e)$ is usually near $10e - 5$. We set the threshold higher than this to also get rid of translations that are not exactly wrong but rather incomplete, for example: 'inspiration' instead of 'source of inspiration'.

Additionally, we set a threshold for $count(e, f)$ to 3 since we want any phrase to occur at least 3 times with a given translation.

It might sometimes happen that none of the candidates satisfies these thresholds. In this case, we gradually lower the thresholds such that at each step there is at least one candidate remaining.

The values we select for thresholds are not optimal, but they were chosen based on the analysis of scores and counts of translations for randomly sampled phrases with different counts.

3.2. Post-processing

Finally, when we have a list of translation candidates, we clean it by removing near duplicates. First, we lower-case all candidates. We did not lower-case the corpora before feeding it to GIZA++, so there might be same translations but in different casing, e.g., 'Stock Exchange' and 'stock exchange'. Second, we detokenize the candidates because the output is still Moses-tokenized. Third, we strip (trim) punctuation from both sides, because very often we can get options like: 'in a sense**,**' and '**,** in a sense**,**'. With lower-casing and stripped punctuation, we can already get rid of some duplicates. The next step is to group same translations which come with different articles ('a', 'an', 'the') and phrases with infinitives that may start with or without 'to' preposition, e.g.: '**to** pave the way' and 'pave the way'. After grouping, we choose the one preferred form and remove the others.

As a result, we obtain a refined list of sorted translations—one-two on average for every source phrase.

4. Data

We took the manually constructed dictionary[2] of n-gram lexical units from Russian National Corpus as a source of phrases for our bilingual dictionary. Namely, it is a compilation of Russian stable lexical phrases grouped by the functions they perform:

- prepositions (190), e.g.:
  согласно с (soglasno s) 'in accordance with',
  во имя (vo imja) 'in the name of';
- adverbs and predicatives (2164), e.g.:
  в итоге (v itoge) 'ultimately',
  в двух словах (v dvuh slovah) 'in a nutshell';
- conjunctions and connective words (59), e.g.:
  а именно (a imenno) 'namely',
  если бы (esli by) 'if only';
- particles (24), e.g.:
  едва не (edva ne) 'nearly',
  как раз (kak raz) 'exactly';
- comment clauses (194), e.g.:
  без сомнения (bez somnenija) 'undoubtedly',
  грубо говоря (grubo govorja) 'roughly speaking'.

We manually removed some phrases from the original dictionary, e.g., the ones which are non-contiguous or too rare. The final number of phrases in each group is indicated in brackets.

We also introduce one more **golden truth dictionary** of Russian-English phrases we built manually to evaluate our approach. We took the first 30 pages

[2] https://ruscorpora.ru/new/obgrams.html

```
глубокое потрясение ||| tremendous shock ||| 0.047619 8.59822e-06 0.015625 0.000186502 ||| 0-0 1-1 ||| 21 64 1 ||| |||
глубокое потрясение ||| with a ||| 1.27533e-06 1.55e-12 0.015625 1.10545e-05 ||| 0-0 1-1 ||| 784108 64 1 ||| |||
государственная облигация ||| 100-year government bond ||| 0.333333 6.33495e-05 0.0714286 3.60143e-09 ||| 0-1 1-2 ||| 3 14 1 ||| |||
государственная облигация ||| Government Bond ||| 0.0714286 2.32599e-06 0.142857 0.000145729 ||| 0-0 1-1 ||| 28 14 2 ||| |||
государственная облигация ||| Treasury ||| 4.02966e-05 8.58728e-09 0.0714286 0.0008367 ||| 0-0 1-0 ||| 24816 14 1 ||| |||
государственная облигация ||| a government bond ||| 0.03125 3.19233e-05 0.142857 0.000790133 ||| 0-0 0-1 1-2 ||| 64 14 2 ||| |||
государственная облигация ||| bond of a government ||| 1 3.16849e-05 0.0714286 0.000979174 ||| 1-0 1-2 0-3 ||| 1 14 1 ||| |||
государственная облигация ||| glossary ||| 0.00115075 2.2591e-07 0.0714286 0.000272 ||| 0-0 1-0 ||| 869 14 1 ||| |||
государственная облигация ||| government bond ||| 0.0060241 6.33495e-05 0.285714 0.0360143 ||| 0-0 1-1 ||| 664 14 4 ||| |||
государственная облигация ||| government bonds ||| 0.00038956 3.08366e-06 0.142857 0.00244474 ||| 0-0 1-1 ||| 5134 14 2 ||| |||
государственный гимн ||| &apos;s National Anthem ||| 0.2 0.000361967 0.000897666 5.66319e-06 ||| 0-1 1-2 ||| 5 1114 1 ||| |||
государственный гимн ||| &apos;s national anthem ||| 0.0793651 0.00217394 0.00448833 0.000149295 ||| 0-1 1-2 ||| 63 1114 5 ||| |||
```

Figure 1: The excerpt of the phrase table generated from the Russian-English sub-corpus of CCMatrix dataset.

of the online Russian-English collocations dictionary[3] as a basis and updated, removed, and added some translations. Mainly, we were replacing some uncommon translations with more common ones and unifying phrase forms. The resulting dictionary consists of various phrase types, including noun phrases ('double agent'), phrasal verbs ('tear apart'), idiomatic expressions ('guinea pig'), comment clauses ('to put it mildly'), etc. Overall, there are 250 entries in the dictionary.

5. Results and Analysis

We first evaluate our approach to translating phrases using the golden truth dictionary that we built. Using our methodology, we obtain translations for each source (Russian) phrase in the dictionary if it is found in the phrase table. Out of 250 phrases, 241 were found and 9 were missing. We consider missing phrases as wrong when calculating the overall translation accuracy. We use two evaluation modes: *top1* mode, where only the first (best) translation is assessed, and *any* mode, where a phrase is considered as translated correctly if at least one of its translations matches the reference.

To have a baseline, we translated the same dictionary with a pretrained Russian-English MarianMT neural translation model (Tiedemann and Thottingal, 2020) implemented in Transformers library[4]. This model (opus-mt-ru-en[5]) was trained on combined Russian-English datasets from OPUS, where CCMatrix is a major one. The same way as with phrase table candidates, we stripped the punctuation from translations. Here, there is always just one translation for any phrase.

We lower-cased both candidate and reference translations and considered a translation correct if it matches the reference as-is or after being adjusted for articles and prepositions ('a', 'the', 'an', 'to'). To clarify, we regard 'a stray dog'/' the stray dog'/'stray dog' or 'to commit a crime'/'commit a crime' as equivalent translations.

[3]https://audio-class.ru/english-collocations/vocabulary-02.php

[4]https://huggingface.co/docs/transformers/model_doc/marian

[5]https://huggingface.co/Helsinki-NLP/opus-mt-ru-en

Method	Accuracy (%)
Our, *any*	69.2
Our, *top1*	62.4
NMT	38.4

Table 1: Accuracy of phrase translations measured against the golden truth dictionary. *Our* is our phrase table based method and *NMT* is a baseline method where translations are obtained from MarianMT model.

$count(f)$	# phrases	Accuracy (%)
< 10	12	25.1
10 - 50	26	69.2
50 - 100	15	86.6
100 - 200	24	62.5
200 - 500	29	82.7
500 - 1k	39	79.1
1k - 5k	50	80.2
5k - 50k	32	56.6
> 50k	14	78.3

Table 2: Accuracy of phrase translations measured against the golden truth dictionary depending on source phrase counts, $count(f)$.

The evaluation results are presented in Table 1. We see that regardless of the mode (*top1/any*), translations obtained using phrase table are significantly more accurate than the ones we got plainly translating using MarianMT, and the difference is at least 24%. We suppose the main reason for the low NMT performance is that the model is not trained to translate phrases, instead being trained on full sentences.

If we take a closer look at the results (Table 3), we will see that in the majority of cases we get correct translations (rows 1-4) for different phrase types: noun phrases ('tough stance'), idioms ('scapegoat'), comment clauses ('simply put'), etc. Sometimes there is more than one candidate, and mostly they represent valid alternatives, e.g., 'simply put' and 'in simple terms'.

The next four rows (5-8) in Table 3 showcase translation candidates that are valid although they do not match the reference. The phrases 'at a loss', 'in dis-

	Source phrase	Candidate translations	Reference translation	$count(f)$	Correct
1	в рамках бюджета v ramkah bjudzheta	within budget, on budget, within the budget, under budget	within budget	957	Yes
2	козёл отпущения kozjol otpushhenija	scapegoat	scapegoat	31	Yes
3	проще говоря proshhe govorja	simply put, to put it simply, in simple terms	simply put	9389	Yes
4	жёсткая позиция zhjostkaja pozicija	tough stance	tough stance	49	Yes
5	в первую очередь v pervuju ochered'	primarily, in the first place, first of all	first and foremost	102472	+-
6	в недоумении v nedoumenii	at a loss, in disbelief	puzzled	1108	+-
7	время от времени vremja ot vremeni	from time to time, occasionally	once in a while	36744	+-
8	полный комплект polnyj komplekt	complete set of, a full set of	full set	1473	+-

Table 3: Phrase translation examples for the test dictionary. The candidates are valid, even if they do not match the reference.

	Source phrase	Candidate translations	Reference translation	$count(f)$	Correct
1	суть рассказа sut' rasskaza	the story	gist of the story	7	No
2	по одному po odnomu	on one	one by one	18409	No
3	устье реки ust'e reki	the mouth of the, the mouth of the river	river mouth	876	+-
4	ни с того ни с сего ni s togo ni s sego	no apparent reason	without any rhyme or reason	210	No
5	аллергия на пыльцу allergija na pyl'cu	are allergic to pollen	pollen allergy	119	+-
6	подопытный кролик podopytnyj krolik	the experimental rabbit	guinea pig	9	No

Table 4: Phrase translation examples for the test dictionary. The candidates are partially valid or wrong.

belief' are synonymous with the word 'puzzled' (row 6); and 'in the first place' (row 5) is actually even more accurate translation for the source phrase than the reference is. The last row illustrates the frequent case when the translation candidate differs from the reference by added preposition or article ('**a** full set **of**').

Let us now turn to more problematic cases demonstrated in Table 4. The first row shows how the main term ('gist') is being lost during translation. This can be attributed to the low phrase count. The next example (row 2) illustrates the challenging case where the source phrase may have several meanings depending on the context. If we consider the source phrase as complete, then the correct translation will be the reference one, 'one by one'. However, if it is a part of the bigger phrase, e.g. 'по одному поводу' (po odnomu povodu) meaning 'on one occasion', then the suggested 'on one' translation is the correct one.

Rows 3 and 4 exemplify the problem of inappropriately trimmed translations: 'the mouth of the' lacks the defining word 'river'; 'no apparent reason' should start with the preposition 'for'. In row 5, 'are allergic to pollen' carries the correct meaning but has a wrong form, whereas 'the experimental rabbit' is an uncommon translation of the Russian phrase that is best translated as 'guinea pig'. The count (9) in the latter case is quite low, though.

Phrase counts for valid translations shown in Table 3 differ from 31 to 102k, yet, there are even less frequent phrases translated correctly, for example, 'turnkey business' with only 9 occurrences. However, if a phrase is very rare, the chances to get a good translation are low. We measured accuracy for phrases with different source counts in Table 2. We see the drastic decrease in accuracy for phrases with $count(f) < 10$, which suggests that 10 can be used as a default threshold when automatically constructing a dictionary. It is also interesting to note that the increase in count does not necessarily imply the increase in accuracy.

To sum up, we see many good translations, sometimes with a fair choice of options. Even if translations do not match the reference, they are mostly valid alternatives. Sometimes the translations are strangely trimmed and have an improper form or represent an uncommon translation. With all that, we almost do not observe any completely irrelevant translations after the performed filtering and post-processing.

Turning to the NMT phrase translations, we see a number of problems. One of them is word-by-word translations of idiomatic expressions: 'single wolf' instead of 'lone wolf', 'beating of infants' instead of 'massacre of the innocents', 'aerial snakes' for 'kite', etc. There are also many sub-optimal translations like 'eastern kitchen' for 'oriental cuisine' and 'artistic literature' for 'fiction' due to the literal translation of the phrases. The other problem is unexpected, lengthy translations: 'i don't know what i'm talking about' for 'pick the nose', 'well, let's just put it that way' for 'simply put', and so forth. Most likely, this happens because the model is trained to produce full sentences. One more important limitation is that the model cannot produce alternative options. Even if beam search with several outputs is used, the variation in translations is quite low.

Let us now focus on the generated bilingual dictionary and assess its overall practical utility. We first note that we set a threshold on $count(f)$, the number of times a source phrase appeared in a corpus, following the above analysis. We set this threshold to minimum 10 occurrences. As a result, from 1% to 26% of phrases, depending on the group, were excluded from the final dictionary.

We went through the resulting translations, and we can say that we are mostly satisfied with the resulting quality. The most common problems we noticed are the ones connected to the phrase context, as with 'one by one' example above. Specifically, some phrases, especially if they are short, should have different translations if they are considered a part of a bigger phrase and if they are considered a complete phrase on their own.

Apart from that, we see that very often good alternatives do not survive filtering by thresholds. Obviously, there is a trade-off between recall and precision, and we choose the latter. A potential solution that can lead to the best possible quality is to use this dictionary (and our method in general) as a basis for manual dictionary creation. Such approach saves a tremendous amount of time and effort required for the search of appropriate translations. Even if individual candidates are a bit noisy and strangely trimmed (like 'good as it gets'), they can come as a tip for a dictionary creator pointing to the right translation ('**as** good as it gets'). This work can be performed by language enthusiasts in a crowd-sourcing manner, for example. In this case, the thresholds should be lowered further such that rare but correct translations do not get omitted. We would like to note that looking at full lists of candidates in a phrase table is not realistic—often there are hundreds of quite irrelevant options.

Another possible improvement is extending the dictionary with parallel sentence examples showcasing a given translation option (highlighting the aligned phrases in a source and target sentences). This can be implemented if the parallel corpus used for phrase table creation is available.

Overall, we evaluate the resulting bilingual Russian-English specialized phrase dictionary as a useful resource for those whose first language is Russian and who learn/use English as a second language. Especially, it can be helpful for those who write in English and has a frequent need to translate common introductory, connective, adverbial, and other above-mentioned types of phrases from Russian to English. We note, however, that this dictionary should be used only as a source of translation options, which should be checked elsewhere if a person is unsure, keeping in mind the automatic nature of this language resource. It also can be used by those who work on creating language learning tools and writing assistants as a raw resource for further processing.

As for the approach in general, we believe that despite its simplicity, it is one of the most affordable ways to automatically compile a bilingual phrase dictionary of decent quality. It can be particularly useful in the low-resource setting, where manually created resources do not exist or are incomplete but there is a parallel corpus available. The minimal size requirements for such corpus is, however, an open research question.

To make our study complete, we need to note that although we did not need it in this work, the important aspect of the automatic dictionary creation is the automatic extraction of meaningful phrases/collocations from text corpora. There exist a number of approaches for this task (Pecina, 2005; Bhalla and Klimcikova, 2019) and we think that their choice depends on the type and the purpose of the dictionary one wants to create.

The constructed dictionary in its current form is publicly available at `https://github.com/bilingual-phrase-dict/ru-en`.

6. Conclusion

This work raises an important issue of phrase translation. We emphasize the need for high-quality phrase translation models for second language learners and users and suggest a simple approach for obtaining phrase translations based on the GIZA++ output. Using this approach, we automatically construct a new Russian-English bilingual phrase dictionary and make it publicly available. We analyze the quality of our approach and highlight its strengths and shortcomings. We also compare it to translating phrases with a state-of-the-art neural machine translation model and show how poor NMT model performs in translating phrases. We see this as a problem and expect that future research will address it by proposing high-quality phrase translation models.

7. References

Bhalla, V. and Klimcikova, K. (2019). Evaluation of automatic collocation extraction methods for language learning. In *Proceedings of the Fourteenth Workshop on Innovative Use of NLP for Building Educational Applications*, pages 264–274, Florence, Italy, August. Association for Computational Linguistics.

Brown, P. F., Pietra, V. J. D., Pietra, S. A. D., and Mercer, R. L. (1993). The mathematics of statistical machine translation: Parameter estimation. *Comput. Linguist.*, 19(2):263–311, jun.

Chen, Y.-J., Yang, C.-Y. H., and Chang, J. S. (2020a). Improving phrase translation based on sentence alignment of Chinese-English parallel corpus. In *Proceedings of the 32nd Conference on Computational Linguistics and Speech Processing (ROCLING 2020)*, pages 6–7, Taipei, Taiwan, September. The Association for Computational Linguistics and Chinese Language Processing (ACLCLP).

Chen, Y., Liu, Y., Chen, G., Jiang, X., and Liu, Q. (2020b). Accurate word alignment induction from neural machine translation. In *Proceedings of the 2020 Conference on Empirical Methods in Natural Language Processing (EMNLP)*, pages 566–576, Online, November. Association for Computational Linguistics.

Daiga Deksne, A. V. (2018). A workflow for supplementing a latvian-english dictionary with data from parallel corpora and a reversed english-latvian dictionary. In *Proceedings of the XVIII EURALEX International Congress: Lexicography in Global Contexts*, pages 127–135, Ljubljana, Slovenia, jul. Ljubljana University Press, Faculty of Arts.

Garcia, M., García-Salido, M., and Alonso-Ramos, M. (2019). Towards the automatic construction of a multilingual dictionary of collocations using distributional semantics.

Jun, Z. (2008). A comprehensive review of studies on second language writing. *HKBU Papers in Applied Language Studies*, 12(2).

Koehn, P., Axelrod, A., Birch, A., Callison-Burch, C., Osborne, M., and Talbot, D. (2005). Edinburgh system description for the 2005 iwslt speech translation evaluation. *International Workshop on Spoken Language Translation*, 01.

Koehn, P., Hoang, H., Birch, A., Callison-Burch, C., Federico, M., Bertoldi, N., Cowan, B., Shen, W., Moran, C., Zens, R., Dyer, C., Bojar, O., Constantin, A., and Herbst, E. (2007). Moses: Open source toolkit for statistical machine translation. In *Proceedings of the 45th Annual Meeting of the Association for Computational Linguistics Companion Volume Proceedings of the Demo and Poster Sessions*, pages 177–180, Prague, Czech Republic, June. Association for Computational Linguistics.

Kupiec, J. (1993). An algorithm for finding noun phrase correspondences in bilingual corpora. In *31st Annual Meeting of the Association for Computational Linguistics*, pages 17–22, Columbus, Ohio, USA, June. Association for Computational Linguistics.

Och, F. J. and Ney, H. (2003). A Systematic Comparison of Various Statistical Alignment Models. *Computational Linguistics*, 29(1):19–51, 03.

Pecina, P. (2005). An extensive empirical study of collocation extraction methods. In *Proceedings of the ACL Student Research Workshop*, pages 13–18, Ann Arbor, Michigan, June. Association for Computational Linguistics.

Richardson, J., Nakazawa, T., and Kurohashi, S. (2014). Bilingual dictionary construction with transliteration filtering. In *Proceedings of the Ninth International Conference on Language Resources and Evaluation (LREC'14)*, pages 1013–1017, Reykjavik, Iceland, May. European Language Resources Association (ELRA).

Rivera, O. M., Mitkov, R., and Corpas Pastor, G. (2013). A flexible framework for collocation retrieval and translation from parallel and comparable corpora. In *Proceedings of the Workshop on Multi-word Units in Machine Translation and Translation Technologies*, Nice, France, September 3.

Schwenk, H., Wenzek, G., Edunov, S., Grave, E., Joulin, A., and Fan, A. (2021). CCMatrix: Mining billions of high-quality parallel sentences on the web. In *Proceedings of the 59th Annual Meeting of the Association for Computational Linguistics and the 11th International Joint Conference on Natural Language Processing (Volume 1: Long Papers)*, pages 6490–6500, Online, August. Association for Computational Linguistics.

Seretan, V. and Wehrli, É. (2007). Collocation translation based on sentence alignment and parsing. In *Actes de la 14ème conférence sur le Traitement Automatique des Langues Naturelles. Articles longs*, pages 375–384, Toulouse, France, June. ATALA.

Smadja, F., McKeown, K., and Hatzivassiloglou, V. (1996). Translating collocations for bilingual lexicons: A statistical approach. *Comput. Linguistics*, 22:1–38.

Tiedemann, J. and Thottingal, S. (2020). OPUS-MT – building open translation services for the world. In *Proceedings of the 22nd Annual Conference of the European Association for Machine Translation*, pages 479–480, Lisboa, Portugal, November. European Association for Machine Translation.

Tiedemann, J. (2012). Parallel data, tools and interfaces in OPUS. In *Proceedings of the Eighth International Conference on Language Resources and Evaluation (LREC'12)*, pages 2214–2218, Istanbul, Turkey, May. European Language Resources Association (ELRA).

Vasiljevic, Z. (2014). Teaching collocations in a second language: Why, what and how. *Elta Journal*, 2(2):48–73.

Zenkel, T., Wuebker, J., and DeNero, J. (2020). End-to-end neural word alignment outperforms GIZA++. In *Proceedings of the 58th Annual Meeting of the Association for Computational Linguistics*, pages 1605–1617, Online, July. Association for Computational Linguistics.

A BERT's Eye View: Identification of Irish Multiword Expressions Using Pre-trained Language Models

Abigail Walsh[1], Teresa Lynn[1], Jennifer Foster[2]
ADAPT Centre
Dublin City University
[1] {firstname.lastname}@adaptcentre.ie
[2] {firstname.lastname}@dcu.ie

Abstract

This paper reports on the investigation of using pre-trained language models for the identification of Irish verbal multiword expressions (vMWEs), comparing the results with the systems submitted for the PARSEME shared task edition 1.2. We compare the use of a monolingual BERT model for Irish (gaBERT) with multilingual BERT (mBERT), fine-tuned to perform MWE identification, presenting a series of experiments to explore the impact of hyperparameter tuning and dataset optimisation steps on these models. We compare the results of our optimised systems to those achieved by other systems submitted to the shared task, and present some best practices for minority languages addressing this task.

Keywords: Irish, BERT, multiword expressions, identification, pre-trained language models, hyperparameter-tuning, supervised learning, low-resource language NLP

1. Introduction

The automatic identification of multiword expressions (MWEs) has been highlighted as one of the two main subtasks of MWE processing (Constant et al., 2017), with their successful identification assisting a number of NLP tasks, such as parsing, machine translation and information retrieval. The PARSEME shared task on the automatic identification of verbal MWEs (vMWEs) (Savary et al., 2017), now in its third iteration, has recognised vMWEs as being of particular interest in this task, due to challenging properties that they can present, such as variability, ambiguity, and discontiguity. Its most recent edition (1.2), further highlighted the challenges inherent to identifying *unseen* vMWEs, that is, vMWEs that did not occur in either the training or development stage of model learning (Ramisch et al., 2020).

In this paper, we present a system for the identification of vMWEs in Irish and compare our results to other systems submitted to the PARSEME shared task. We use multilingual and monolingual language models, and demonstrate that monolingual models can lead to superior results, even compensating for small amounts of data. We also explore some of the optimisation steps that allow for lower-resourced languages, such as Irish, to fully exploit such resources, and report on patterns we find in these optimisation experiments.

2. Background

The Irish language is a minority language of the Celtic family of languages. Despite its status as the official language of Ireland, and an official working language of the European Union, it is recognised as a low resource language, particularly in the field of NLP (Judge et al., 2012; Lynn, 2022). Many NLP tasks lack the necessary resources for research in Irish, and the development of these resources has been an ongoing initiative for the past several years. Research into MWEs is one of those areas.

The PARSEME shared task on the identification of verbal MWEs came about as demand for a multilingual framework for the treatment of MWEs in NLP increased. Verbal MWEs, or vMWEs, are MWEs with a head verbal component, and include Light Verb Constructions ('LVCs') such as '***make a decision***', and Verbal Idioms 'VIDs' such as '***a little birdie told me***'. The latest edition (1.2) saw 14 languages included, as systems attempted to tackle the problem of *unseen* vMWEs, which has been recognised as a significant challenge in the task of MWE identification to date. Irish was one of the languages included, with the creation of the PARSEME annotated corpus of verbal MWEs for Irish (Walsh et al., 2020).

Of the nine systems participating in the shared task, five systems made use of neural networks: MultiVitaminBooster (Gombert and Bartsch, 2020), TRAVIS-mono and TRAVIS-multi (Kurfalı, 2020), MTLB-STRUCT (Taslimipoor et al., 2020) and ERMI (Yirmibeşoğlu and Güngör, 2020). Three used methods based on filtering using association measures: HMSid (Colson, 2020), Seen2Seen (Pasquer et al., 2020b) and Seen2Unseen (Pasquer et al., 2020a), while one system used a rule-based joint parsing and MWE identification system: FipsCo. Of the systems using neural networks, four of them included the use of pre-trained language models, those being multilingual BERT, monolingual BERT (Devlin et al., 2019) and XLM-Roberta (Conneau et al., 2020).

Pre-trained language models have become the defacto standard language resource for many NLP tasks, with

Proceedings of the 18th Workshop on Multiword Expressions (MWE 2022) n@LREC2022, pages 89–99

a track record of beating previous SOTA results (Min et al., 2021). The MTLB-STRUCT system, which uses multilingual BERT fine-tuned for joint parsing and identification, achieved the best results for the open track in both the tasks of the identification of vMWES, and the subtask of identifying *unseen* vMWEs, when averaged across all languages. For individual languages, the only system in the open track to outperform the MTLB-STRUCT system was the TRAVIS-mono system, which uses a monolingual BERT model with a classification layer for MWE identification, where that language had a monolingual BERT model.

2.1. BERT and gaBERT

Bidirectional Encoder Representations from Transformers (BERT) is the transformer-based pre-trained language model that has seen applications in a wide variety of NLP tasks (Devlin et al., 2019). It is trained on two tasks: (1) a masked language modelling task, where words are masked and then predicted from their context, and (2) next sentence prediction, where the task is to determine if the second sentence in a pair follows the first one. These two tasks have proven to be sufficiently general that the resulting language model can be fine-tuned on a large number of NLP tasks, through the addition of a classification layer, and the adjustment of model parameters.[1] Two English language BERT models (BERT-base and BERT-large) were released, along with a multilingual BERT model (mBERT), which had been trained on a concatenation of Wikipedia data for 104 languages. Since the release of BERT, monolingual models have been built for many other languages, including Irish.

gaBERT (Barry et al., 2022) is a monolingual language model for Irish trained on approximately 7.9 million sentences in Irish. The training process and hyperparameters were largely kept the same as that of BERT, with the distinction of a smaller batch size to accommodate memory size limitations. gaBERT was evaluated on dependency parsing and a cloze test, and the results were compared with mBERT, showing that gaBERT was more effective than mBERT for both these tasks.

2.2. Irish in the PARSEME Shared Task

Until recently, Irish research on MWEs has been mostly limited to the field of theoretical linguistics or corpus linguistics. Developments on this topic for NLP include the publication of the Peadar Ó Laoghaire collection of idioms (Ní Loingsigh and Ó Raghallaigh, 2016), and the creation of a lexicon of Irish MWEs for research purposes (Walsh et al., 2019). The Irish UD treebank (Lynn and Foster, 2016) recently saw a unified treatment of MWEs applied to the data (McGuinness et al., 2020). The release of the PARSEME annotated corpus of verbal MWEs for Irish was the first corpus to be manually annotated for these types of verbal MWEs in Irish (Walsh et al., 2020). The corpus[2] consists of 1700 sentences originally from the Irish UD Treebank[3], which includes gold-standard POS-information, morphological features, and dependency relations. These sentences are manually annotated with seven categories of verbal MWEs: Light verb constructions ('LVC.full' and 'LVC.cause'), Inherently Adpositional Verbs ('IAV'), Verbal Idioms ('VID'), Verb-Particle constructions ('VPC.full' and 'VPC.semi'), and Inherently Reflexive Verbs ('IRV').

'LVCs' are the most numerous label in the Irish corpus, including constructions such as the 'LCV.full' *déan iarracht* 'make an attempt/try', or the 'LVC.cause' *cuir tús* 'put a start/start'. 'IAVs' are also frequent in Irish, such as *buail le* (lit. hit with) 'meet' or *éirigh le* (lit. rise with) 'succeed'.

The corpus was split according to the specifications of the PARSEME shared task (Ramisch et al., 2020), with a training dataset size of 257 sentences (100 vMWEs) and a development dataset size of 322 sentences (126 vMWEs), with the rest of the data in the test set (1120 sentences, and 442 vMWEs). Compared to the other languages in the shared task, the Irish corpus is small, with only Hindi (1684 sentences) being smaller. The number of vMWEs annotated in the corpus was also low, with only 662 vMWEs in total, compared to 1034 for Hindi. This, combined with the high ratio of *unseen* vMWEs present (69% of the vMWEs occurring in the test set were not present in either the training data or development data), as well as the relatively high numbers of categorisation labels used (7 labels, compared to a language average of 5), makes the task of vMWE identification in Irish particularly challenging.

3. Experiment Design

Approaching the task of vMWE identification as a sequence labelling task, we follow the example of the TRAVIS system and fine-tune both a multilingual BERT model (mBERT) and a monolingual BERT model (gaBERT) with a classification layer on this task, and compare the results. The classification layer is a linear layer connected to the language models' hidden states to perform token-level classification. The HuggingFace Transformers library (Wolf et al., 2020) provides both the mBERT (Devlin, J. et. al., 2018) and gaBERT (Barry, J. et. al., 2021) models, which can be integrated with their tokenising library to easily fine-tune language models.

The data we use is in `cupt` format, which is a combination of `CoNLL-U` format and `parseme-tsv` format. For this sequence labelling task, we only required

[1]While the precise reason for this ability for language models to generalise across many tasks is not well understood due to the black box nature of the pre-training, Zhang and Hashimoto (2021) suggests that the MLM task encourages the LM to capture statistical dependencies, which corresponds to general syntactic information.

[2](Walsh, A. et. al., 2020)

[3](Lynn, T. et. al., 2015)

Hyperparameter	Default	Tuning range
Number of epochs	20	5, 10, 15, 20, 25, 30, 35, 40
Batch size	8	1, 2, 3, 4, 5, 6, 8, 10, 12, 14, 16, 20
Learning rate	2e-5	1e-6, 2e-6, 1e-5, 2e-5, 1e-4, 2e-4, 1e-3, 2e-3, 1e-2, 2e-2, 0.1, 0.2
Random seed	10	5, 10, 15, 20, 25, 30, 35, 40, 45, 50, 55, 60, 65, 70, 75, 80, 85, 90, 95, 100

Table 1: Default values used and range for tuning each hyperparameter.

the tokens and the MWE labels, so the data was processed into a `json` format containing this information. For labelling the vMWES, we used a modified *IOB2* scheme, as described in Section 3.2.1.

3.1. Series 1: Hyperparameter Optimisation

Fine-tuning hyperparameters is an important step in optimising a model's performance on a task, and even small adjustments to the hyperparameters can have a huge impact on model performance. There are many options to consider when tuning hyperparameters, from the selection of which hyperparameters to adjust, to the range of values being evaluated, to the method of hyperparameter optimisation being applied.

In this first series of experiments, we explore the impact that adjusting certain key hyperparameters has on our dataset, which is notably small. To best analyse the impact of this tuning, we opted to tune the hyperparameters **manually** and **individually**, selecting a combination of the best performing hyperparameters to fine-tune an optimised system for both the mBERT and gaBERT models.

We selected *learning rate*, *batch size*, *number of training epochs*, *the number of layers being fine-tuned*, and the *random seed variable* as our tunable parameters, defaulting to the values used by Devlin et al. (2019) for all other hyperparameters. We train both the mBERT and gaBERT models on three settings of layers: (i) fine-tuning all layers of the model, (ii) freezing layers 1-8 and only fine-tuning on the top-most 4 layers, (iii) freezing all layers and fine-tuning only the classification layer. The default values and range of values for tuning are represented in Table 1. To avoid over-fitting with the test data, we evaluated the model performance on the development set, and selected the best performing parameters based on these results.

3.1.1. Transformer Instability

A known issue in the training of transformer models is the tendency for instability of those models (Dodge et al., 2020; Bouscarrat et al., 2021; Mosbach et al., 2021), where the selection of a random seed value can have a significant impact on model performance. This effect appears to be magnified when training on small datasets, although, as Mosbach et al. (2021) find, this may be in fact due to the reduced number of iterations that training on smaller datasets may produce. To demonstrate the effects of this factor, we trained 10 mBERT-based models with a different random seed each time, which resulted in 2 models that failed to predict any MWEs at all.

Accounting for this instability, we perform the hyperparameter tuning first on the *number of epochs*, *batch size* and *learning rate*, before selecting the best performing hyperparameters and tuning this model on the *random seed value*, selecting the best performing random seed as our optimised hyperparameter. While the random seed value does not provide information on the model's structure as with the other hyperparameters, the selection of this value can drastically affect the performance of the model. The goal of our first series of experiments is to select an optimised model for comparison with the systems submitted at the PARSEME shared task so we have elected to tune this variable also.

3.2. Series 2: Data and Labelling

The second series of experiments focuses on some of the challenges for this task that are related to the data, such as data scarcity, relatively high number of labels, and the labelling scheme applied. We attempt to address these issues through optimising the data and comparing the baseline results to the models trained on these adjusted datasets.

3.2.1. Labelling Scheme

The labelling scheme used for the first series of experiments was a modified *IOB2* scheme, which is a version of the Inside-Outside-Beginning (*IOB*) format designed for chunking tasks such as NER detection (Ramshaw and Marcus, 1995). This required a conversion from the labels used in `cupt`, where vMWES are tagged with a number corresponding to the order the vMWE occurs within the sentence, to which a category label was appended for the first token of the vMWE. Our initial method was simply to select the first MWE label attached to each token, and discard any subsequent labels, a solution which was not always adequate. For instance, in converting from the *cupt* (Example 1) to the *IOB2* labelling (Example 2), the two LVCs *dhein staidéir* 'did study' and *dhein taighde* 'did research' have been incorrectly reduced to what appears to be a single LVC *dhein staidéir taighde* 'did study research'.

(1) **dhein** sé an-chuid **staidéir** agus
1:LVC.full;2:LVC.full * * 1 *
taighde
2

(2) **dhein** sé an-chuid **staidéir** agus **taighde**
B-LVC.full O O I-LVC.full O I-LVC.full
'he did a lot of study and research'

To address this, we propose a modified scheme *IOB2-double*, which uses the same labels as *IOB2*, but attempts to represent these 'doubly-annotated' tokens by adjusting the usage of the 'B-' labels: when encountering a token which has more than one vMWE label, the 'B-' prefix can be applied to both the initial token (vMWE #1), and the first subsequent token in the second vMWE (vMWE #2), as in Example 3. Using this scheme, the two LVCs are represented as 'did study' and 'research', which still does not capture the full picture, but prevents the loss of vMWEs through merging labels.

(3) **dhein** sé an-chuid **staidéir** agus
B-LVC.full O O I-LVC.full O
taighde
B-LVC.full

This labelling scheme does not address the discontiguity of *dhein, staidéir* and *taighde*, which are interleaved with non-lexicalised components. Berk et al. (2019) discuss this issue, and propose an alternative labelling scheme, *bigappy-unicrossy*, which uses lower case labels and label prefixes ('b-', 'i-', 'o') to allow for one level of nested MWEs, two levels of discontinuity of MWEs (including nested discontinuous MWEs), and one level of crossing MWEs. Their scheme does not address the issue of double-tagged tokens or overlapping vMWEs, so we apply our adjusted 'B-' criteria. In this scheme, the previous text is annotated as in Example 4. The lower case labels indicate that the vMWE *dhein staidéir* 'do study' is partially nested, as elements of it come between construction *dhein taighde* 'do research'.

(4) **dhein** sé an-chuid **staidéir** agus **taighde**
B-LVC.full o o i-LVC.full o B-LVC.full

3.2.2. Data Optimisation

The data-optimisation experiments address potential challenges that the Irish dataset presents over other languages: (i) the number of tags in the tagset, (ii) the complexity of the data, and (iii) the small size of the training and development datasets. To address these challenges, Exp 2A reduces the number of tags through first merging the two fine-grained labels ('LVC.full' and 'LVC.cause' → 'LVC'; 'VPC.full' and 'VPC.semi' → 'VPC'), and Exp 2B merges all tags into a single 'MWE' tag. Exp 3 reduces the complexity of the data through removing two challenging vMWE labels ('IRV' and 'VID'), while Exp 4 increases the size of the training and development datasets through re-splitting of the data, with 219 vMWEs annotated in the training data (+119 vMWEs), 216 vMWEs annotated in development data (+90 vMWEs) and 230 vMWEs in the test data (-212 vMWEs).

Of note, one of the so-called challenging vMWE labels, the 'IRV' label (e.g. ***iompair*** *mé* ***mé féin*** 'I **behaved myself**'), was identified previously (Walsh et al., 2020) as a label potentially worth removing due to the scarcity of this label occurring in the data (only 6 instances of this label were annotated) and the controversial nature of the label. The 'VID' label (e.g. ***cuir isteach sa chomhrá*** (lit. put into the conversation) 'intervene', ***dar le*** 'according to') presents the most syntactically and semantically diverse of the vMWE categories, given the highly variable nature of verbal idioms, whose lexicalised components can differ by part-of-speech, number, open-slots, etc.

4. Results and Analysis

4.1. Evaluation Metrics

We use both the evaluation library provided by seqeval (Nakayama, 2018), as well as the evaluation algorithm used in the PARSEME Shared Task (Ramisch et al., 2018) to evaluate our models, reporting *precision*, *recall* and *F1* scores. Two important differences between these algorithms are noted: (i) discontinuous MWE chunks are counted as separate MWEs by the seqeval calculations, and (ii) the PARSEME shared task evaluation metrics allow for partial matches of predicted vMWEs that share tokens with the gold annotated vMWEs ('Token-based' measures). When comparing our systems with those submitted for the PARSEME shared task, we limit the evaluation to the metrics calculated by the evaluation script provided for that task.

4.1.1. Analysis of Series 1

We trained each language model on the three layer settings mentioned in Section 3.1, resulting in six models for each hyperparameter tuning step: `mBERT-0` and `gaBERT-0` (layers 1-12 frozen, fine-tuned on 0 layers of language model), `mBERT-4` and `gaBERT-4` (layers 1-8 frozen, fine-tuned on final 4 layers of language model), and `mBERT-12` and `gaBERT-12` (no layers frozen, fine-tuned on all 12 layers).

`mBERT-12` and `gaBERT-12` models generally performed the best across our experiments, while `mBERT-0` and `gaBERT-0` generally performed the worst. From our experiments, we found training the models for more epochs improved performance, while batch size was inversely correlated with performance. The range of values containing the optimal learning rate varies depending on the layer settings, with `mBERT-0` and `gaBERT-0` requiring a larger learning rate. These trends are explained in more detail.

Number of Epochs: Training `mBERT-4` and `mBERT-12` for less than 5 epochs almost always produced a model that failed to predict any vMWE labels at all, with the same applying to `gaBERT-4` and `gaBERT-12`. This tendency to not predict labels decreased significantly as the number of epochs approached 15, while the $F1$ score for the models increased. This increase in $F1$ score continued an upwards trend to our upper bound of 40 epochs, though improvement slowed after 20 epochs.

Batch Size: The $F1$ score followed an inverse trend for batch size, with the peak $F1$ score achieved when batch size was between 1-4 for models `mBERT-4`, `mBERT-12`, `gaBERT-4` and `gaBERT-12`. Of note, when training with batch size of 20 for `mBERT-12`, the training halted due to memory limitations, highlighting the impact of hardware limitations on such experiments.

Learning Rate: Initially, the learning rates tuned were those described in Table 1. Noting the range of values that yielded the best performing models, we conducted a secondary tuning experiment using these optimised learning rates as anchor values for each of the layer settings, and training on a range of values on either side of these initial values. For `mBERT-4`, `mBERT-12`, `gaBERT-4` and `gaBERT-12`, when combined with the other default parameters, learning rates needed to be small; if the learning rate was larger than $8e$-4 it invariably produced a model that failed to predict any MWE labels. The best performing models used a learning rate of $4e$-5 for `mBERT-4` and `mBERT-12`, and $2e$-4 for `gaBERT-4` and `gaBERT-12`.
For `mBERT-0` and `gaBERT-0`, a larger learning rate was necessary to train a model that predicted MWE labels (greater than $2e$-4), and even learning rates as large as 0.8 will result in an $F1$ score of 10.1 (`mBERT-0`) and 23.2 (`gaBERT-0`). Combining this larger learning rate with the other hyperparameter tuning steps may result in even better performance.
Following these investigative experiments, we selected the best performing hyperparameter values from each trial and performed a series of experiments tuning the random seed value. As the best results for both models was consistently achieved for `mBERT-12` and `gaBERT-12`, we limited tuning to these layer settings. When using a combination of the best learning rate and batch size for `gaBERT-12`, we found that none of the models across any of the seed values succeeded in predicting any MWE labels, indicating that this particular combination of hyperparameters was not useful for our task. To find an optimised mode, we trained one series of models using the optimised learning rate parameter (`gaBERT-12-rate`) and one series of models using the optimised batch size (`gaBERT-12-batch`), with the values for the other hyperparameters taken from the default values in Table 2.

Random Seed: The box plot average of $F1$ scores from random seed tuning experiments are shown in Figure 1. We can see from the diagram that the `gaBERT-12-batch` model was more sensitive to instability than the `gaBERT-12-rate`, with the highest performing model achieving an $F1$ score of 43.0, but several seed values yielded a model that gave an $F1$ score of 0.0. The optimised gaBERT model was found with `gaBERT-12-rate` trained on random seed 10, while the optimised mBERT model (`mBERT-12`) was found on random seed 75.

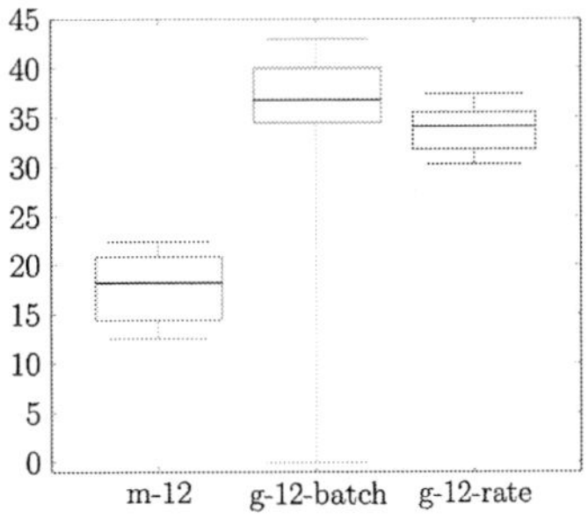

Figure 1: Box plot of $F1$ scores generated by mBERT-12, gaBERT-12-batch and gaBERT-12-rate models trained across 20 random seed values.

4.1.2. Analysis of Series 2

In our data optimisation experiments, we compare the results of models trained with the optimised hyperparameters of Series 1 on the baseline dataset (Exp 1), and datasets modified to address the challenges outlined in Section 4.1.2 (Exps 2A, 2B, 3 and 4). For each experiment, we apply the three labelling schemes discussed in Section 3.2.1: *IOB2*, *IOB2-double*, and *bigappy-unicrossy*. The $F1$ scores for each of these three datasets are displayed in Figure 2 (Exp 1), Figures 3 and 4 (Exp 2A and Exp 2B), Figure 5 (Exp 3) and Figure 6 (Exp 4). The precision, recall and $F1$ scores for each of these experiments are displayed in full in Table 3.
No clear discernible pattern emerges as to which labelling scheme produces the best results. In Figure 6 we see the results of models trained on reshuffled data (Exp 4) appears to show the *IOB2-double* labelling scheme out-performing *IOB2* labelling, with *bigappy-unicrossy* labelling giving the best results, however this trend was reversed for the mBERT model in Exp 2B, and for gaBERT in Exp 1.
The results of experiments 2A, 2B and 3 show that while modifying the dataset impacts the results of the model, it is difficult to predict whether this impact will be positive or negative. The results for Exp 2A demonstrate that the mBERT model trained on *IOB2-double* data failed to predict any MWE labels, again highlighting the model's susceptibility to instability. The experiments indicate that the language models' sensitivity to changes in dataset make it difficult to draw conclusions regarding the impact of the dataset optimisation, without further investigation into hyperparameter tuning.

4.2. Manual Inspection of Data

After inspecting the predicted labels, a large number of single-token predicted vMWEs were found. While single-token vMWEs did occur in the data as a result of converting from doubly-annotated tokens (see Section 3.2.1), these are relatively rare occurrences, and will only ever occur in combination with a multi-token vMWE. In contrast, the predicted single-token vMWEs would often occur with no other vMWE in context.

Parameter	mBERT-12	gaBERT-12-rate	gaBERT-12-batch
Number of epochs	30	30	30
Batch size	4	8	2
Learning rate	$4e$-5	$2e$-4	$2e$-5

Table 2: Hyperparameter settings for random seed tuning experiments.

Experiment	Model	Labelling	Precision	Recall	$F1$
Exp 1: Baseline dataset	mBERT-op	IOB2	16.09	12.93	14.34
		IOB2-d	20.05	17.09	14.34
		bi-uni	17.96	13.86	15.65
	gaBERT-op	IOB2	41.67	35.80	38.51
		IOB2-d	39.37	29.10	33.47
		bi-uni	39.59	26.79	31.96
Exp 2A: Fine-grained MWE labels merged	mBERT-op	IOB2	12.85	9.51	10.93
		IOB2-d	0.00	0.00	0.00
		bi-uni	12.83	9.05	10.61
	gaBERT-op	IOB2	46.21	31.09	37.17
		IOB2-d	45.25	37.59	41.06
		bi-uni	48.55	42.69	45.43
Exp 2B: All MWE labels merged	mBERT-op	IOB2	22.83	14.55	17.77
		IOB2-d	20.19	14.55	16.91
		bi-uni	16.86	10.16	12.68
	gaBERT-op	IOB2	41.83	33.72	37.34
		IOB2-d	36.75	25.64	30.20
		bi-uni	41.69	33.03	36.86
Exp 3: VID and IRV removed	mBERT-op	IOB2	15.69	12.83	14.12
		IOB2-d	9.35	8.82	9.08
		bi-uni	14.33	11.23	12.59
	gaBERT-op	IOB2	43.43	29.15	34.88
		IOB2-d	41.56	27.01	32.74
		bi-uni	48.28	41.18	44.44
Exp 4: Data resplit	mBERT-op	IOB2	18.06	16.96	17.49
		IOB2-d	22.47	22.17	22.32
		bi-uni	32.00	24.35	27.65
	gaBERT-op	IOB2	42.51	38.26	40.27
		IOB2-d	46.03	37.83	41.53
		bi-uni	46.53	40.87	43.52

Table 3: Precision, recall and $F1$ scores for the mBERT and gaBERT models trained on experiment data from Experiments 1–4, using optimised hyperparameters found in Series 1. Results obtained using the PARSEME ST evaluation script for global MWE-based evaluation, before the post-processing script was applied.

A post-processing script was added to each system where these single-token vMWEs were removed from the data, and this resulted in improved MWE-based precision and $F1$ scores for both models, an increase of 5.59 and 7.15 for global MWE-based $F1$ scores for mBERT- and gaBERT-optimised models respectively.

Between the models, this tendency to predict single-token vMWEs is more prevalent with the mBERT-based models than with gaBERT-based models, with the rate of single-token to multi-token MWE predictions almost double for the mBERT models, across all labelling schemes. Additionally, generating a bag-of-words of the predicted tokens of both models shows gaBERT-based models predict labels attached to a wider variety of tokens than mBERT-based models, particularly for 'LVC' type vMWEs.

Certain patterns in predictions were consistent across all experiments. Most of the 'VPC' label predictions were assigned to the tokens *bain* + *amach* (extract out) 'get', or some variation of these tokens, which make up the majority of the 'VPC' annotations in the training and development data. Verbs such as *cuir* 'put' were highly associated with 'LVC.cause' labels, reflecting the use of this verb in causative constructions, e.g. *cuir fearg (ar)* (put anger (on)) 'anger', while *déan* and *tabhair* ('make/do' and 'give') are highly associated with 'LVC.full', e.g. *déan iarratas* 'make an application'.

On examining individual categories of vMWES, it ap-

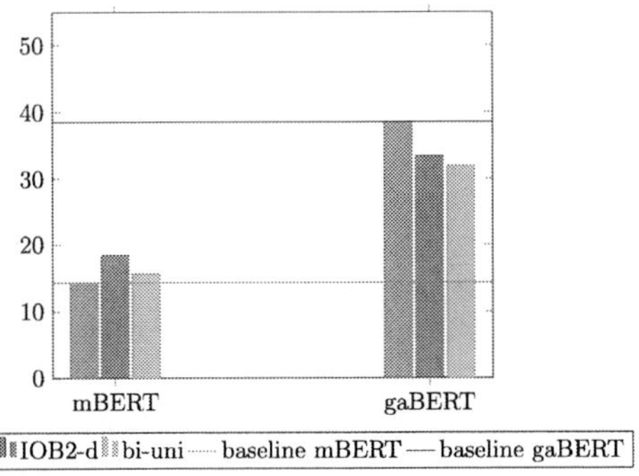

Figure 2: $F1$ scores for mBERT and gaBERT models for Exp 1: Using baseline data and comparing performance of labelling schemes (*IOB2*, *IOB2-double* and *bigappy-unicrossy*).

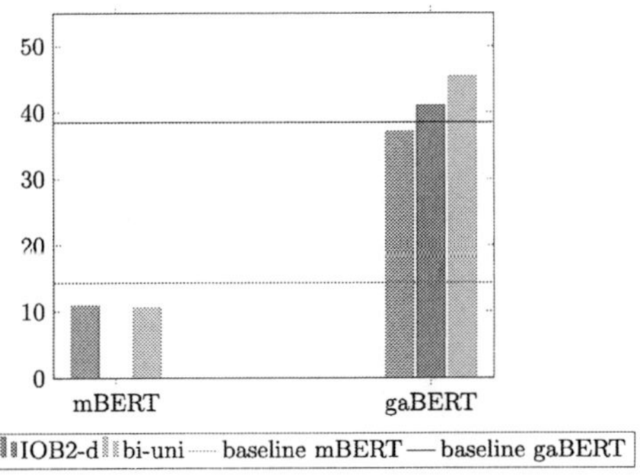

Figure 3: $F1$ scores for mBERT and gaBERT models for Exp 2A: Simplifying tagset by merging 'LVC' and 'VPC' sub-tags. Data labelled using *IOB2*, *IOB2-double* and *bigappy-unicrossy*.

mBERT	Freq	gaBERT	Freq
le	35	*le*	39
cuir	25	*cuir*	23
déan	23	*ar*	18
déanamh	16	*déan*	18
ar	14	*déanamh*	15
bain	12	*cur*	14
éirigh	11	*bain*	13
amach	10	*tabhair*	11
as	9	*éirigh*	11
tabhair	8	*i*	10

Table 4: Table showing 10 most frequently labelled words for mBERT-optimised and gaBERT-optimised models.

pears some labels were easier to predict than others. Both gaBERT and mBERT appear to achieve high precision but low recall for 'VPC.full' MWEs, reflecting the scarcity of this label in the training data. gaBERT-based models appear to perform better on predicting

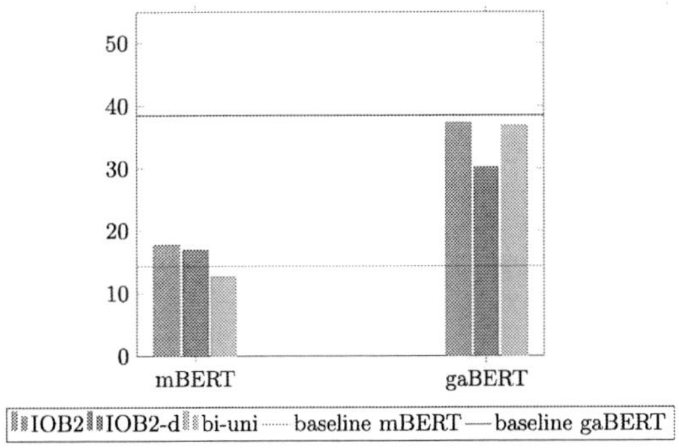

Figure 4: $F1$ scores for mBERT and gaBERT models for Exp 2B: Simplifying tagset by merging all vMWE labels. Data labelled using *IOB2*, *IOB2-double* and *bigappy-unicrossy*.

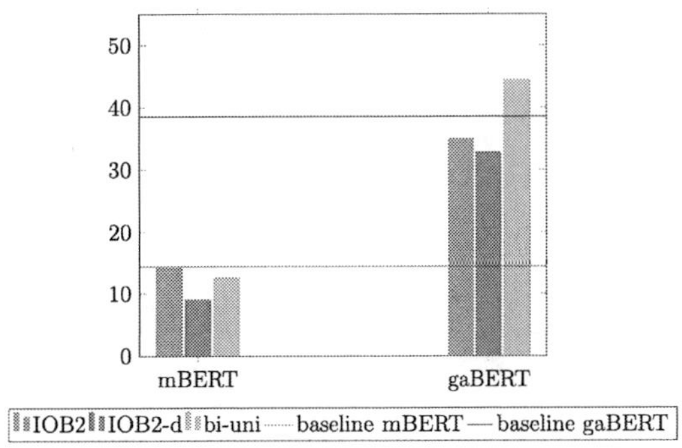

Figure 5: $F1$ scores for mBERT and gaBERT models for Exp 3: Simplifying dataset by removing challenging vMWEs 'IRV' and 'VID'. Data labelled using *IOB2*, *IOB2-double* and *bigappy-unicrossy*.

both 'LVC.full' and 'LVC.cause' MWEs than mBERT-based models, with the baseline results showing a difference of 27.86 and 41.71 in the MWE-based $F1$ scores, respectively. 'VID' vMWEs proved challenging for both models to predict, with mBERT-based models outperforming gaBERT-based models, with an MWE-based $F1$ score of 12.35 vs 10.64.[4] These scores decreased further with the reshuffled dataset, with the mBERT-based model achieving an $F1$ score of 5.56 and the gaBERT-based model scoring 4.48.[4]

4.3. Optimised Model

When comparing the results of Exp 4 with the results of our optimised baseline model, we noted that the mBERT-based model sees a significant improvement for each of the evaluation metrics with the additional data, however, the gaBERT-based model actually saw a slight decline in the token-based and unseen MWE-based scores, particularly in precision scores. This result may be due to the addition of a larger variety of

[4]MWE-based $F1$ scores after removing single-token predictions.

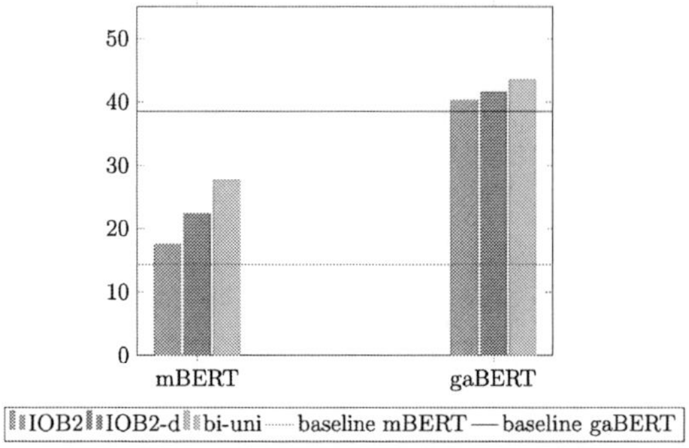

Figure 6: $F1$ scores for mBERT and gaBERT models for Exp 4: Increasing training and development data by reshuffling dataset splits. Data labelled using *IOB2*, *IOB2-double* and *bigappy-unicrossy*.

certain vMWEs such as 'VPCs', which in turn may prompt the model to attempt to predict these vMWEs attaching to a wider variety of tokens, making some incorrect predictions.

4.3.1. Comparison with Systems Submitted to the PARSEME Shared Task

Table 5 displays the results of systems submitted to the open track of the PARSEME shared task 1.2 for the Irish language. We see that our fine-tuned mBERT model from Series 1 compares favourably with the systems submitted for this task in Irish. Our mBERT-based system, if hypothetically submitted to the open track for Irish, would rank 3rd for unseen MWE identification, as well as MWE-based and token-based rankings. Our gaBERT-based system outperforms all other systems in this track, ranking 1st across all metrics, beating the MTLB-STRUCT system's MWE-based $F1$ score by 20.79 for unseen vMWE identification.

On the multilingual level, MTLB-STRUCT, the overall highest-performing system, achieved an MWE-based $F1$ score of 38.53 on unseen MWEs, a global MWE-based $F1$ score of 70.14, and a Token-based $F1$ score of 74.14, when averaged across all 14 languages. Even with the improvement in scores generated by the gaBERT-based model, Irish is still the language with the lowest performance score for global MWE-based and Token-based scores. However, the unseen MWE-based $F1$ score given by gaBERT is actually higher than the language average, and gaBERT outperforms the best system for several other languages (Basque, Hebrew, Italian, Portuguese and Romanian). This could be due to many Irish vMWE constructions consisting of common verbs (*bain* 'extract', *cuir* 'put', *tabhair* 'give', *faigh* 'get') and the language's proclivity for 'LVC' and 'IAV' constructions, which follow regular syntactic patterns.

4.4. Lessons Learned for Low-Resource MWE Identification

Following these experiments, we draw some conclusions from our method, and hope these learnings will be applicable to other lower-resourced languages tackling this task.

The results demonstrate the value of **monolingual language models** in such tasks. Our gaBERT-based models outperformed the mBERT-based models in almost all experiments conducted, barring some models which failed to predict any MWEs at all. This significant increase in performance is particularly reflected in the case of unseen VMWEs, which by their nature, present a great challenge to low-resource languages, as they are likely to be more prevalent where there is a scarcity of data/resources. Our experiments show how even a very small dataset can yield results similar to languages with much larger datasets (e.g. Portuguese, which had 6437 annotated vMWEs, almost 10 times the number annotated in the Irish dataset).

Clearly, such monolingual language models are expensive to train, both in language resources and in hardware required, and may be a challenge for lower-resource languages to build. However, our experiments show that multilingual models such as mBERT show promising capabilities to capture even unseen vMWES, and even small additions to the data can dramatically improve these results. These experiments also highlighted the importance of careful **hyperparameter tuning**, as the manual explorations of the hyperparameter space resulted in an improvement of 4.73 (8.86 after single-tokens were removed) in the unseen MWE-based $F1$ score compared to the mBERT-based system submitted by TRAVIS-multi.

Our experiments confirm the susceptibility of transformer-based models to **instability**, where even small variations in the data or in the hyperparameters selected (particularly the varying of the random seed variable) can result in a model that fails to predict any labels whatsoever. This problem seems to be exacerbated by the small size of the training data. However, our experiments indicate that the issue can be combatted through increasing the number of epochs trained for, and by varying the learning rate. This finding of ours parallels the work of Mosbach et al. (2021) who, upon investigating the topic of instability in fine-tuning BERT, recommend using small learning rates with bias correction to avoid vanishing gradients early in training, and increasing the number of iterations considerably and training to near zero training loss. However, as discussed in Section 4.1.1, some combinations of hyperparameters may result in unexpected model behaviour during training. As such, a random search hyperparameter tuning approach may be the most effective, as there is little guarantee that a well-performing hyperparameter setting will still perform well when combined with a different well-performing hyperparameter.

Category	Model	Precision	Recall	$F1$
Unseen MWE-based	gaBERT-optimised	53.30	32.44	**40.33**
	MTLB-STRUCT	23.08	16.94	19.54
	Seen2Unseen	21.74	9.97	13.67
	mBERT-optimised	25.88	07.36	11.46
	Travis-multi	3.75	1.99	2.6
	MultiVitaminBooster	0.0	0.0	0.0
Global MWE-based	gaBERT-optimised	63.01	35.80	**45.66**
	MTLB-STRUCT	37.72	25	30.07
	Seen2Unseen	44.16	23.39	30.58
	mBERT-optimised	43.41	12.93	19.93
	Travis-multi	12.36	5.05	7.17
	MultiVitaminBooster	0.0	0.0	0.0
Global Token-based	gaBERT-optimised	74.31	42.89	**54.38**
	MTLB-STRUCT	65.02	33.79	44.47
	Seen2Unseen	50.41	24.11	32.62
	mBERT-optimised	65.76	19.30	29.85
	Travis-multi	65.48	16.3	26.11
	MultiVitaminBooster	0.0	0.0	0.0

Table 5: Precision, recall and $F1$ scores for unseen MWE-based, global MWE-based and global Token-based metrics for open-track systems submitted to the PARSEME shared task 1.2 for the Irish annotated corpus, with our optimised gaBERT and mBERT-based models included for comparison.

We also investigated the potential for **alternative sequence labelling schemes** that more accurately capture the vMWE labels. Our experiments on this topic are inconclusive, as there is no guarantee that the results we found are consistent when applied to a model trained on different hyperparameter settings. However, these alternative labelling schemes do allow for capturing doubly-annotated tokens, which previously would have been lost when using a traditional *IOB2* labelling scheme.

5. Conclusion & Future Work

In this paper we report on an exploration of the application of pre-trained language models (both multilingual and monolingual) for the task of vMWE identification in Irish. Following the example of the TRAVIS systems submitted to the PARSEME shared task 1.2, we fine-tune language models to perform sequence labelling classification of the tokens, describing two series of experiments, exploring hyperparameter tuning, and data modifications addressing potentially challenging issues. We briefly discuss the labelling scheme used, focusing on the issue of labelling doubly-annotated (overlapping) tokens.

Our results reveal patterns in hyperparameter tuning, and these insights lead us to developing an optimised mBERT and gaBERT-based model. Five experiments exploring data modification and labelling of the data show inconclusive patterns with $F1$ scores achieved. A manual inspection of the data reveals some patterns in predicted MWEs by model and category. A comparison of our optimised systems for both mBERT and gaBERT with the PARSEME shared task results demonstrate the importance of careful hyperparameter tuning.

These experiments particularly highlight the value of monolingual language models in this task, as the gaBERT-based model achieved unseen MWE-based $F1$ scores that outperformed other systems submitted for the Irish corpus, and even outperformed systems submitted for other, higher-resourced languages, indicating that high-quality language-specific resources can compensate for a lack of language data in certain NLP tasks.

Future work includes continuing hyperparameter optimisation following the data optimisation strategies explored in this work and application of alternative labelling schemes, to investigate the full impact of these changes to a potentially optimised MWE identification model. We would also consider experiments in joint-learning tasks, such as the joint parsing and MWE identification systems trained by MTLB-STRUCT, which showed promising results. Such experiments allow for exploitation of other linguistically rich Irish resources, such as the Irish UD Treebank.

6. Acknowledgements

This research is funded by the Irish Government Department of Tourism, Culture, Arts, Gaeltacht, Sport and Media under the GaelTech Project. This work is also supported by Science Foundation Ireland in the ADAPT Centre (Grant 13/RC/2106) (`http://www.adaptcentre.ie`) at Dublin City University. The authors would like to thank the anonymous reviewers for their helpful feedback and suggestions.

7. Bibliographical References

Barry, J., Wagner, J., Cassidy, L., Cowap, A., Lynn, T., Walsh, A., Ó Meachair, M. J., and Foster, J. (2022). gaBERT – an Irish Language Model. In *Proceedings of the 13th Language Resources and Evaluation Conference*, Marseille, France, June.

Berk, G., Erden, B., and Güngör, T. (2019). Representing overlaps in sequence labeling tasks with a novel tagging scheme: bigappy-unicrossy. Computational Linguistics and Intelligent Text Processing, Springer International Publishing.

Bouscarrat, L., Bonnefoy, A., Capponi, C., and Ramisch, C. (2021). AMU-EURANOVA at CASE 2021 Task 1: Assessing the stability of multilingual BERT. In *Proceedings of the 4th Workshop on Challenges and Applications of Automated Extraction of Socio-political Events from Text (CASE 2021)*, pages 161–170, Online, August. Association for Computational Linguistics.

Colson, J.-P. (2020). HMSid and HMSid2 at PARSEME shared task 2020: Computational corpus linguistics and unseen-in-training MWEs. In *Proceedings of the Joint Workshop on Multiword Expressions and Electronic Lexicons*, pages 119–123, online, December. Association for Computational Linguistics.

Conneau, A., Khandelwal, K., Goyal, N., Chaudhary, V., Wenzek, G., Guzmán, F., Grave, E., Ott, M., Zettlemoyer, L., and Stoyanov, V. (2020). Unsupervised cross-lingual representation learning at scale. In *Proceedings of the 58th Annual Meeting of the Association for Computational Linguistics*, pages 8440–8451, Online, July. Association for Computational Linguistics.

Constant, M., Eryiğit, G., Monti, J., van der Plas, L., Ramisch, C., Rosner, M., and Todirascu, A. (2017). Survey: Multiword Expression Processing: A Survey. *Computational Linguistics*, 43(4):837–892, December.

Devlin, J., Chang, M.-W., Lee, K., and Toutanova, K. (2019). BERT: Pre-training of deep bidirectional transformers for language understanding. In *Proceedings of the 2019 Conference of the North American Chapter of the Association for Computational Linguistics: Human Language Technologies, Volume 1 (Long and Short Papers)*, pages 4171–4186, Minneapolis, Minnesota, June. Association for Computational Linguistics.

Dodge, J., Ilharco, G., Schwartz, R., Farhadi, A., Hajishirzi, H., and Smith, N. A. (2020). Fine-tuning pretrained language models: Weight initializations, data orders, and early stopping. *ArXiv*, abs/2002.06305.

Gombert, S. and Bartsch, S. (2020). MultiVitaminBooster at PARSEME shared task 2020: Combining window- and dependency-based features with multilingual contextualised word embeddings for VMWE detection. In *Proceedings of the Joint Workshop on Multiword Expressions and Electronic Lexicons*, pages 149–155, online, December. Association for Computational Linguistics.

Judge, J., Ní Chasaide, A., Ní Dhubhda, R., Scannell, K. P., and Uí Dhonnchadha, E. (2012). *The Irish Language in the Digital Age*. Springer Publishing Company, Incorporated.

Kurfalı, M. (2020). TRAVIS at PARSEME shared task 2020: How good is (m)BERT at seeing the unseen? In *Proceedings of the Joint Workshop on Multiword Expressions and Electronic Lexicons*, pages 136–141, online, December. Association for Computational Linguistics.

Lynn, T. and Foster, J. (2016). Universal Dependencies for Irish. In *Proceedings of the Second Celtic Language Technology Workshop*, pages 79–92, Paris, July.

Lynn, T. (2022). Report on the Irish language. https://european-language-equality.eu/deliverables/. Technical Report D1.20, European Language Equality Project.

McGuinness, S., Phelan, J., Walsh, A., and Lynn, T. (2020). Annotating MWEs in the Irish UD treebank. In *Proceedings of the Fourth Workshop on Universal Dependencies (UDW 2020)*, pages 126–139, Barcelona, Spain (Online), December. Association for Computational Linguistics.

Min, B., Ross, H., Sulem, E., Veyseh, A. P. B., Nguyen, T. H., Sainz, O., Agirre, E., Heinz, I., and Roth, D. (2021). Recent advances in natural language processing via large pre-trained language models: A survey.

Mosbach, M., Andriushchenko, M., and Klakow, D. (2021). On the stability of fine-tuning bert: Misconceptions, explanations, and strong baselines. In *International Conference on Learning Representations*, pages 847–869, Vienna, Apr.

Nakayama, H. (2018). seqeval: A python framework for sequence labeling evaluation. Software available from https://github.com/chakki-works/seqeval.

Ní Loingsigh, K. and Ó Raghallaigh, B. (2016). Starting from scratch – the creation of an Irish-language idiom database. In George Meladze Tinatin Margalitadze, editor, *Proceedings of the 17th EURALEX International Congress*, pages 726–734, Tbilisi, Georgia, sep. Ivane Javakhishvili Tbilisi University Press.

Pasquer, C., Savary, A., Ramisch, C., and Antoine, J.-Y. (2020a). Seen2Unseen at PARSEME shared task 2020: All roads do not lead to unseen verb-noun VMWEs. In *Proceedings of the Joint Workshop on Multiword Expressions and Electronic Lexicons*, pages 124–129, online, December. Association for Computational Linguistics.

Pasquer, C., Savary, A., Ramisch, C., and Antoine, J.-Y. (2020b). Verbal multiword expression identification: Do we need a sledgehammer to crack a nut? In *Proceedings of the 28th International Conference on Computational Linguistics*, pages 3333–

3345, Barcelona, Spain (Online), December. International Committee on Computational Linguistics.

Ramisch, C., Cordeiro, S. R., Savary, A., Vincze, V., Barbu Mititelu, V., Bhatia, A., Buljan, M., Candito, M., Gantar, P., Giouli, V., Güngör, T., Hawwari, A., Iñurrieta, U., Kovalevskaitė, J., Krek, S., Lichte, T., Liebeskind, C., Monti, J., Parra Escartín, C., QasemiZadeh, B., Ramisch, R., Schneider, N., Stoyanova, I., Vaidya, A., and Walsh, A. (2018). Edition 1.1 of the PARSEME shared task on automatic identification of verbal multiword expressions. In *Proceedings of the Joint Workshop on Linguistic Annotation, Multiword Expressions and Constructions (LAW-MWE-CxG-2018)*, pages 222–240, Santa Fe, New Mexico, USA, August. Association for Computational Linguistics.

Ramisch, C., Savary, A., Guillaume, B., Waszczuk, J., Candito, M., Vaidya, A., Barbu Mititelu, V., Bhatia, A., Iñurrieta, U., Giouli, V., Güngör, T., Jiang, M., Lichte, T., Liebeskind, C., Monti, J., Ramisch, R., Stymne, S., Walsh, A., and Xu, H. (2020). Edition 1.2 of the PARSEME shared task on semi-supervised identification of verbal multiword expressions. In *Proceedings of the Joint Workshop on Multiword Expressions and Electronic Lexicons*, pages 107–118, online, December. Association for Computational Linguistics.

Ramshaw, L. and Marcus, M. (1995). Text chunking using transformation-based learning. In *Third Workshop on Very Large Corpora*.

Savary, A., Ramisch, C., Cordeiro, S., Sangati, F., Vincze, V., QasemiZadeh, B., Candito, M., Cap, F., Giouli, V., Stoyanova, I., and Doucet, A. (2017). The PARSEME shared task on automatic identification of verbal multiword expressions. In *Proceedings of the 13th Workshop on Multiword Expressions (MWE 2017)*, pages 31–47, Valencia, Spain, April. Association for Computational Linguistics.

Taslimipoor, S., Bahaadini, S., and Kochmar, E. (2020). MTLB-STRUCT @parseme 2020: Capturing unseen multiword expressions using multi-task learning and pre-trained masked language models. In *Proceedings of the Joint Workshop on Multiword Expressions and Electronic Lexicons*, pages 142–148, online, December. Association for Computational Linguistics.

Walsh, A., Lynn, T., and Foster, J. (2019). Ilfhocail: A lexicon of Irish MWEs. In *Proceedings of the Joint Workshop on Multiword Expressions and WordNet (MWE-WN 2019)*, pages 162–168, Florence, Italy, August. Association for Computational Linguistics.

Walsh, A., Lynn, T., and Foster, J. (2020). Annotating verbal MWEs in Irish for the PARSEME shared task 1.2. In *Proceedings of the Joint Workshop on Multiword Expressions and Electronic Lexicons*, pages 58–65, online, December. Association for Computational Linguistics.

Wolf, T., Debut, L., Sanh, V., Chaumond, J., Delangue, C., Moi, A., Cistac, P., Rault, T., Louf, R., Funtowicz, M., Davison, J., Shleifer, S., von Platen, P., Ma, C., Jernite, Y., Plu, J., Xu, C., Le Scao, T., Gugger, S., Drame, M., Lhoest, Q., and Rush, A. (2020). Transformers: State-of-the-art natural language processing. In *Proceedings of the 2020 Conference on Empirical Methods in Natural Language Processing: System Demonstrations*, pages 38–45, Online, October. Association for Computational Linguistics.

Yirmibeşoğlu, Z. and Güngör, T. (2020). ERMI at PARSEME shared task 2020: Embedding-rich multiword expression identification. In *Proceedings of the Joint Workshop on Multiword Expressions and Electronic Lexicons*, pages 130–135, online, December. Association for Computational Linguistics.

Zhang, T. and Hashimoto, T. B. (2021). On the inductive bias of masked language modeling: From statistical to syntactic dependencies. In *Proceedings of the 2021 Conference of the North American Chapter of the Association for Computational Linguistics: Human Language Technologies*, pages 5131–5146, Online, jun. Association for Computational Linguistics.

8. Language Resource References

Barry, J. et. al. (2021). *gaBERT Irish language model.* distributed via Huggingface Library: DCU-NLP/bert-base-irish-cased-v1.

Devlin, J. et. al. (2018). *BERT multilingual language model.* distributed via Huggingface Library: bert-base-multilingual-cased.

Lynn, T. et. al. (2015). *Irish UD Treebank.* distributed via LINDAT/CLARIAH-CZ: `http://hdl.handle.net/11234/1-4611`.

Walsh, A. et. al. (2020). *PARSEME corpus for Irish.* distributed via LINDAT/CLARIAH-CZ: `http://hdl.handle.net/11234/1-3367`.

Enhancing the PARSEME Turkish Corpus of Verbal Multiword Expressions

Yağmur Öztürk[1], Najet Hadj Mohamed[2], Adam Lion-Bouton[2], Agata Savary[1]
Paris-Saclay University - LISN[1], University of Tours - LIFAT[2]
{yagmur.ozturk, agata.savary}@universite-paris-saclay.fr
{najat.hadjmohamed, adam.lion-bouton}@etu.univ-tours.fr

Abstract

The PARSEME (Parsing and Multiword Expressions) project proposes multilingual corpora annotated for multiword expressions (MWEs). In this case study, we focus on the Turkish corpus of PARSEME. Turkish is an agglutinative language and shows high inflection and derivation in word forms. This can cause some issues in terms of automatic morphosyntactic annotation. We provide an overview of the problems observed in the morphosyntactic annotation of the Turkish PARSEME corpus. These issues are mostly observed on the lemmas, which is important for the approximation of a type of an MWE. We propose modifications of the original corpus with some enhancements on the lemmas and parts of speech. The enhancements are then evaluated with an identification system from the PARSEME Shared Task 1.2 to detect MWEs, namely Seen2Seen. Results show increase in the F-measure for MWE identification, emphasizing the necessity of robust morphosyntactic annotation for MWE processing, especially for languages that show high surface variability.

Keywords: multiword expressions, morphosyntax, agglutinative languages, lemmatization, natural language processing

1. Introduction

Natural language processing tasks come with the challenge of working across languages. Meeting this challenge, both Universal Dependencies (UD)[1] and PARSEME[2] are multilingual projects with the aim of unifying linguistic descriptions across languages. Languages that are typologically distant from some of the high-resourced Germanic and Romance languages can be a challenge to adapt into this unified typology made for linguistic annotation. Since PARSEME annotations are done on previously annotated UD treebanks, problems occurring in the treebanks are persistent in the PARSEME corpora.

In the scope of this case study, we have examined the Turkish corpus (Erden et al., 2018) of PARSEME due to its rich morphology realized with inflectional and derivational suffixes. This corpus was automatically annotated for morphosyntax with UDPipe (Straka, 2018) and manually annotated (Berk et al., 2018) for verbal multiword expressions (VMWEs) with PARSEME's annotation guidelines[3]. In the PARSEME Shared Task 1.1 (Ramisch et al., 2018), a MWE is defined as a group of lexicalized words displaying lexical, morphological, syntactic and/or semantic idiosyncrasy. Traditionally, lexicalisation refers to the process in which a word acquires the status of an autonomous lexical unit. Expanding the scope of this definition, in MWEs, PARSEME considers lexicalisation applying not only to the whole unit of an MWE, but also its individual components. The reason for this is the need of precising the span of an MWE. Thus, we only annotate the lexically fixed components of an MWE, and these components are referred to as lexicalized within a given MWE (Markantonatou et al., 2018).

MWEs are represented as multisets of lemmas of their components, e.g. the English MWE ***let bygones be bygones*** is represented as {be, bygone, bygone, let} and the Turkish ***geri adım attılar*** (lit. 'they took a step back') 'they retreated' as {adım, at, geri}. Many VMWEs exhibit a certain degree of morphosyntactic flexibility, which is displayed by their various forms. For instance, ***geri adım attılar*** 'they took a step back', and ***geri adım atabilirlerdi*** 'they could have taken a step back' are occurrences of the VMWE, represented as {geri, adım, at}{back, step, throw}. A type is the set of all occurrences of the same MWE, and is formally represented as a multiset of lemmas of its lexicalized components. In practice, approximating types as multisets of lemmas can be helpful for MWE identification by neutralizing morphosyntactic variability, e.g. by conflating different forms and occurrences of the same MWE. For MWE types to be correctly identified, correct lemmatization of occurrences is important. In languages with higher rate of inflection and derivation, this issue can be more visible.

For this case study, examination of the Turkish corpus was made using a corpus visualization tool provided by PARSEME. This tool enables the user to see all occurrences of annotated VMWE types and their categories defined by the PARSEME annotation guide. The most notable issue observed in the Turkish corpus is the frequent incorrect/incomplete lemmatization of highly inflected verbs. Issues are further discussed in section 4. After the manual enhancement of most of these lemmas, one of the best performing systems of the PARSEME shared task 1.2, called Seen2Seen, was trained and tested on the enhanced data to show the impact of enhanced lemmatization.

2. Related Works

One of the first works on annotating Turkish MWEs was done by (Adalı et al., 2016) to define a comprehensive annotation guide. The authors mention specific constructions such as duplication and named entities. This guide is referenced in the first edition of PARSEME. Annotation from this edition was adapted to the updated version of the unified guidelines on the same corpus in the following editions of PARSEME.

Pertaining to the morphosyntactic annotation of treebanks

[1] `https://universaldependencies.org/`

[2] `https://gitlab.com/parseme/corpora/-/wikis/home`

[3] `https://parsemefr.lis-lab.fr/parseme-st-guidelines/1.2/`

Proceedings of the 18th Workshop on Multiword Expressions (MWE 2022) n@LREC2022, pages 100–104

in Turkish, it is important to mention manual annotation work in progress, which aims to increase the number of derivational representations. With this manual annotation, (Türk et al., 2019) aim to increase the accuracy of annotation not only for Turkish but also for other agglutinative languages. For future works, this corpus can be annotated for MWEs, which will help build a better corpus for PARSEME. In the PARSEME project, most of the language data is annotated for morphosyntax using automatic tools trained on treebanks, such as UDPipe[4]. The Turkish corpus is also automatically annotated for morphosyntax with UDPipe, and manually annotated for VMWEs. Turkish data have existed in PARSEME since edition 1.0 and went through changes in terms of annotation guidelines. Edition 1.1 uses the ITU NLP Tool[5] for morphosyntactic annotation. In the latest edition, re-parsing was executed relying on a model in UDPipe version 2.4 based on IMST[6] (Sulubacak et al., 2016). This treebank was first manually annotated in non-UD style and then converted to UD. Manual annotations of VMWEs from edition 1.1 were updated to match the new annotation guidelines of PARSEME edition 1.2. The raw[7] Turkish corpus of PARSEME consists of newspaper articles, which is the same genre of text used in the IMST.

In addition, UD currently has 9 Turkish treebanks. These treebanks have followed slightly different annotation processes from one another, therefore teams focusing on Turkish are working on the unification (Türk et al., 2019) of annotation guidelines for UD. Moreover, shortcomings of UD in expressing the derivational nature of languages as a more general problem have been studied by (Bedir et al., 2021).

In UD 2.0, the lemmatizer works with a guesser that produces (lemma rule, UPOS) pairs, where the lemma rule generates a lemma from a word by stripping some prefixes and suffixes and prepending and appending new prefixes and suffixes. The lemmatization rules look at the last four characters of a word, but also at the word prefix, and the disambiguation is performed by an averaged perceptron tagger (Straka and Straková, 2017). However, we cannot exactly know where this system fails to perform optimally in Turkish lemmatization.

Lemmatization is especially important for languages like Turkish, which have rich inflectional morphology, with possibly many inflectional suffixes agglutinated to a single verb or noun. It is also possible to come across verb constructions of inflected forms that were not observed in the training and development corpora. This property was touched upon by (Oflazer et al., 2004), where Turkish word forms that consist of morphemes concatenated to a root morpheme or to other morphemes were compared to beads on a string. Works have been made to contribute to the representation of Turkish and other agglutinative languages in UD-based treebanks, which in turn helps to develop more accurately annotated datasets for such languages.

3. Verbal Multiword Expressions in Turkish

VMWEs are the main type of MWEs in question for the PARSEME project. VMWEs are seen as a bigger challenge than non-verbal MWEs since they exhibit higher surface variability (Pasquer et al., 2020). Taking on this challenge, the PARSEME framework defines a VMWE as an expressions: (i) with at least two lexicalized components, including a head word and at least one other syntactically related word, (ii) whose head (in a canonical form) is a verb, and (iii) which functions as a verbal phrase (Ramisch et al., 2018). In the final annotation guidelines, PARSEME also defines VMWE categories for better identification of their occurrences. Three of the main five categories exist in Turkish, more frequently Light Verb Constructions (LVC) and Verbal Idioms (VID), more rarely Multi Verb Constructions (MVC)[8] as in examples (1)–(3), respectively[9] Differences between these categories lie in the role of the component words. Fundamentally, LVCs occur with light verbs and predicative nouns, VIDs have at least two lexicalized components including a head verb and at least one of its dependents, and MVCs are constructed with more than one verb.

(1) **şüphe et-ti** (category: *LVC*)
şüphe et-PAST
doubt do-PAST
'(someone) doubted'

(2) **kulak as-ma-dı** (cat.: *VID*)
kulak as-NEG-PAST
ear hang-NEG-PAST
'(someone) did not pay attention'

(3) **gid-ip gel-ir-ken** (cat.: *MVC*)
git-CONV gel-HAB-CONV
go-CONV come-HAB-CONV
'going in between'

MWE occurrences do not have a balanced distribution among all types and most of the types rarely occur in a given corpus, since it only represents a small part of the natural language.

In a language such as Turkish, we can see a lot of inflection and derivation which causes some issues for this task. In the VID example (2), both of the components can get suffixes in various occurrences of this type, such as ***kulak assalardı*** 'ear hang-CND-PLUR-PAST'. In the case of incorrect lemmatization, this MWE can be found more than once with different lemmas, therefore erroneously increasing the number of VMWE types (as approximated by

[4] https://ufal.mff.cuni.cz/udpipe

[5] http://tools.nlp.itu.edu.tr/index.jsp

[6] https://universaldependencies.org/treebanks/tr_imst/index.html

[7] Raw corpora, i.e. large corpora automatically annotated for morphosyntax, but not annotated for VMWEs, were published in the PARSEME suite to boost automatic discovery of new VMWEs in edition 1.2 of the shared task.

[8] https://parsemefr.lis-lab.fr/parseme-st-guidelines/1.2/?page=030_Categories_of_VMWEs

[9] The hyphens are used in the examples to signal the agglutinative nature of inflected forms. Here, *ti* is the suffix for past tense. Since there is no other suffix, we know that it is the 3rd person singular form.

PARSEME) in the Turkish corpus. This wrong representation can also endanger future studies that use this corpus. Specific issues are explained in more detail in the following section.

4. Issues in the Morphosyntactic Annotation of the Turkish Corpus

This section provides an overview of the issues observed in the PARSEME Turkish corpus regarding morphosyntactic annotation realized by UDPipe. Three main issues were observed and are discussed below with examples.

Sound change produced in the stem by suffixation Some stems ending with voiceless consonants, go through the process of sound change produced in the stem by suffixation. In this process, the ending ('p', 't', 'k', 'ç') changes to its voiced counterpart ('b', 'd', 'g', 'c') before adjoining a suffix that commences with a vowel (Goksel, 2005).

For instance the lemma *et* 'to do', when receiving the suffix *-ecek* signalling future tense, yields *edecek* 'will do'. This lemma has a very high surface variability, both inside and outside of VMWEs. Since it is more of a challenge for automatic systems to identify lemmas that go through this type of change, we frequently see incorrectly lemmatized word forms in the corpus caused by this issue.

Consider examples (4)–(6) showing various morphological variants of the same LVC. In (4), the suffix *-ti* does not start with a vowel, so the voicing does not take place and the lemmatization is correct (cf. the UD lemma in the second line of the example). In (5), conversely, the voicing of the lemma does take place and the lemmatizer fails to restore the correct lemma. This challenge may be even harder when several suffixes are adjoined, as in (6).

(4) **istifa et-ti**
istifa et-PAST (UD lemma: *et*)
resignation do-PAST
'(someone) resigned'

(5) **istifa ed-ecek**
istifa et-FUT (UD lemma: **ed*)
resignation do-FUT
'(someone) will resign'

(6) **istifa ed-ebil-ir-di**
istifa et-POT-HAB-PAST (UD lem.: **edebil*)
resignation do-POT-HAB-PAST
'(someone) could have resigned'

Suffixation MWE occurrences vary in inflectional forms and in Turkish we observe high surface variability. In general, suffixation can be observed in all components of a Turkish MWE. An example of suffixation in one component can be the occurrences of *dava aç* 'to sue' in the examples (8) and (9).

(7) **dava aç-tı**
dava aç-PAST (UD lemma: *aç*)
lawsuit open-PAST
'(someone) commenced lawsuit'

(8) **dava aç-ıl-abil-ir**
dava aç-PASS-POT-HAB (UD lemma: **açılab*)
lawsuit open-PASS-POT-HAB
'lawsuit could be commenced'

(9) **dava aç-ıl-acak**
dava aç-PASS-FUT (UD lemma: **açıla*)
lawsuit open-PASS-FUT
'lawsuit will be commenced'

In (8)–(9), we observe wrongly stripped series of suffixes in the verb component of the VMWE. We can also note that there can be more than one example of insufficient suffix stripping in a given verb, as illustrated above.

We occasionally came across the opposite issue, namely with too many, rather than too few, suffixes hypothesized by the lemmatizer. For instance, the first component of the VMWE ***rehin alındı*** 'hostage take-PASS-PAST', was lemmatized as **reh*, instead of the correct *rehin*.The reason for this can be the resemblance between the ending of this word with the possessive suffix *-in* '-yours' in Turkish.

Nominalization Some commonly used derived nouns are components of LVCs and they play the roles of predicative nouns (i.e. describe actions or states). In the IMST, these nominal derivations are mostly assigned the VERB POS and lemmatized into infinitives. Their nominal nature is retrievable from the morphological feature VERBFORM=VNOUN, as in example (10).

(10) **açıkla-ma yap-tı**
açıkla-VNOUN yap-PAST (UD. lem.: *açıkla*)
to.state-VNOUN make-PAST
'(someone) made (a) statement'

Here, the first component *açıklama* is the result of a derivation realized with suffix *-ma*, which turns the verb *açıkla* 'to state' into a noun *açıklama* 'statement'. This analysis, notwithstanding its defensibility, is incompatible with the PARSEME definition of an LVC as a verb-noun combination, since (10) is represented as a combination of verbs instead.

5. Enhancement Process

The issues described in the preceding section were observed via the PARSEME annotation consistency checker[10]. All problems of voicing and suffixation, illustrated in section 4., spotted in this way, were manually corrected both within VMWE components and in other occurrences of the same verbs. Cases like (10) were more difficult to decide on since they lie on the fuzzy border between inflection and derivation. Ideally, on the one hand, we would expect a more elaborate morphosyntactic representation of nominalizations in UD, and a more flexible definition of LVCs in PARSEME on the other. In the meantime, we changed the lemmas of only the clearly lexicalized nominalizations, functioning as standalone nouns independently of the verbs they stem from, like *açıklama* 'statement'. The enhancements were made manually on the training, development and test corpora, which are in

[10] https://grew.fr/download/PARSEME/tr.html

Data	Global MWE-based			Global Token-based		
	P	R	F1	P	R	F1
ST TRAIN/DEV/TEST	61.69	65.33	**63.46**	63.1	65.69	**64.37**
Enhanced TRAIN/DEV, ST TEST	61.33	63.94	62.61	62.86	64.52	63.68
Enhanced TRAIN/DEV/TEST	61.43	70.98	**65.86**	62.90	71.60	**66.97**

Table 1: The overall results of Seen2Seen evaluation for the shared task and the enhanced data.

Data	LVC			VID		
	P	R	F1	P	R	F1
ST TRAIN/DEV/TEST	59.87	65.57	**62.59**	61.77	63.41	**62.58**
Enhanced TRAIN/DEV, ST TEST	58.54	65.93	62.02	62.33	60.26	61.28
Enhanced TRAIN/DEV/TEST	59.36	74.91	**66.23**	61.72	65.40	**63.50**

Table 2: The results of global-MWE based Seen2Seen evaluation per MWE category.

the CUPT[11] format. In total, 3116 tokens were affected by the enhancements. As a result we obtained a more accurate count of VMWE types. Namely, previously there were 2826 types of VMWEs, with 2.74 occurrences per type on average, whereas the enhancement reduced the number of types to 2310 and increased the occurrences per type to 3.34. This is because, with incorrect lemmas, occurrences of the same VMWE, as in examples (5)–(6), could be wrongly split into different clusters of types.

6. System Results

To see the impact of the corrections, we used one of the MWE identification systems from the edition 1.2 of the PARSEME shared task. This system, namely Seen2Seen[12], ranked first in the global F-measure in the closed track (where no external resources were allowed) and second across both the closed and the open track.[13] Seen2Seen reads all MWEs annotated as such in the training corpus, and extracts all candidate occurrences of the same multisets of lemmas in the test corpus. These candidates then go through a set of morphosyntactic filters. In total, 8 filters are defined, and the training phase allows us to decide which filter to activate for which language, based on the performances on the development corpus.

Seen2Seen was used to annotate the original and the enhanced data. Tables 1 and 2 show the results of this experiment. The first line of each table corresponds to the system trained and evaluated on the original shared task (ST) data. In the second line, the system is trained on the enhanced TRAIN and DEV files but tested on the original TEST. In the last line, the system is both trained and tested on the enhanced files. Note that, while results of the three scenarios of testing are shown next to each other in tables 1 and 2, scores shown in line 3 cannot be directly compared to those shown in lines 1 and 2 since they are computed on different version of the TEST.[14] Table 1 shows the macro-average results for Turkish on the general metrics, namely the MWE-based (correctly identifying a VMWE as a whole) and the token-based (correctly identifying the individual components of a VMWE), recall, precision and F-measure. In Table 2, the results of the MWE-based metrics can be compared per category: LVC and VID.[15]

The results show a difference of 2.5 and 2.6 in the global MWE-based and token-based F-measure, respectively. This is mainly due to two factors. Firstly, with enhanced lemmas, the number of VMWE occurrences considered seen[16] in TEST grows from 812 to 911, while Seen2Seen has a stable performance on the seen VMWEs[17] Secondly, while precision slightly drops between line 1 and 3, the recall significantly increases. This is probably because the variants of seen VMWEs were previously omitted by the system if their lemmas spuriously diverged from seen VMWEs. Now, with more accurate lemmas, the system does see them as valid VMWE candidates. When the lines 1 and 2 are compared, we see a minor decrease in the F-measure by 0.85 and 0.69, which was expected since it is not optimal for a system to be tested on a data set which was annotated according to different principles than those in the training data.

Per-category results show that the Recall for LVCs increased by 9.34 which was expected since our enhancements were very frequent in light verbs. This also resulted in an increase of 3.64 in the F-measure. Conversely, we observe, only an increase of 1.99 in the Recall and 1.8 in the F-measure of VIDs, which might point out that components of VIDs might not vary in surface forms as much as LVCs due to their idiomatic nature.

7. Conclusion

We examined a corpus of VMWEs in Turkish, annotated for the PARSEME project.We detected some shortcomings in terms of morphosyntactic annotation. We focused on enhancing the lemmas in the corpus for better MWE processing. One of the best performing systems from the

[11] http://multiword.sourceforge.net/cupt-format

[12] https://gitlab.com/cpasquer/st_2020

[13] http://multiword.sourceforge.net/sharedtaskresults2020

[14] For the same reason statistical significance tests would not be truly meaningful either.

[15] MVCs are ignored in this table since only one such MWE occurs in both corpora, and it was not affected by our corrections.

[16] An expression is defined as seen if the multiset of lemmas of its lexicalized components was annotated in the training and development sets (Ramisch et al., 2020).

[17] F=0.7329 and F=0.7303 for the ST and the enhanced data, respectively.

PARSEME shared task was trained and tested on the enhanced data to compare the impact of our corrections. The results showed an increase of F-measure for MWE identification when the system was trained and tested on the new corpus when compared to the ST results. We also observed an increase of F-measure in the LVCs, which emphasized the amount of enhancement made in the LVC components.

Our results and the new data establish a new benchmark for the Turkish MWE identification. They also show the necessity for a high-quality morphosyntactic annotation for better MWE processing, especially in morphologically rich corpora. Our observations can also pave the way to some future studies with the examination of other agglutinative languages for MWE processing to see if enhancements of the same nature can be made.

8. Bibliographical References

Adalı, K., Dinç, T., Gökırmak, M., and Eryiğit, G. (2016). Comprehensive annotation of multiword expressions in turkish. In *TurCLing 2016 The First International Conference on Turkic Computational Linguistics at CICLING.*

Bedir, T., Şahin, K., Gungor, O., Uskudarli, S., Özgür, A., Güngör, T., and Ozturk Basaran, B. (2021). Overcoming the challenges in morphological annotation of Turkish in universal dependencies framework. In *Proceedings of The Joint 15th Linguistic Annotation Workshop (LAW) and 3rd Designing Meaning Representations (DMR) Workshop*, pages 112–122, Punta Cana, Dominican Republic, November. Association for Computational Linguistics.

Berk, G., Erden, B., and Güngör, T. (2018). Turkish verbal multiword expressions corpus. In *2018 26th Signal Processing and Communications Applications Conference (SIU)*, pages 1–4.

Goksel, A. (2005). *Turkish: A comprehensive grammar.* Routledge Comprehensive Grammars. Routledge, London, England, May.

Stella Markantonatou, et al., editors. (2018). *Multiword expressions at length and in depth.* Number 2 in Phraseology and Multiword Expressions. Language Science Press, Berlin.

Oflazer, K., Çetinoğlu, Ö., and Say, B. (2004). Integrating morphology with multi-word expression processing in Turkish. In *Proceedings of the Workshop on Multiword Expressions: Integrating Processing*, pages 64–71, Barcelona, Spain, July. Association for Computational Linguistics.

Pasquer, C., Savary, A., Ramisch, C., and Antoine, J.-Y. (2020). Verbal multiword expression identification: Do we need a sledgehammer to crack a nut? In *Proceedings of the 28th International Conference on Computational Linguistics*, pages 3333–3345, Barcelona, Spain (Online), December. International Committee on Computational Linguistics.

Ramisch, C., Cordeiro, S. R., Savary, A., Vincze, V., Barbu Mititelu, V., Bhatia, A., Buljan, M., Candito, M., Gantar, P., Giouli, V., Güngör, T., Hawwari, A., Iñurrieta, U., Kovalevskaitė, J., Krek, S., Lichte, T., Liebeskind, C., Monti, J., Parra Escartín, C., QasemiZadeh, B., Ramisch, R., Schneider, N., Stoyanova, I., Vaidya, A., and Walsh, A. (2018). Edition 1.1 of the PARSEME shared task on automatic identification of verbal multiword expressions. In *Proceedings of the Joint Workshop on Linguistic Annotation, Multiword Expressions and Constructions (LAW-MWE-CxG-2018)*, pages 222–240, Santa Fe, New Mexico, USA, August. Association for Computational Linguistics.

Ramisch, C., Savary, A., Guillaume, B., Waszczuk, J., Candito, M., Vaidya, A., Barbu Mititelu, V., Bhatia, A., Iñurrieta, U., Giouli, V., Güngör, T., Jiang, M., Lichte, T., Liebeskind, C., Monti, J., Ramisch, R., Stymne, S., Walsh, A., and Xu, H. (2020). Edition 1.2 of the PARSEME shared task on semi-supervised identification of verbal multiword expressions. In *Proceedings of the Joint Workshop on Multiword Expressions and Electronic Lexicons*, pages 107–118, online, December. Association for Computational Linguistics.

Straka, M. and Straková, J. (2017). Tokenizing, POS tagging, lemmatizing and parsing UD 2.0 with UDPipe. In *Proceedings of the CoNLL 2017 Shared Task: Multilingual Parsing from Raw Text to Universal Dependencies*, pages 88–99, Vancouver, Canada, August. Association for Computational Linguistics.

Straka, M. (2018). UDPipe 2.0 prototype at CoNLL 2018 UD shared task. In *Proceedings of the CoNLL 2018 Shared Task: Multilingual Parsing from Raw Text to Universal Dependencies*, pages 197–207, Brussels, Belgium, October. Association for Computational Linguistics.

Türk, U., Atmaca, F., Özateş, Ş. B., Köksal, A., Ozturk Basaran, B., Gungor, T., and Özgür, A. (2019). Turkish treebanking: Unifying and constructing efforts. In *Proceedings of the 13th Linguistic Annotation Workshop*, pages 166–177, Florence, Italy, August. Association for Computational Linguistics.

9. Language Resource References

Erden, B., Berk, G., and Gungor, T. (2018). Turkish verbal multiword expressions corpus. In *26th IEEE Signal Processing and Communications Applications Conference, SIU 2018*, pages 1–4, İzmir, Turkey, May.

Sulubacak, U., Gokirmak, M., Tyers, F., Coltekin, C., Nivre, J., and Eryigit, G. (2016). Universal dependencies for turkish. In *Proceedings of COLING 2016, the 26th International Conference on Computational Linguistics*, pages 3444–3454, Osaka, Japan, December. The COLING 2016 Organizing Committee.

Sample Efficient Approaches for Idiomaticity Detection

Dylan Phelps, Xuan-Rui Fan, Edward Gow-Smith,
Harish Tayyar Madabushi, Carolina Scarton, Aline Villavicencio

Department of Computer Science,
University of Sheffield
United Kingdom
{drsphelps1, lhsu1, egow-smith1, h.tayyarmadabushi, c.scarton, a.villavicencio}
@sheffield.ac.uk

Abstract

Deep neural models, in particular Transformer-based pre-trained language models, require a significant amount of data to train. This need for data tends to lead to problems when dealing with idiomatic multiword expressions (MWEs), which are inherently less frequent in natural text. As such, this work explores *sample efficient* methods of idiomaticity detection. In particular we study the impact of Pattern Exploit Training (PET), a few-shot method of classification, and BERTRAM, an efficient method of creating contextual embeddings, on the task of idiomaticity detection. In addition, to further explore generalisability, we focus on the identification of MWEs not present in the training data. Our experiments show that while these methods improve performance on English, they are much less effective on Portuguese and Galician, leading to an overall performance about on par with vanilla mBERT. Regardless, we believe sample efficient methods for both identifying and representing potentially idiomatic MWEs are very encouraging and hold significant potential for future exploration.

Keywords: Idiomaticity Detection, Sample Efficient MWE Detection, Pre-Trained Language Models

1. Introduction and Motivation

The handling of idiomaticity is an important part of natural language processing, due to the ubiquity of idiomatic multiword expressions (MWEs) in natural language (Sag et al., 2002). As such, it is an area where the performance of state-of-the-art Transformer-based models has been investigated (Yu and Ettinger, 2020; Garcia et al., 2021b; Nandakumar et al., 2019), with the general finding being that, through pre-training alone, these models have limited abilities at handling idiomaticity. However, these models are extremely effective at transfer learning through fine-tuning, and thus are able to perform much better on supervised idiomatic tasks (Fakharian and Cook, 2021; Kurfalı and Östling, 2020), where significant amounts of labelled data is provided.

Unfortunately, individual MWEs tend to occur infrequently in natural text, making it harder to train models to capture the idiomatic meaning due to the lack of available training data. As such it is important to be able to find methods of identifying potentially idiomatic MWEs using relatively less data. To address this question we focus on *sample efficient* methods for the task, taking two perspectives. The first is an evaluation of a few-shot method on the task of zero-shot idiomaticity detection. In particular we evaluate Pattern Exploit Training (PET) (Schick and Schütze, 2021a), which has been shown to be an effective few-shot method on other tasks (Schick and Schütze, 2021b). The second is an evaluation of the effectiveness of better representations of MWEs, created using a sample efficient strategy, namely BERTRAM (Schick and Schütze, 2020). Both of these are explored in the zero-shot context, where training data does not include MWEs present in the test data. So as to ensure reproducibility and to enable others to build upon this work, we make the programme code and models publicly available[1].

1.1. Research Questions and Contributions

Given the need for sample efficient methods when dealing with idiomaticity, this work is aimed at exploring the following questions:

- How effective are few-show methods on the task of zero-shot idiomaticity detection? In particular we evaluate Pattern Exploit Training (PET) (Schick and Schütze, 2021a), which has been shown to be an effective few-shot method on other tasks (Schick and Schütze, 2021b).

- Given that prior work has shown pre-trained language models do not adequately capture multiword expressions, in particular those which are idiomatic, how effective is improving their representations on the task of detecting idiomaticity? In particular, we use BERTRAM (Schick and Schütze, 2020) as a sample efficient strategy for creating representations of MWEs.

From our experiments, we find that both BERTRAM and PET are able to outperform mBERT (Devlin et al., 2019) significantly on the English portion of the test

[1] https://github.com/drsphelps/idiom-bertram-pet

Proceedings of the 18th Workshop on Multiword Expressions (MWE 2022) n@LREC2022, pages 105–111
Marseille, 25 June 2022.

data, which is a promising result. However, both of these models perform worse overall due to their significantly lower performance on Portuguese. We explore potential reasons for this poor performance on non-English languages: for PET our patterns are all in English and a multilingual model is used instead of a language specific one. However, an error analysis (Section 5.1) suggests that these are not the reasons for the lower performance on non-English languages. In BERTRAM, however, a monolingual model is used for each language which might have contributed to the drop in performance. We believe that these results point to the need for further exploration in languages other than English.

Additionally, our exploration using BERTRAM is, to the best of our knowledge, the first work to explore the relation between the representation and detection of idiomaticity.

The rest of this paper is structured as follows. We begin in Section 2 by presenting a quick overview of work related to MWE identification, before presenting more details of the methods we make use of in this work. We then provide an overview of the data and task we use for our evaluation in Section 3, before presenting the methods in Section 4. We then present our results and a discussion of what these results imply in Section 5, before concluding in Section 6.

2. Related Work

Despite idiomaticity detection being a problem that has been widely explored (Constant et al., 2017), the impact of better MWE representations, especially within contextualised models, has not been well studied. To this end we use BERT for Attentive Mimicking (BERTRAM) (Schick and Schütze, 2020), which has been shown to perform well on idiom representation tasks (Phelps, 2022), to evaluate the effect idiom representations have on detection. Additionally, we apply a few-shot learning technique Pattern Exploit Training (PET) (Schick and Schütze, 2021a), to assess whether the relatively new paradigm of few-shot learning can be applied to this task successfully.

2.1. PET

PET (Schick and Schütze, 2021a; Schick and Schütze, 2021b) is a semi-supervised training method that improves performance in few-shot settings by integrating task descriptions into examples.

A Pattern is used to map each example into a cloze-style question with masked out tokens, for example *'X. It was [MASK]'*, where X is the input example, could be used for a sentiment classification task. A Verbaliser maps the task classes into outputs from the masked language model (MLM), for example positive/negative labels map to the words 'good'/'bad' in the MLM's vocabulary (label tokens), and is combined with the pattern to form a Pattern Verbaliser Pair (PVP). The probability of each class is then calculated using softmax over the logits for each label token.

For each PVP, an MLM can be fine-tuned on the small amount of labelled data. Knowledge is distilled from multiple PVPs by combining the predictions on the unlabelled data and using it as a larger labelled dataset to train another classifier. This allows for multiple patterns and verbalisers to be used without having to choose the best performer for each task, which may also change depending on the data split.

2.1.1. iPET

iPET (Schick and Schütze, 2021a) is a variation where each PVP's model is trained iteratively using a gradually increasing training set made up of labelled examples from another model's predictions in the previous iteration. Despite using the same PVPs and MLMs, iPET has been shown to improve the performance on a number of tasks (Schick and Schütze, 2021b).

2.2. BERTRAM

BERTRAM (Schick and Schütze, 2020) is a model for creating embeddings for new tokens within an existing embedding space, from a small number of contexts. To create an embedding for a token with a number contexts, a form embedding is first created using embeddings trained for each of the n-grams in the token. This form embedding is then passed as an input, alongside the embeddings for words in the context, into a BERT model. An attention layer is then applied over the contextualised embedding output from BERT for each context to create the final embedding for the token.

The model is trained using embeddings for common words as 'gold standard' embeddings, with the distance from the embedding created by the model and the 'gold standard' embedding being used as the loss function.

3. Dataset and Task Description

In evaluating the models presented in this work we use the Task 2 of SemEval 2022: Multilingual Idiomaticity Detection and Sentence Embedding (Tayyar Madabushi et al., 2022). This task aims at stimulating the development and evaluation of improved methods for handling potentially idiomatic MWEs in natural language. While there exist datasets for evaluating models' ability to identify idiomaticity (Haagsma et al., 2020; Korkontzelos et al., 2013; Cook et al., 2008; Cordeiro et al., 2019; Garcia et al., 2021b; Shwartz and Dagan, 2019), these are often not particularly suited to investigating a) the transfer learning capabilities across different data set-ups b) the performance of pre-trained contextualised models.

The task consists of two subtasks: Subtask A, which is focused on the detection of idiomaticity, and Subtask B, which is focused on the representation of idiomaticity. In this work we are interested in the task of idiomaticity classification, since we wish to investigate how our models can identify idiomaticity in text without having to generate semantic similarity scores. As such, we restrict our attention to Subtask A. We also want to see how our models perform when MWEs

Pattern Number	Pattern	Literal Token	Idiom Token
P1	X: ____	literal	phrase
P2	(____) X	literal	phrase
P3	X. [IDIOM] is ____ literal.	actually	not
P4	X. ____, [IDIOM] is literal.	yes	no
P5	X. [IDIOM] is ____ $[\text{IDIOM}]_2$	actually	not

Table 1: Pattern Verbaliser Pairs used in the task. X represents the example sentence, [IDIOM] is the idiom found in the example, and $[\text{IDIOM}]_2$ represents the nth component word of the idiom

in the test data are disjoint from those in the training data, as we argue this means the models cannot so easily leverage statistical information garnered from the training data, but must instead have some 'knowledge' of idiomaticity in general. As such, we also restrict our attention to the zero-shot setting of the SemEval task. The dataset consists of three languages: English, Portuguese and Galician. In the training data there are 3,327 entries in English, and 1,164 entries in Portuguese. There is no Galician training (or development) data in the zero-shot setting, to test the ability of models at cross-lingual transfer. In the test set, there are 916 English, 713 Portuguese, and 713 Galician examples, and macro F1 score is used as an evaluation metric.

It should be noted that the dataset provided by Tayyar Madabushi et al. (2022) consists of four data splits: The training set, two development sets and the test set. Of the two development sets, the first - called the 'dev' split - includes gold labels and the second - called the 'eval' split - does not include gold labels but requires submission to the competition website. We report our results on the 'eval' set to maintain consistency with the SemEval task.

4. Methods

In this section we detail our use of PET, iPET and BERTRAM for the task of idiomaticity detection.

4.1. PET and iPET

During our experiments with PET and it's variants, we define and test 5 Pattern Verbaliser Pairs, shown in table 2. P1 and P2 are generic prompts which do not give the model much more information about the example, whereas P3, P4, and P5 include the whole idiom within the prompt. We hypothesise that this will allow the model to understand which part of the example it should be focusing on. Each of the patterns we define is in English, even when the example sentence and idiom are in Portuguese or Galician — we will investigate the effect that this has on the final performance across the languages, as we hypothesise this may not have an impact given our use of a multilingual model.

For each PVP, we train a classification model using mBERT as the MLM. Furthermore, we train a standard PET model using all of the patterns. An iPET model is also trained, however to evaluate how using only generic prompts affects the results, we only train our iPET model using PVPs P1 and P2, for 2 iterations. Each of the model setups is trained 3 times using different random seeds, and the final distilled model is then used to produce the presented results.

Additionally, we investigate how the number of labelled examples affects the achieved performance for each of the model setups discussed. We train the models using 10, 100, and 1000 labelled examples separately, with the examples chosen randomly across English and Portuguese, but with the split of idiomatic and literal uses being kept at 50/50. The PET and iPET models then have access to 3,000 unlabelled examples to use within their training tasks.

We evaluate each model setup and labelled example set size combination on the *eval* set, before choosing the best-performing combination for each PET variant to evaluate on the test set. The results from the *eval* set can be seen in Table 2. Here we see that PET-all trained on 1000 labelled examples performs best overall, beating the individual pattern models, a result also seen in the original paper (Schick and Schütze, 2021a). The lack of example specific prompts causes iPET to perform poorly when compared to the individual task specific patterns, and when compared to the best PET-all model. The highest scoring PET model (PET-all) and our iPET model are evaluated on the test dataset in Section 5.

4.2. BERTRAM

To evaluate the effect that improved idiom representations have on this idiom detection task, we use the same BERTRAM setup as presented in Phelps (2022), that was shown to give greatly improved performance over the baseline system for Subtask B, the task of representing idiomaticity. We use the same BERTRAM models: the English model presented in the original BERTRAM paper (Schick and Schütze, 2020), and the Portuguese and Galician models that were trained for Subtask B from data in the CC100 corpus. Unlike the English BERTRAM model, Phelps (2022) does not use one token approximation when training the Portuguese and Galician models. Embeddings for each of the idioms in the task datasets were generated with the appropriate BERTRAM model using 150 examples scraped from the CC100 dataset. 150 examples were chosen as this was shown to have the highest performance on Subtask B. It should be noted that the BERTRAM models were used to create representations of MWEs in the test set. While this does not require labelled data asso-

Model	EN	PT	Overall
mBERT (Tayyar Madabushi et al., 2021)	0.7420	0.5519	0.6871
PET-all (10 labelled)	0.4365	0.2901	0.4267
PET-all (100 labelled)	0.5908	**0.5718**	0.5888
PET-all (1000 labelled)	**0.7820**	0.5619	**0.7164**
PET-P1 (1000 labelled)	0.6386	0.5507	0.6278
PET-P2 (1000 labelled)	0.6905	0.5495	0.6607
PET-P3 (1000 labelled)	0.7493	0.5474	0.6981
PET-P4 (1000 labelled)	0.7441	0.5315	0.6860
PET-P5 (1000 labelled)	0.7551	0.5680	0.7032
iPET (1000 labelled) [P1 & P2]	0.6701	0.5648	0.6522

Table 2: The F1 Score (Macro) on the *eval* set, broken down into each language, for each of the models. Highest score for each language (or overall) shown in bold.

Model	EN	PT	GL	Overall
mBERT (Tayyar Madabushi et al., 2022)	0.7070	**0.6803**	0.5065	**0.6540**
BERTRAM	**0.7769**	0.5017	0.4994	0.6455
PET-all (10 labelled)	0.5197	0.2634	0.2090	0.4128
PET-all (100 labelled)	0.6777	0.5014	0.4902	0.5694
PET-all (1000 labelled)	0.7281	0.6253	**0.5110**	0.6446
iPET (1000 labelled) [P1 & P2]	0.6604	0.5676	0.4735	0.5879

Table 3: The F1 Score (Macro) on the *test* set, broken down into each language, for each of the models. Highest score for each language (or overall) shown in bold.

ciated with MWEs (thus remaining a zero-shot task), it does require knowledge of which phrases need to have explicit representations created.

As we have separate BERTRAM models for each language that are trained to mimic embeddings from single language BERT models, we split the system and data into English, Portuguese and Galician. The English model uses BERT base (Devlin et al., 2019), and is trained on the 3,327 English training examples found in the training set. The Portuguese model uses BERTimbau (Souza et al., 2020), and Galician uses BERTinho (Vilares et al., 2021), and as there is no Galician training data available, both are trained on the 1,164 Portuguese examples. Each model has the MWEs from the relevant language added to its embedding matrix.

5. Results and Discussion

Table 3 presents the results of our best PET-based models alongside our BERTRAM-based model on the test set, as well as the mBERT system presented in (Tayyar Madabushi et al., 2022), for comparison. For each model we present the F1 macro score on the test set for each language, as well as the overall F1 macro score.

An increase in performance over mBERT by our BERTRAM model is seen for the English split, with the score on the Galician split not seeing a significant change. The overall score for BERTRAM is brought down by a much lower score on the Portuguese data, however, meaning no overall increase in performance is seen. A similar picture is seen for the PET-all (1000 examples) model, with a higher F1 score in both English and Galician, and a lower score in Portuguese, leading to an overall lower F1 score across the entire test dataset. As found on the example data, the iPET model which was only trained on the non-example specific prompts (P1 and P2) performs very poorly.

The significant boost from using BERTRAM on English seems to indicate that the improved representations also lead to better classification, despite the lacklustre performance on Galician and Portuguese. We believe that this drop in performance is either because one-token approximation was not used in creating the non-English BERTRAM models, or because mBERT, trained on all three languages simultaneously, is trained on more data than each of our monolingual models. This lack of training data does not affect our English model as there is a more training data in English than in Portuguese and none at all in Galician. We perform a language specific error analysis to explore the causes of this drop in performance (Section 5.1).

It is interesting to note that pre-trained language models can identify idiomaticity in a zero-shot and sample efficient context *even when prior work has shown that they do not encode idiomaticity very well* (Garcia et al., 2021a). We believe that this implies that, while these models do not encode idiomaticity, they encode enough related information to be able to *infer* idiomaticity from relatively little data.

Unsurprisingly, 'highlighting' the phrase that is potentially idiomatic by adding the phrase to the pattern, as in patterns P3, P4 and P5 (see Table 2), significantly improves a model's ability to identify idiomatic-

Language	Pattern	Literal Token	Idiom Token
EN	X. ____, [IDIOM] is literal.	yes	no
PT	X. ____, [IDIOM] é literal.	sim	não
GL	X. ____, [IDIOM] é literal.	si	non

Table 4: The translations of P4 into Portuguese and Galician

Model	Prompt Language	EN	PT	GL	Overall
mBERT (Tayyar Madabushi et al., 2022)	N/A	0.7070	0.6803	0.5065	0.6540
PET-P4 (1000 labelled)	EN	0.7161	0.6373	0.5365	0.6581
PET-P4 (1000 labelled)	PT	0.6994	0.6260	0.4964	0.6283
PET-P4 (1000 labelled)	GL	0.7040	0.5997	0.5154	0.6279

Table 5: The F1 Score (Macro) on the *test* set, broken down into each language, for PET using prompts in each of the task languages.

ity, which is consistent with results presented by Tayyar Madabushi et al. (2021).

Research Questions The results presented herein suggest that few-shot learning methods are indeed effective on the task of idiomaticity detection despite the lower accuracy on Portuguese and Galician. Similarly, our results support the conclusion that improved MWE representations does have an impact on improved detection.

5.1. Error Analysis

The effectiveness of PET on the English split of the task suggests that pre-trained language models can effectively identify idiomatic MWEs in a sample efficient manner. However, the overall drop in performance on the task can be attributed to lower performance on non-English languages when compared to the results achieved by Tayyar Madabushi et al. (2021).

One possibility for the decrease in performance is the use of English prompts across all the languages. This leads to the inputs for English examples being monolingual and the inputs for non-English examples to be multilingual, which may cause confusion in the output logits for the verbalizer tokens from which PET draws it's predictions.

To investigate this further we translate one of our patterns, P4, into both Portuguese and Galician and evaluate the performance on the entire *test* split. P4 was chosen as it was one of the better performing patterns for English in our initial experiments (Table 2), and was easily translated into the two languages. The translations can be seen in table 4.

As shown in table 5, the use of Portuguese and Galician prompts does not increase the performance in the respective language. For Portuguese the model with Portuguese prompts achieves 0.6260 F1 score compare to 0.6373 for that with English prompts. Galician shows similar results, with 0.5154 F1 score for the model with prompts in Galician and 0.5365 for that in English.

Additionally, we use multilingual BERT which was trained on a lot more English training data than Portuguese or Galician language. To investigate the impact of this on our results, we extract only the Portuguese section of the training and test data and compare the performance of multilingual BERT with Portuguese BERT (Souza et al., 2020). Surprisingly, we find that the there isn't a significant difference between the performance of multilingual BERT and Portuguese BERT, with overall F1 (macro) scores of 0.4541 and 0.4621, respectively.

6. Conclusions and Future work

This work presented our exploration of *sample efficient* methods for idiomaticity detection, crucial given the infrequent occurrence of specific MWEs in natural language text. Our experiments show that these methods are extremely promising and have great potential.

In future work, we intend to raucously evaluate and find solutions to the problem of lower performance on non-English test splits. We also intend to explore other variations of BERTRAM (e.g. one-token approximation) in bridging the performance gap between English and the other languages.

As noted earlier, we show that pre-trained language models can identify idiomaticity in a zero-shot and sample efficient context *even when prior work has shown that they do not encode idiomaticity very well.* As such, an important avenue of future exploration is the generalisation of these methods to develop models capable of identifying *the notion of idiomaticity*, much like humans are able to grasp that certain phrases are clearly non-compositional.

Acknowledgements

This work is partially supported the Healthy Lifespan Institute (HELSI) at The University of Sheffield and is funded by the Engineering and Physical Sciences Research Council (EPSRC) [grant number EP/T517835/1]. This work was also partially supported by the UK EPSRC grant EP/T02450X/1 and the CDT in Speech and Language Technologies and their Applications funded by UKRI [grant number EP/S023062/1].

7. Bibliographical References

Constant, M., Eryiğit, G., Monti, J., van der Plas, L., Ramisch, C., Rosner, M., and Todirascu, A. (2017). Survey: Multiword expression processing: A Survey. *Computational Linguistics*, 43(4):837–892, December.

Cook, P., Fazly, A., and Stevenson, S. (2008). The vnc-tokens dataset. In *Proceedings of the LREC Workshop Towards a Shared Task for Multiword Expressions (MWE 2008)*, pages 19–22.

Cordeiro, S., Villavicencio, A., Idiart, M., and Ramisch, C. (2019). Unsupervised compositionality prediction of nominal compounds. *Computational Linguistics*, 45(1):1–57.

Devlin, J., Chang, M.-W., Lee, K., and Toutanova, K. (2019). BERT: Pre-training of deep bidirectional transformers for language understanding. In *Proceedings of the 2019 Conference of the North American Chapter of the Association for Computational Linguistics: Human Language Technologies, Volume 1 (Long and Short Papers)*, pages 4171–4186, Minneapolis, Minnesota, June. Association for Computational Linguistics.

Fakharian, S. and Cook, P. (2021). Contextualized embeddings encode monolingual and cross-lingual knowledge of idiomaticity. In *Proceedings of the 17th Workshop on Multiword Expressions (MWE 2021)*, pages 23–32.

Garcia, M., Kramer Vieira, T., Scarton, C., Idiart, M., and Villavicencio, A. (2021a). Probing for idiomaticity in vector space models. In *Proceedings of the 16th Conference of the European Chapter of the Association for Computational Linguistics: Main Volume*, pages 3551–3564, Online, April. Association for Computational Linguistics.

Garcia, M., Vieira, T. K., Scarton, C., Idiart, M., and Villavicencio, A. (2021b). Probing for idiomaticity in vector space models. In *Proceedings of the 16th conference of the European Chapter of the Association for Computational Linguistics*. Association for Computational Linguistics (ACL).

Haagsma, H., Bos, J., and Nissim, M. (2020). Magpie: A large corpus of potentially idiomatic expressions. In *Proceedings of The 12th Language Resources and Evaluation Conference*, pages 279–287.

Korkontzelos, I., Zesch, T., Zanzotto, F. M., and Biemann, C. (2013). Semeval-2013 task 5: Evaluating phrasal semantics. In *Second Joint Conference on Lexical and Computational Semantics (* SEM), Volume 2: Proceedings of the Seventh International Workshop on Semantic Evaluation (SemEval 2013)*, pages 39–47.

Kurfalı, M. and Östling, R. (2020). Disambiguation of potentially idiomatic expressions with contextual embeddings. In *Proceedings of the Joint Workshop on Multiword Expressions and Electronic Lexicons*, pages 85–94, online, December. Association for Computational Linguistics.

Nandakumar, N., Baldwin, T., and Salehi, B. (2019). How well do embedding models capture non-compositionality? a view from multiword expressions. In *Proceedings of the 3rd Workshop on Evaluating Vector Space Representations for NLP*, pages 27–34, Minneapolis, USA, June. Association for Computational Linguistics.

Phelps, D. (2022). drsphelps at semeval-2022 task 2: Learning idiom representations using bertram.

Sag, I. A., Baldwin, T., Bond, F., Copestake, A., and Flickinger, D. (2002). Multiword expressions: A pain in the neck for nlp. In *International conference on intelligent text processing and computational linguistics*, pages 1–15. Springer.

Schick, T. and Schütze, H. (2020). BERTRAM: Improved word embeddings have big impact on contextualized model performance. In *Proceedings of the 58th Annual Meeting of the Association for Computational Linguistics*, pages 3996–4007, Online, July. Association for Computational Linguistics.

Schick, T. and Schütze, H. (2021a). Exploiting cloze-questions for few-shot text classification and natural language inference. In *Proceedings of the 16th Conference of the European Chapter of the Association for Computational Linguistics: Main Volume*, pages 255–269, Online, April. Association for Computational Linguistics.

Schick, T. and Schütze, H. (2021b). It's not just size that matters: Small language models are also few-shot learners. In *Proceedings of the 2021 Conference of the North American Chapter of the Association for Computational Linguistics: Human Language Technologies*, pages 2339–2352, Online, June. Association for Computational Linguistics.

Shwartz, V. and Dagan, I. (2019). Still a pain in the neck: Evaluating text representations on lexical composition. *Transactions of the Association for Computational Linguistics*, 7:403–419.

Souza, F., Nogueira, R., and Lotufo, R. (2020). BERTimbau: pretrained BERT models for Brazilian Portuguese. In *9th Brazilian Conference on Intelligent Systems, BRACIS, Rio Grande do Sul, Brazil, October 20-23 (to appear)*.

Tayyar Madabushi, H., Gow-Smith, E., Scarton, C., and Villavicencio, A. (2021). AStitchInLanguageModels: Dataset and methods for the exploration of idiomaticity in pre-trained language models. In *Findings of the Association for Computational Linguistics: EMNLP 2021*, pages 3464–3477, Punta Cana, Dominican Republic, November. Association for Computational Linguistics.

Tayyar Madabushi, H., Gow-Smith, E., Garcia, M., Scarton, C., Idiart, M., and Villavicencio, A. (2022). SemEval-2022 Task 2: Multilingual Idiomaticity Detection and Sentence Embedding. In *Proceedings of the 16th International Workshop on Semantic Evaluation (SemEval-2022)*. Association for Computational Linguistics.

Vilares, D., García, M., and Gómez-Rodríguez, C. (2021). Bertinho: Galician BERT representations. *CoRR*, abs/2103.13799.

Yu, L. and Ettinger, A. (2020). Assessing phrasal representation and composition in transformers. *arXiv preprint arXiv:2010.03763*.

mwetoolkit-lib: Adaptation of the mwetoolkit as a Python Library and an Application to MWE-based Document Clustering

Fernando Rezende Zagatti* [‡], **Paulo Augusto de Lima Medeiros***, **Esther da Cunha Soares***, **Lucas Nildaimon dos Santos Silva*** [‡], **Carlos Ramisch**[†], **Livy Real***

*americanas s.a

{paulo.medeiros, esther.soares, livy.coelho}@b2wdigital.com

[‡]Federal University of São Carlos

{fernando.zagatti, lucas.nildaimon}@estudante.ufscar.br

[†]Aix Marseille Univ, CNRS, LIS, Marseille, France

carlos.ramisch@lis-lab.fr

Abstract

This paper introduces the mwetoolkit-lib, an adaptation of the mwetoolkit as a python library. The original toolkit performs the extraction and identification of multiword expressions (MWEs) in large text bases through the command line. One of the contributions of our work is the adaptation of the MWE extraction pipeline from the mwetoolkit, allowing its usage in python development environments and integration in larger pipelines. The other contribution is the execution of a pilot experiment aiming to show the impact of MWE discovery in data professionals' work. Thus, we propose a textual clustering experiment in which we compare using single-word and MWE features. This experiment found that the addition of MWE knowledge to the Term Frequency-Inverse Document Frequency (TF-IDF) vectorization altered the word relevance order, improving the linguistic quality of the clusters returned by k-means.

Keywords: Multiword expressions, Python library, Clustering, k-means

1. Introduction

According to the literature, multiword expressions (MWEs) are combinations of two or more words that present some characteristic behavior when occurring together, having a different behavior when compared to the words used individually (such as 'hot dog' and 'human resources'). This difference can be at any given linguistic level(s), including morphology, syntax, semantics and/or pragmatics (Baldwin and Kim, 2010). Moreover, MWEs often present statistical salience with respect to the distributions of the words that compose them. Due to their unpredictable nature, from a computational perspective, it is challenging to know how to deal with such terms, and often they end up generating errors in Natural Language Processing (NLP) tasks. Therefore, in the industrial context, data analysts and scientists need to be able to process such multiword units in order to enhance their analysis and interpretation of textual data.

As explained by Constant et al. (2017) and Watrin and François (2011), MWE processing is essential for several NLP tasks, such as parsing, machine translation, information extraction and retrieval. Also, MWE processing can be divided into MWE discovery and identification (Constant et al., 2017); the former focuses on extracting MWE candidates from corpora and building a lexicon, and the latter targets labelling word combinations as MWEs in context. Although usually explored in academic research contexts, the task of MWE discovery may also turn out relevant in industrial contexts. Thus, tools like the research-oriented `mwetoolkit` (Ramisch, 2014) could be adapted to benefit not only NLP researchers, but also data analysts working on applied text-related problems.

For that reason, we developed a wrapper for the Multiword Expressions toolkit, the `mwetoolkit-lib`[1], aiming at the MWE discovery task. It is a python library which can be seamlessly imported into any external python code, including jupyter notebooks, and it is integrated with `pandas` (Wes McKinney, 2010), a widely used python library for data analysis.

Such as `mwetoolkit` proposes to easily identify MWEs within a given corpus, our library allows its use outside the command lines. As it is a library that can be easily integrated into pipelines, the `mwetoolkit-lib` main target audience is developers and data scientists, but it can still be used by different professionals, such as lexicographers and translators to find terms of interest.

Furthermore, this paper proposes a pilot experiment on how MWE discovery may impact data scientists and analysts' daily work. We observed that a generalist scope encompasses multiple domains that, in turn, have their own specific MWEs. Therefore, it may be that a word combination in one domain is not an MWE in other domains. To avoid potential domain ambiguities and maximize our knowledge and control of the results, we focus on terminological MWEs relevant to our con-

[1] `https://gitlab.com/fernandozagatti/mwetoolkit-lib/`

Proceedings of the 18th Workshop on Multiword Expressions (MWE 2022) n@LREC2022, pages 112–117

text only, delimiting our experiments to texts in the Human Resources (HR) domain.
The pilot experiment consists in analyzing the impact of discovering MWEs as key terms from an HR corpus and clustering the corpus documents using the k-means algorithm (MacQueen and others, 1967) on the extracted MWE features. We choose such task because it is prototypical in the daily work of both data scientists and analysts, who often have to face the lack of annotated data required for supervised learning methods. In addition, there seems to be considerably less literature on MWE-aware applications based on unsupervised methods. Aiming to automatize an applied data processing pipeline using morphosyntactic patterns for MWE discovery and unsupervised techniques to work with corpora, the main contributions of this paper are:

- Development of the `mwetoolkit-lib`, a freely available python library based on the `mwetoolkit`, which ensures larger usability and integration with resources widely used in academia and industry.
- A pilot experiment to check the impact of the use of MWE knowledge (so linguistic/symbolic knowledge) on unsupervised clustering algorithms results.

2. Related work

Usually, state-of-the-art techniques for automatic identification of MWEs use morphosyntactic patterns combining linguistic and statistical information, rarely resorting to explicit representations of the meaning of words (Seretan, 2011; Ramisch, 2014; Constant et al., 2017). The literature is extensive and there are works in different domains and tasks related to MWE, such as discovery, identification and MWE-aware applications. For discovery, also using `mwetoolkit` as the basis of their work, Cordeiro et al. (2016) presented an extension to `mwetoolkit`, named `mwetoolkit+sem`. They add a new metric for MWE discovery/extraction which tries to estimate a combination's compositionality using word embeddings. In general, the score is calculated through the cosine distance between the MWE term and the words that make up the MWE.
Dubremetz and Nivre (2014) used the `mwetoolkit` on a sample of the French Europarl corpus and the French MWE lexicon Delac for training binary classifiers aiming at MWE discovery. They obtained a maximum precision of 74% in a manual evaluation of this classification task, i.e. 74% of the candidate MWEs classified as correct MWEs were indeed MWEs. Also, approximately half of the correctly discovered MWEs were not present in Delac, contributing to the enrichment of the French MWE lexicon.
Unsupervised methods for MWE discovery have been employed in the past, including clustering techniques (Tutubalina, 2015; Chakraborty et al., 2011). Though, MWE discovery supporting unsupervised text analytics remains understudied to the best of our knowledge.

3. The mwetoolkit-lib

Existing tools for MWE discovery propose sub-optimal interfaces for data analysts, specially considering the use of linguistic and domain-specific knowledge. Hence, we aim to integrate the consolidated methodology with these tools daily used by data scientists. Based on the `mwetoolkit`, a robust framework for processing MWEs, it was necessary to adapt the existing code to integrate the methods and commands used in the terminal into any python script, including notebooks, broadly used by data analysts and scientists.

3.1. The mwetoolkit

The `mwetoolkit` (Ramisch, 2014) is a robust toolkit for MWE processing which proposes a command line interface and is organized as a set of python scripts. It allows text preprocessing while supporting different tagger and parser file formats, complex morphosyntactic user-defined pattern searching using multi-level regular expressions, efficient word and n-gram counting, and statistical measures for MWE discovery. In addition, the toolkit has modules for MWE identification based on lexicon matching and on Conditional Random Fields, but these are out of scope given that we focus on MWE extraction.
The MWE discovery task is tackled using the statistical salience that MWEs may have and common morphosyntactic patterns they share. This pipeline is the following: (I) MWE candidates are searched within the corpus' n-grams using the user-defined patterns; (II) the absolute frequency for each candidate is computed; (III) statistical Association Measures (AMs) are computed; and (IV) the discovered candidates are filtered and ranked according to such measures. These steps are detailed below:

I **Pattern searching:** Given a list of morphosyntactic patterns which comprises lemmas, surface forms, POS tags and/or syntactic dependencies, all n-grams that match these patterns are extracted from the input corpus.

II **MWE candidates counting and word indexing:** Occurrences of each MWE candidate and their component words need to be counted in order to compute the final AMs. A suffix array was implemented for word indexing and thus handling this task efficiently.

III **Statistical Association Measures:** Different AMs are computed using both n-gram and component words' counts as input: maximum likelihood estimator, dice's coefficient, pointwise mutual information and student's t-score. Such AMs are key for the lexicometric analysis of the data professional.

IV **Ranking and filtering:** As its name suggests, MWE candidates might not be MWEs. As a post-processing step, filtering such candidates can be done by using their counts or AMs. Also, candidate ranking using AMs is supported.

3.2. Adaptation to a python library

The code proposed in the `mwetoolkit` for achieving the MWE discovery pipeline is robust and finely organized. Each step is handled by a single script or a pair of scripts: (I) `candidates.py`; (II) `index.py` and `counter.py`; (III) `feat_association.py`; (IV) `sort.py` and `filter.py`. All these scripts make up the internal library `mwetk` which comprises shared functions and classes.

Aiming to adapt this pipeline to the `mwetoolkit-lib`, we first identified the functionalities that should be shared between the proposed library and the aforementioned scripts. Then, the corresponding methods were moved to an internal library `mwetk`, and the scripts were updated accordingly, so that they keep functional after the refactoring.

The main method of the `mwetoolkit-lib`, to be called by the user in a python script, was built inside the `mwetoolkitlib.py` file and must be accessed by calling the `get_candidates_dataframe` method. The idea here is to encapsulate all intermediate steps into a single function, hiding unimportant details about the tool's internal architecture from the users, leaving the pipeline less prone to human errors.

It is necessary to pass two parameters to the method, namely: (1) a corpus file containing the corpus from which the MWEs will be discovered with the POS tags, lemmas and surface forms for each token and (2) a file containing the morphosyntactic patterns that the user wants to extract from the text. Both files can be presented in any format supported by the `mwetoolkit`. This method will return a `pandas` dataframe with MWE candidates and their info. As in the original `mwetoolkit`, candidates are shown in their normalized form (lemmas) alongside with their POS tags, occurrences count and AMs. Ranking and filtering can now be easily done using `pandas` and data can be integrated with other python libraries.

4. Experimental evaluation

For making sure we properly reproduced all the steps of the `mwetoolkit`, we proposed an experimental evaluation considering an industry daily task: creating representative textual datasets using unsupervised techniques. We want to show that `mwetoolkit-lib` does not miss any detail of the `mwetoolkit` and to check how the use of linguistic knowledge through making the textual clustering a MWE-aware task improves the quality of our results.

For this evaluation, we used a private dataset of texts of the HR domain provided by americanas s.a, describing employees activities in Brazilian Portuguese, and containing 20,000 documents.

The first step in the evaluation was to run tests to confirm that the command-line `mwetoolkit` and our python library were extracting the same results. After ensuring that both were extracting the same 8,300 MWEs and generating the same list of candidates, we investigated the impact of MWEs on the k-means clustering algorithm in this data.

4.1. Term Frequency-Inverse Document Frequency

Among different techniques for converting text into numeric vectors, we chose the *Term Frequency-Inverse Document Frequency* (TF-IDF) since this is a straightforward and consolidated technique in the literature. Pimpalkar and Raj (2020) define this technique as a quantitative metric used to determine the relevance of terms in a document. The formulas for calculating the TF-IDF used in this project, taken from scikit-learn[2], are represented by Equations 1 and 2.

$$tfidf(t,d) = tf(t,d) * idf(t) \quad (1)$$

$$idf(t) = log[(1+n)/(1+df(t))] + 1 \quad (2)$$

The following topics define the meaning of each term in Equations 1 and 2:

- **tf-idf(t, d):** "Term Frequency-Inverse Document Frequency" of term "t" in document "d".
- **idf(t):** "Inverse Document Frequency" which measures how common a word is among all documents.
- **tf(t, d):** Computes "term frequency" which is the number of times a word "t" appears in a document "d".
- **n:** Total number of documents available.
- **df(t):** Number of documents in which the term "t" appears.

4.2. K-means clustering

K-means is a clustering algorithm proposed by MacQueen and others (1967). Its main process is the partitioning of its N-dimensional dataset into k distinct groups based on samples. It manages to provide partitions that are reasonably efficient in terms of cluster variation, mainly because it is an unsupervised technique and does not require expert considerations.

As reported by Xiong et al. (2016), after initializing the algorithm and imputing the dataset and the value of k, k samples are randomly selected as centroids, one for each cluster. Then, at each step, the algorithm calculates the distance of the dataset samples from each of the k centroids, assigning the sample to the closest centroid and, once all samples are classified in a cluster, the centroids are recalculated; this process is repeated iteratively until the clusters do not undergo major changes.

[2] `https://scikit-learn.org/`

4.3. The experiment

Since this algorithm does not consider any linguistic feature, we want to test whether imputing the data with MWE analysis would improve the quality of the clusters found by k-means. The pipeline for the experiments, seen in Figure 1, was performed with and without the MWE extraction step.
Firstly, we conducted the textual preprocessing (tokenization, transformation of the text into lowercase, removal of diacritics and stopwords), and vectorization with TF-IDF. Then, the k-means method was applied with 8 clusters. The number of clusters was defined by the Elbow method.[3]
Secondly, the MWE discovery step was inserted before preprocessing and, when tokenization was performed, NLTK's MWETokenizer (Bird et al., 2009) was used to merge the discovered MWEs into single tokens. The morpho-syntactic patterns used by the `mwetoolkit-lib` can be seen in Table 1. These patterns were defined by linguists based on related works such as Boos et al. (2014) and experimental tests within HR domain. Lemmas and POS tags used by the MWE extraction pipeline were computed using the `stanza` library(Qi et al., 2020).

Pattern	Examples
NOUN ADP NOUN	atendimento ao cliente (customer service)
NOUN ADJ ADJ	planejamento orçamentário anual (annual budget planning)
NOUN NOUN ADJ	inglês nível intermediário (intermediate English)
NOUN NOUN NOUN	Supremo Tribunal Federal (Federal Supreme Court)
NOUN ADJ	nota fiscal (invoice)
NOUN NOUN	vale transporte (transportation allowance)

Table 1: Morphosyntactic patterns used for discovery.

4.4. Evaluation results

Using vectorization with TF-IDF, it was possible to extract the degree of relevance of the words and to rank them according to their value. Extracting the top-5 words (Table 2) for vectorization using the knowledge of MWE, the token "atendimento ao cliente" ('customer service') was identified as something very relevant to the text. In the clusters without MWEs, this information was lost and the TF-IDF considered "service" and "customer" as distinct features. It may look very simple, but having this MWE identified, we could obtain a single cluster in which it is very salient, while, in the clusters without MWEs knowledge, the words "atendimento" and "cliente" appeared in all the other clusters within the 15 most common unigrams.

Rank	With MWE	Without MWE
Top1	atividades	atendimento
Top2	responsavel	responsavel
Top3	principais	atividades
Top4	atendimento	area
Top5	atendimento_ao_cliente	cliente

Table 2: Relevance of words and MWEs by TF-IDF.

For clustering, in the first run, without MWE, k-means created a cluster with the word "atendimento" (service) in which it brought texts about services in general, customer service, public service, telephone service, among others. In parallel, when we applied MWE discovery in the pipeline, a cluster was created specifically for the MWE "atendimento_ao_cliente" (customer service) and another for activities and services in general.
Adding the knowledge of MWE, 1282 MWEs appeared among the most frequent terms in the clusters. Without this information, only 48.60% had appeared among the most frequent terms. These MWEs are in the HR domain, such as "producao_de_conteudo" ('content creation') and "fechamento_de_caixa" ('financial close'). With one of the groups being more specifically about 'customer service', we were able to better differentiate the other clusters. In the MWE-aware version of this experiment, we obtain a cluster that deals specifically with financial tasks with terms such as "notas_fiscais" ('invoices'), "controle_de_contas" ('billing control') and "emissao_de_notas" ('invoice issuance') that were not representative in any cluster in the 'flat' version of the experiment.
It is important to emphasize that using unsupervised methods impose some difficulty on having highly trustful evaluation. Thus, our pilot experiment still requires a more in-depth quantitative evaluation in other datasets to observe the real effects of MWE on unsupervised clustering. However, it already showed the usability of `mwetoolkit-lib` and how it was easy to integrate the linguistic knowledge of `mwetoolkit` with other methods in a larger pipeline, bringing up an easy way to have hybrid approaches implemented for textual clustering.

5. Conclusions and future work

We implemented the `mwetoolkit` (Ramisch, 2014) as a python library, aiming to make this MWE module easier for data scientists to use in non-academic R&D contexts. We conducted some experiments to demonstrate the impact of using MWE knowledge in clustering methods and how MWEs extracted by `mwetoolkit-lib` can be used in an unsupervised method.
The adoption of hybrid approaches (such as MWE + clustering) brings advantages to the automatizing meth-

[3]This method tests the algorithm with different numbers of clusters in order to identify the optimal value of k.

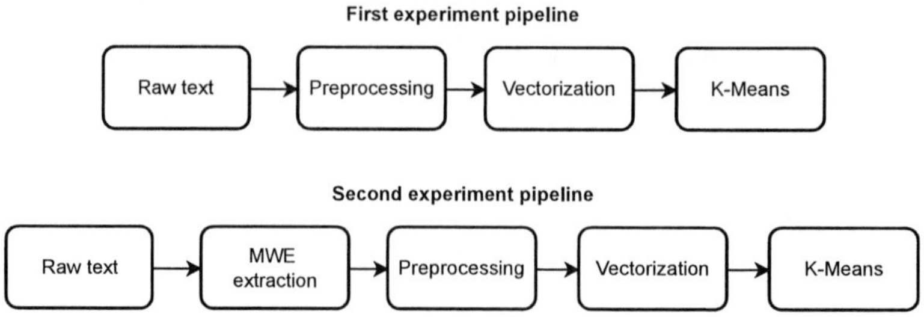

Figure 1: Difference between the pipeline of experiment 1 (top, no MWEs) and experiment 2 (bottom, with MWEs)

ods, in a way that the data does not need any previous human annotation to be used. We do believe that the future of NLP is based on bringing together linguistics/logic knowledge within the big data knowledge we can access together, and making these sources of information dialogue with each other.

The use of hybrid methods with MWEs can also bring domain knowledge that is implicit in the data. This knowledge can be extracted more easily when applying the techniques together with human experts to analyze the results individually.

As future work, extensions in both `mwetoolkit-lib` and experiments can be explored. The `mwetoolkit-lib` can benefit from the implementation of the MWE identification pipeline from the `mwetoolkit`, thus allowing training, evaluating and execution of the labelling of MWEs in running text. Furthermore, benefiting from the rich python environment, different Machine Learning algorithms can be used to tackle this new task by integrating the `mwetoolkit-lib` with other python libraries such as `scikit-learn` (Pedregosa et al., 2011) and `keras` (Chollet and others, 2015).

Concerning the experiments, we would like to carry out clustering using other algorithms (such as MiniBatch k-Means or HDBSCAN) and in new datasets, ensuring that the linguistic quality improvement we found generalizes over other architectures and domains.

6. Acknowledgements

This research was supported by americanas s.a. We thank our colleagues Helena de Medeiros Caseli, Diego Furtado Silva, Daniel Lucrédio, Lucas Cardoso Silva and Bruno Silva Sette from Federal University of São Carlos who provided insights and expertise that assisted this research. This work has been funded by the French Agence Nationale pour la Recherche, through the SELEXINI project (ANR-21-CE23-0033-01), and is part of the UFSCar extension project "Dos dados ao conhecimento: extração e representação de informação no domínio do e-commerce" (#23112.000186/2020-97)

7. Bibliographical References

Baldwin, T. and Kim, S. N. (2010). Multiword expressions. *Handbook of natural language processing*, 2:267–292.

Bird, S., Klein, E., and Loper, E. (2009). *Natural language processing with Python: analyzing text with the natural language toolkit.* " O'Reilly Media, Inc.".

Boos, R., Prestes, K., and Villavicencio, A. (2014). Identification of multiword expressions in the brwac. In *LREC*, pages 728–735.

Chakraborty, T., Das, D., and Bandyopadhyay, S. (2011). Semantic clustering: an attempt to identify multiword expressions in Bengali. In *Proceedings of the Workshop on Multiword Expressions: from Parsing and Generation to the Real World*, pages 8–13, Portland, Oregon, USA, June. Association for Computational Linguistics.

Chollet, F. et al. (2015). Keras. `https://keras.io`.

Constant, M., Eryiğit, G., Monti, J., van der Plas, L., Ramisch, C., Rosner, M., and Todirascu, A. (2017). Survey: Multiword expression processing: A Survey. *Computational Linguistics*, 43(4):837–892, December.

Cordeiro, S., Ramisch, C., and Villavicencio, A. (2016). mwetoolkit+sem: Integrating word embeddings in the mwetoolkit for semantic MWE processing. In *Proceedings of the Tenth International Conference on Language Resources and Evaluation (LREC'16)*, pages 1221–1225, Portorož, Slovenia, May. European Language Resources Association (ELRA).

Dubremetz, M. and Nivre, J. (2014). Extraction of nominal multiword expressions in french. In *MWE@EACL*.

MacQueen, J. et al. (1967). Some methods for classification and analysis of multivariate observations. In *Proceedings of the fifth Berkeley symposium on mathematical statistics and probability*, volume 1, pages 281–297. Oakland, CA, USA.

Pedregosa, F., Varoquaux, G., Gramfort, A., Michel, V., Thirion, B., Grisel, O., Blondel, M., Prettenhofer, P., Weiss, R., Dubourg, V., Vanderplas, J., Passos, A., Cournapeau, D., Brucher, M., Perrot, M., and Duchesnay, E. (2011). Scikit-learn: Machine learning in Python. *Journal of Machine Learning Research*, 12:2825–2830.

Pimpalkar, A. P. and Raj, R. J. R. (2020). Influence of pre-processing strategies on the performance of ml classifiers exploiting tf-idf and bow features. *ADCAIJ: Advances in Distributed Computing and Artificial Intelligence Journal*, 9(2):49–68.

Qi, P., Zhang, Y., Zhang, Y., Bolton, J., and Manning, C. D. (2020). Stanza: A Python natural language processing toolkit for many human languages. In *Proceedings of the 58th Annual Meeting of the Association for Computational Linguistics: System Demonstrations*.

Ramisch, C. (2014). *Multiword expressions acquisition: A generic and open framework*. Springer.

Seretan, V. (2011). *Syntax-based collocation extraction*, volume 44. Springer Science & Business Media.

Tutubalina, E. (2015). Clustering-based approach to multiword expression extraction and ranking. In *Proceedings of the 11th Workshop on Multiword Expressions*, pages 39–43, Denver, Colorado, June. Association for Computational Linguistics.

Watrin, P. and François, T. (2011). An n-gram frequency database reference to handle MWE extraction in NLP applications. In *Proceedings of the Workshop on Multiword Expressions: from Parsing and Generation to the Real World*, pages 83–91, Portland, Oregon, USA, June. Association for Computational Linguistics.

Wes McKinney. (2010). Data Structures for Statistical Computing in Python. In Stéfan van der Walt et al., editors, *Proceedings of the 9th Python in Science Conference*, pages 56 – 61.

Xiong, C., Hua, Z., Lv, K., and Li, X. (2016). An improved k-means text clustering algorithm by optimizing initial cluster centers. In *2016 7th International Conference on Cloud Computing and Big Data (CCBD)*, pages 265–268. IEEE.

Handling Idioms in Symbolic Multilingual Natural Language Generation

Michaelle Dubé François Lareau
OLST, Université de Montréal
C.P. 6128 succ. Centre-Ville, Montréal QC, H3C 3J7, Canada
{michaelle.dube, francois.lareau}@umontreal.ca

Abstract

While idioms are usually very rigid in their expression, they sometimes allow a certain level of freedom in their usage, with modifiers or complements splitting them or being syntactically attached to internal nodes rather than to the root (e.g., *take something with a big grain of salt*). This means that they cannot always be handled as ready-made strings in rule-based natural language generation systems. Having access to the internal syntactic structure of an idiom allows for more subtle processing. We propose a way to enumerate all possible language-independent n-node trees and to map particular idioms of a language onto these generic syntactic patterns. Using this method, we integrate the idioms from the French Lexical Network (LN_{fr}) into GenDR, a multilingual realizer. Our implementation covers nearly 98% of LN_{fr}'s idioms with high precision, and can easily be extended or ported to other languages.

Keywords: idioms, multilingual natural language generation, lexicalization

1. Introduction

Idioms are notoriously difficult for natural language processing (NLP) (Sag et al., 2002; Constant et al., 2017). In this paper, we will focus on the task of rule-based natural language generation (NLG), and on the most prototypical type of idioms, which have namely been called *fixed expressions* by Sag et al. (2002) or *full idioms* by Mel'čuk (2012). To put it in a nutshell, such idioms can be defined as non-compositional multiword expressions (MWEs) where each word has been emptied of its meaning and rendered non-referential. They show a high degree of syntactic cohesion that typically forbids alteration. For example, UNDER THE WEATHER doesn't refer to any weather at all but means 'sick', and the noun WEATHER here cannot be modified without breaking the idiomatic interpretation of the whole. This is not to say that idioms cannot have complements or modifiers, but these are normally attached to the syntactic head of the phrase (here, UNDER), and they complement or modify the whole expression, not one of its internal words.

Because idioms behave somewhat like simple words from a syntactic point of view, they can very well be processed as ready-made blocks in symbolic NLG. For example, if a system is able to produce *Mary felt a bit sick that day*, it is trivial to replace the string `"sick"` with `"under the weather"` somewhere in the process and produce *Mary felt a bit under the weather that day*. Indeed, this has been the prevalent approach so far (cf. §2). However, there are several ways idioms can wreak havoc in an NLG system:

1. An idiom can be split by its modifier. For example, in French, DONNER SA LANGUE AU CHAT ('give up guessing', lit. 'give one's tongue to the cat'), when combined with ENCORE ('again') yields *donner encore sa langue au chat*.
2. Modifiers do not always attach to the syntactic head of an idiom. For example, to intensify TAKE (y) WITH A GRAIN OF SALT, you can modify the noun GRAIN instead of the head TAKE: *Take it with a big grain of salt.*
3. An idiom can be split by its complement, as in *You have to take whatever he says with a grain of salt.*
4. Complements do not always attach to the syntactic head of an idiom. This is particularly common with (but not exclusive to) idioms that contain body part words. For example, the second actant of PULL (y'S) LEG is expressed as a syntactic complement of the noun LEG, not as an object of the verb: *He's just pulling your leg.*
5. Inflection can be messy. This is especially true of nominal idioms in languages where agreement exists, because an inflected head triggers the inflection of internal determiners and adjectives. The problem is further exacerbated in languages with grammatical case. For example, in Lithuanian, LIETUVOS APELIACINIS TEISMAS ('court of appeal of Lithuania', lit. 'appellate court of Lithuania') has a nominal head TEISMAS 'court' with an adjective APELIACINIS 'appellate', and when the noun varies in case or number, so does the adjective. This requires access to individual words within the idiom (Dubinskaitė, 2017).
6. Idioms can sometimes "loosen up" and allow some syntactic freedom, with component words becoming referential, as in *It was a pretty big bullet to bite*, where BULLET acts as if it actually meant something like 'situation', although there is no such sense for that word in any other context.

Solving these problems elegantly in a symbolic NLG system requires access to the internal syntactic structure of idioms. In this paper, we propose a solution to represent that internal structure, which addresses the first five issues above. It is language-independent and designed for multilingual natural language generation

Proceedings of the 18th Workshop on Multiword Expressions (MWE 2022) n@LREC2022, pages 118–126

(MNLG), but it requires detailed lexical resources that we had only for French. Therefore, the discussion will draw from French data. As for the sixth issue, it has been explored in detail by Pausé (2017) from a theoretical point of view, but we have no elegant solution for it in the context of MNLG.

This paper is structured as follows. First, we will make a distinction between superficial and deep realizers in NLG and discuss briefly how idioms have been handled in existing systems (§2). Then, we will present the lexical data on which we rely and explain Pausé's (2017) idiom classification, which is central to our solution (§3). The main section will present our implementation (§4), which will be followed by an evaluation (§5) and a conclusion (§6).

2. Idioms in Linguistic Realizers

We should emphasize that in this paper we will only discuss the problem of idioms in rule-based realizers. Statistical and neuronal language models typically reproduce MWEs with relative ease, since they are very good at capturing recurrent patterns in a corpus. Yet, they are rambling machines that are very hard to harness. Thus, for many practical NLG applications where high precision and full control are needed, symbolic realizers are still the way to go.

While NLG refers to the whole pipeline from data collection to text delivery, realizers focus on the linguistic part of the process. Most realizers expect an input where both lexical choice and syntactic structure have already been computed, leaving the user with two particularly complex tasks. This is the case for FUF/SURGE (Elhadad, 1993; Elhadad and Robin, 1996), RealPro (Lavoie and Rambow, 1997; CoGenTex, 1998), SimpleNLG (Gatt and Reiter, 2009), its bilingual version, SimpleNLG-EnFr (Vaudry and Lapalme, 2013) and its Spanish version, SimpleNLG-ES (Ramos-Soto et al., 2017), JSReal (Daoust and Lapalme, 2015) and its bilingual version, JSRealB (Molins and Lapalme, 2015; Lapalme, 2020), as well as ATML3 (Weißgraeber and Madsack, 2017). KPML (Bateman, 1996) and OpenCCG (White, 2008) both start from a more abstract representation of the text's meaning, but they tend to focus on the grammar more than the lexicon, resulting in well-formed sentences that somehow lack lexical flexibility. The same goes for the bilingual (French/English) realizer FLAUBERT (Meunier and Danlos, 1998; Danlos, 2000)—not the be confused with the language model FlauBERT (Le et al., 2020). More recently, statistical approaches have been applied to text generation from logical forms (Basile, 2015) or semantic structures (Mille, 2014), but again lexical choice is rather rigid.

MARQUIS (Wanner et al., 2010) was a multilingual data-to-text generator used to produce air quality bulletins. It was designed to have a reusable text realization component that takes as input semantic representations, thus taking charge of lexical choice. Its lexicalization module was designed to produce natural-sounding collocations and to be as generic as possible (Lareau and Wanner, 2007; Wanner and Lareau, 2009). However, it handled full idioms as blocks of text, lacking the flexibility required for the cases discussed in §1. Its successor FORGe (Mille and Wanner, 2017) significantly improved the lexical coverage of MARQUIS, but also takes a rigid approach to idioms. Another successor, GenDR (Lareau et al., 2018) significantly expanded the range of collocation patterns it can handle (Lambrey and Lareau, 2015), but it also treats idioms as blocks with no internal structure.

To sum up, as far as we know, there is no generic, largish-scale deep realizer that takes idioms for what they are: premade phrases with internal syntactic structure. Hence, our goal is to incorporate such a functionality into a deep realizer. We picked GenDR for that purpose, because it already had a strong focus on nontrivial lexicalizations, in particular collocations. We will explain in this paper how we extended its lexicalization module to handle idioms in a way that reflects both their non-compositional semantic nature and their internal syntactic structure.

3. Lexical Data

We take our lexical data from the LN_{fr} (Polguère, 2009; Polguère, 2014; Ollinger and Polguère, 2020), a rich, open resource based on the principles of Explicative Combinatorial Lexicology (ECL) (Mel'čuk et al., 1995; Mel'čuk, 1995; Apresjan, 2000; Mel'čuk, 2006). Since GenDR itself is based on Meaning-Text Theory (MTT) (Žolkovskij and Mel'čuk, 1965; Kahane, 2003; Mel'čuk, 2016), an ECL-based resource was an obvious choice for our purposes. Each of LN_{fr}'s ~20k entries corresponds to a specific word sense that has its own lexicographic record with morphological, semantic and syntactic information, examples, and relations with other lexical units via lexical functions (LFs) (Wanner, 1996; Apresjan et al., 2002).

Our work is based on **Pausé's (2017) idiom classification**, in which she proposed linear syntactic patterns for French idioms. To avoid any confusion with our own generic patterns, we will henceforth use the term **linguistic patterns** to refer to them. These patterns are sequences of part of speech (POS) tags that represent each word of an idiom. For example, the idiom JOINDRE LES DEUX BOUTS ('make ends meet', lit. 'join the two ends') is assigned the pattern `V Det Num N`.

If necessary, function markers are used to distinguish patterns that have the same POS sequence but different syntactic structures. For example, while CRACHER DANS LA SOUPE ('bite the hand that feeds you', lit. 'spit in the soup') and BATTRE DE L'AILE ('be on the skids', lit. 'flap from the wing') both correspond to the sequence `V Prep Det N`, they don't have the same syntactic structure because the preposition is a circumstantial in the former but an oblique in the latter, so they have been assigned, respectively,

V Prep.circ Det N and V Prep.obl Det N. Obviously, this is tied to an underlying syntactic analysis, as determined by the lexicographers.

These patterns can further specify the syntactic position of an idiom's complements, which is useful when they do not attach to the syntactic head of the idiom, but to an arbitrary node within the idiom. For example, in PARLER DANS LE DOS (DE y) ('talk behind (y's) back'), the second complement of the idiom is expressed as a complement of the noun DOS ('back'), not as a complement of the head PARLER ('talk'). This is encoded as V Prep Det N (Prep_$2), where (Prep_$2) refers to the second complement and its preposition.

Pausé's classification was incorporated into LN_{fr}, which contained 2919 idioms classified between 514 different patterns when we conducted our study. Table 1 gives the frequency of the most common patterns, with an example for each. Note the zipfian distribution, with only eight patterns accounting for half of the data.

Idiom pattern	Example	#	%
N Prep N	TÊTE DE MULE	409	14%
N Adj	TERRE FERME	377	13%
Prep N	DE JUSTESSE	222	8%
N Prep.circ N	CORPS À CORPS	138	5%
Adj N	JOLI CŒUR	100	4%
Prep Det N	DANS LE VENT	98	3%
V Det N	LEVER LE PIED	79	3%
N Prep Det N	ART DE LA TABLE	79	3%
Others	...	1417	49%
Total		**2919**	**100%**

Table 1: Most frequent idiom patterns in LN_{fr}

4. Implementation

As said in §2, we implemented our solution in the multilingual deep realizer GenDR (Lareau et al., 2018), which follows the principle of resource sharing across languages (Bateman et al., 2005). This realizer is built on top of the graph transducer MATE (Bohnet and Wanner, 2010). It is based on MTT and only handles the semantics-syntax interface: it takes as input a graph-based semantic representation (SemR) (Mel'čuk, 2012) and produces first an abstract dependency tree called a deep syntactic representation (DSyntR), from which it then derives a full-dependency tree called a surface syntactic representation (SSyntR) (Mel'čuk, 1988). A DSyntR is roughly similar to a Universal Dependency tree (de Marneffe et al., 2021), without functional words and with idioms collapsed into single nodes, while a SSyntR is analogous to a Surface-syntactic Universal Dependency (SUD) tree (Gerdes et al., 2018). Only the second transduction is relevant to us, since idioms are represented as single nodes in the DSyntR (thus, the SemR⇒DSyntR mapping is trivial), but as multiple nodes in the SSyntR. Figure 1 presents an input example (SemR) and a sample of possible outputs (SSyntR), in which the meaning 'courtiser' ('to court') can be lexicalized as the lexeme COURTISER or as the idiom FAIRE LA COUR (lit. 'do the court').

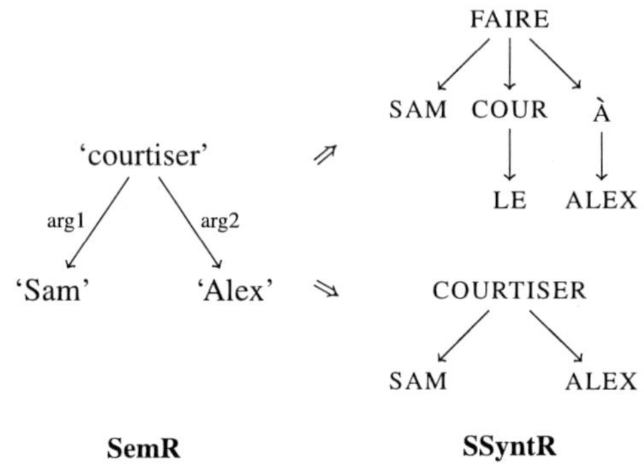

Figure 1: Alternative outputs for a simple SemR

4.1. Template Lexicalization Rules

The process of mapping a single DSyntR node onto multiple SSyntR nodes is called **template lexicalization** within GenDR (Lareau et al., 2018). Figure 2 is an example of such a rule for JOINDRE LES DEUX BOUTS ('make ends meet', lit. 'join the two ends').[1]

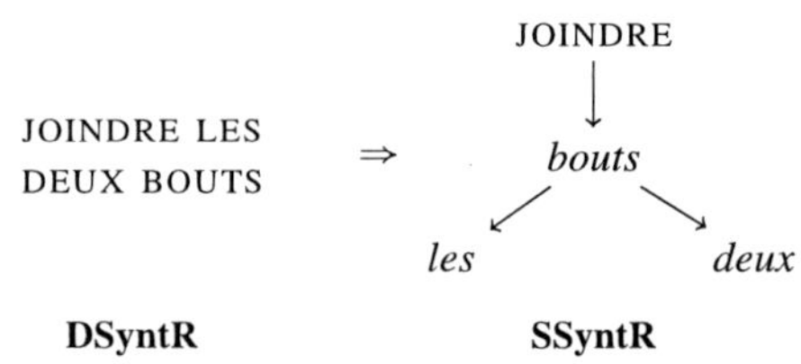

Figure 2: A simple template lexicalization rule

A full grammar would require rules like this one for each idiom in a given language. Obviously, a great number of these rules would resemble each other, thus the goal is to generalize them. Our solution is to create a set of template lexicalization rules that generalize Pausé's linguistic patterns (cf. §3). Each of these rules describes a generic pattern of syntactic tree with placeholders that are filled with lexical stock from our dictionary. The latter is derived from LN_{fr} and enhanced with our own data, as explained below. The idea behind these rules is to generalize linguistic patterns into more generic, language-independent patterns defined by the number of nodes in an idiom's subtree.

[1] Note that we omit relation names from our discussion. The choice of relation names is beyond the scope of our work, since they are language-specific. These decisions are thus left to the lexicographers working on LN_{fr}.

4.2. Generic Tree Patterns

We grouped idioms that had identical structures. For example, four-nodes idioms like JOINDRE LES DEUX BOUTS, ENFONCER UNE PORTE OUVERTE ('state the obvious', lit. 'kick an open door') and DANS DE BEAUX DRAPS ('in trouble', lit. 'in some nice bedsheets') have different linguistic patterns, but share the same structure, as illustrated in Figure 3.

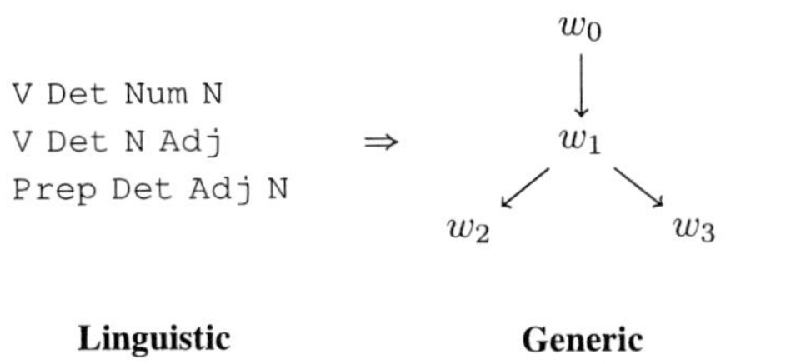

Figure 3: Linguistic patterns with the same structure

This pattern is not the only possibility for a four-node tree. Giving SSyntRs only represent hierarchy and not word order, two trees that differ solely by word order are equivalent. Therefore, there are four theoretically possible patterns for a four-node tree, to which we assigned IDs 4_01 to 4_04, as shown in Figure 4.

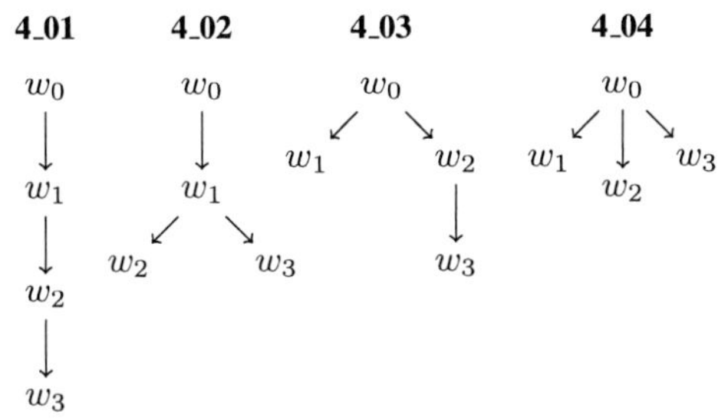

Figure 4: Generic patterns for a four-node tree

To systematically enumerate all possible generic patterns, we rely on number theory, which defines an integer's **partition** as its decomposition into a sum of positive integers (Andrews, 1998). For example, 3 has three different partitions: 3, 2 + 1, and 1 + 1 + 1. Each summand of the partition is called a **part**. The integer partitions thus correspond to all possible configurations of a root's (direct and indirect) dependents in a tree, with the number of parts in a partition corresponding to the number of direct dependents of the root.

To illustrate this, consider a three-node tree. It comprises a root and two dependents. The root's position is fixed, but there are two ways we can configure the other two nodes: either one depends on the root, and the other depends on the first (forming a chain), or both depend directly on the root. This corresponds to the two partitions of the integer 2: as 2 (a two-node subtree is attached to the root) or 1 + 1 (two single-node subtrees are attached to the root).

	Partitions	**#Trees**
2 nodes	1	1
		= 1
3 nodes	2	1
	1 + 1	1
		= 2
4 nodes	3	2
	2 + 1	1
	1 + 1 + 1	1
		= 4
5 nodes	4	4
	3 + 1	2
	2 + 2	1
	2 + 1 + 1	1
	1 + 1 + 1 + 1	1
		= 9
6 nodes	5	9
	4 + 1	4
	3 + 2	2
	3 + 1 + 1	2
	2 + 2 + 1	1
	2 + 1 + 1 + 1	1
	1 + 1 + 1 + 1 + 1	1
		= 20
7 nodes	6	20
	5 + 1	9
	4 + 2	4
	4 + 1 + 1	4
	3 + 3	3
	3 + 2 + 1	2
	3 + 1 + 1 + 1	2
	2 + 2 + 2	1
	2 + 2 + 1 + 1	1
	2 + 1 + 1 + 1 + 1	1
	1 + 1 + 1 + 1 + 1 + 1	1
		= 48

Table 2: Number of different n-node trees

As one can see, the enumeration of all node configurations for a tree of size n boils down to enumerating the partitions of the integer $n - 1$. Hence, the nodes of a four-node tree can be configured according to the partitions of 3, since its root has three (direct or indirect) dependents:

- a root linked to a three-node subtree (3);
- a root linked to a one-node subtree and a two-node subtree (2 + 1);
- a root linked to three one-node subtrees (1 + 1 + 1).

We have established above that a three-node subtree can be configured in two ways, thus yielding a total of four different configurations for a four-node tree. Now that we have computed the configurations for a four-node tree, we can compute those of a five-node tree, and so on, recursively. Table 2 gives the partitions and corresponding number of configurations for trees with up to seven nodes.

Let us pay special attention to the 3 + 3 partition for the

dependents of a seven-node tree, highlighted in Table 2. This partition is composed of two three-node subtrees. As seen previously, with $n = 3$, there are two possible trees for this part. Thus, one might expect to get $2 + 2$ trees for a $3 + 3$ partition. However, this is not the case. To demonstrate this, let us identify the two variants of a three-node tree as A and B. If you have two of them, the possible combinations are AA, AB, BA and BB. However, since our trees are unordered, AB and BA are actually identical. Therefore, there are only three possible configurations for a $3 + 3$ partition.

4.3. Mapping Linguistic Patterns onto Generic Patterns

Since our generic patterns are essentially empty trees, they must be filled with lexical information specific to each language, which we retrieved from LN_{fr} in this case. Therefore, we need to map each linguistic pattern used for French idioms (cf. §3) onto one of our generic patterns. This pattern mapping involves establishing each idiom's SSyntR; therefore, it requires good knowledge of the formalism and high precision. Consequently, it was performed manually. For this purpose, we differentiated each generic pattern with a unique ID, as seen in Figure 4. In addition, we annotated each linguistic pattern with a word-to-node mapping code that describes the position in the tree of all the words of an idiom's pattern, as in Table 3.
For example, the four-node idiom JOINDRE LES DEUX BOUTS ('make ends meet', lit. 'join the two ends') follows the generic tree pattern `4_02`. Using its linguistic pattern `V Det Num N`, we established a mapping between the idioms' words and the nodes of the tree, which we express as a code: `0231`. Figure 5 illustrates the procedure we followed.

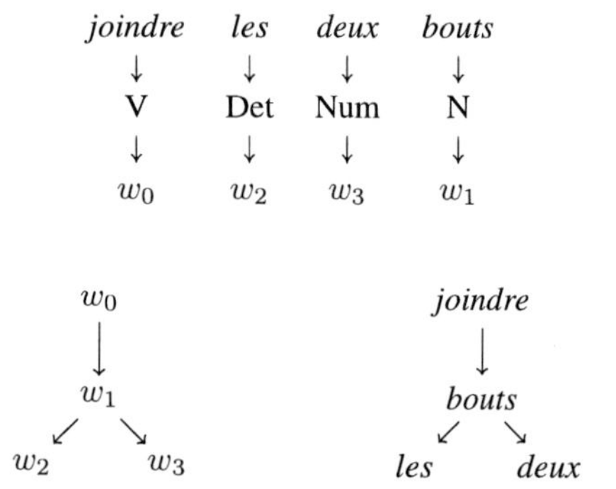

Figure 5: Example of an idiom's word mapping

The mapping code tells our realizer which word to assign to each of the tree's nodes during lexicalization. Each node in a tree is identified by an ID (w_0, w_1, w_2, etc.). Furthermore, we refer to an idiom's words by their linear order in the citation form. In sum, the mapping code takes this ordinal numbering and rearranges it according to the words' position in the tree.

Idiom pattern	Tree pattern	Word mapping
Adj N	2	10
N Prep N	3_01	012
Prep Det N	3_01	021
V Det Num N	4_02	0231

Table 3: Pattern mapping

Thus, in this case, `0231` means that w_0 will be filled by `"joindre"`, node w_2 by `"les"`, node w_3 by `"deux"` and node w_1 by `"bouts"`.
Following this procedure, we determined the mapping codes for each pair of patterns. This had to be done manually for each of the 514 linguistic patterns. Table 3 gives a few examples.
The mapping between specific idioms and one of Pausé's patterns is already given in the LN_{fr}, as this is part of the dictionary's structure. Hence, each of the 2919 French idioms are mapped onto one of 514 patterns. Table 4 presents some examples.

Idiom	Idiom pattern
JOLI CŒUR	Adj N
FEUILLE DE MATCH	N Prep N
DANS LE VENT	Prep Det N
JOINDRE LES DEUX BOUTS	V Det Num N

Table 4: Idiom pattern mappings from LN_{fr}

All this information was compiled into a dictionary format compatible with GenDR (Lareau and Lambrey, 2016). The process was relatively straightforward, except in the case of amalgams (such as *des=de+les*), as they are single words but correspond to two nodes in the SSyntR. Other forms that required special attention were reflexive pronouns, compounds and linguistic patterns containing embedded idioms.

5. Evaluation

The evaluation of our implementation focuses on the surface lexicalization of idioms in GenDR. The assessment is based on two criteria. First, we evaluate the coverage of the implementation, i.e., the percentage of LN_{fr}'s idioms that we can regenerate. Second, we evaluate the precision of the implementation, i.e., the proportion of generated structures that are correctly formed.

5.1. Coverage

The coverage of our implementation is measured by calculating the number of idioms that we process out of the total number of idioms associated with a linguistic pattern in LN_{fr}. Our dataset was composed of 2919 idioms from LN_{fr}, classified between 514 linguistic patterns (cf. §3). Most of the data (93%) were nominal (48%), prepositional (22%) and verbal (22%) idioms.

	Coverage	# total	%
Idioms	2846	2919	97,5%
Linguitic patterns	452	514	87,9%
Generic patterns	29	36	80,6%

Table 5: Coverage against LN_{fr}

Our implementation is currently limited to idioms of six words or fewer, which corresponds to a **97.5%** coverage of the idioms in LN_{fr}, i.e., 2846 idioms. As seen in Table 5, only 73 idioms (divided into 62 patterns) are not covered by our implementation and overall 29 of our 36 generic patterns are exploited by LN_{fr}'s idioms.

Table 6 lists the coverage of LN_{fr} idioms classified by POS. We notice a high coverage of all POS, except for clausal idioms (67%), such as CE N'EST PAS LA MER À BOIRE ('it's no big deal', lit. 'it is not the sea to drink'). This is due to their length, which tends to be greater than other idioms, thus often exceeding our limit of six.

POS	Coverage	# idioms	%
Nominal	1409	1414	99,6%
Prepositional	650	655	22%
Verbal	601	646	93%
Conjunctive	84	87	97%
Clausal	28	42	67%
Adjectival	35	35	100%
Adverbial	21	21	100%
Propositional	7	8	88%
Numeral	5	5	100%
Interjectional	4	4	100%
Pronominal	2	2	100%
Total	2856	2919	97,5%

Table 6: Coverage by part of speech against LN_{fr}

The decision to limit our coverage to six-node idioms was based on two factors. First, the number of possible trees (or generic patterns) grows exponentially with the number of nodes. Figure 6 shows the relationship between the number of trees and the frequency in LN_{fr} for idioms of different sizes. Notice that the number of possible trees quickly becomes higher than the number of idioms in the dictionary.

Secondly, we observe a recursion among the generic patterns. A tree being an intrinsically recursive structure, a subtree is itself a tree. Thus, we can compare the internal structure of idioms to Russian dolls, one embedded in the other. As a result, we can group an idiom's words into clusters that do not necessarily correspond to anything from a lexicological point of view, but that can operate as a string from a computational point of view. In other words, it is possible to describe a long idiom as a combination of smaller idioms corresponding to implemented generic patterns. For example, METTRE LES PETITS PLATS DANS LES GRANDS ('put on a big spread', lit. 'put the small dishes in the large') has seven nodes in its structure. In order to simplify this tree, we can reconfigure it into a three-node tree where *les petits plats* and *dans les grands* themselves form two three-node subtrees that depend on the root METTRE (Figure 7).

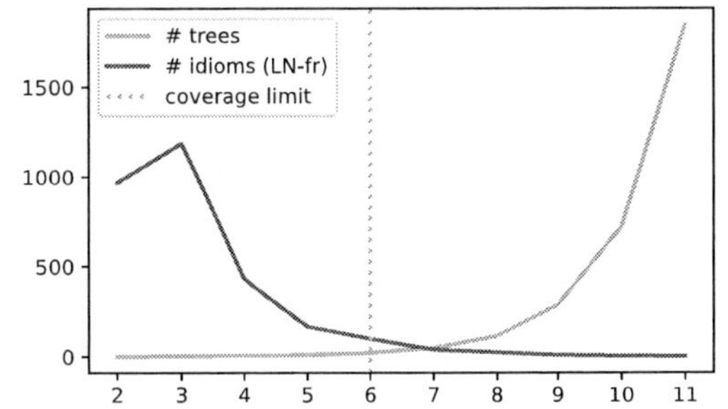

Figure 6: Number of trees vs. number of actual idioms in LN_{fr} (y-axis) with n nodes (x-axis), shown with our coverage cutoff

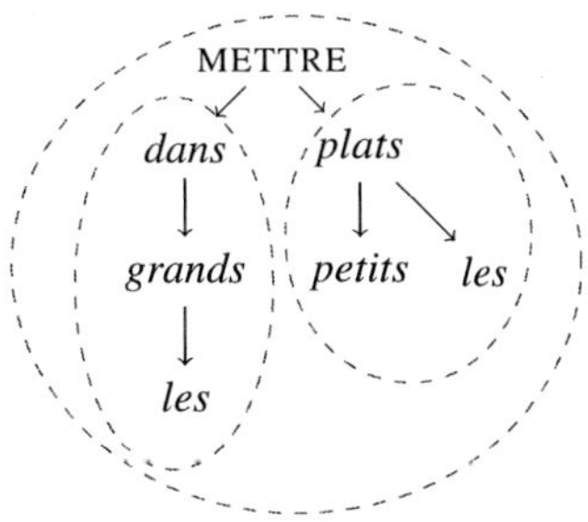

Figure 7: METTRE LES PETITS PLATS DANS LES GRANDS ('put on a big spread', lit. 'put the small dishes in the large') seen as a recursive structure

The verb (METTRE) is the only element of this idiom that can be freely inflected, hence the only one that needs to be isolated from the others. Note that this reconfiguration is not implemented for the moment. However, this solution will allow us to reuse our work as a design basis for processing longer idioms.

5.2. Precision

We automatically generated DSyntRs in MATE format for each of the 2846 idioms in LN_{fr}, together with placeholders for their complements. We then randomly selected three samples without overlap for human evaluation by two annotators: samples 1 and 2 each contained 100 structures (3.5% of the data) and were respectively evaluated by annotators A and B; sample 3 had 300 structures (10.6% of the data) and underwent double evaluation. The annotators were graduate students in linguistics with extensive training in GenDR and MTT. They used our grammar rules to process the DSyntRs and evaluated the resulting SSyntRs. An out-

Sample	n	Judge A	Judge B	κ
Sample 1	100	98 (98%)		
Sample 2	100		97 (97%)	
Sample 3	300	295 (98.3%)	294 (98%)	0.91

Table 7: Precision evaluation results

put structure was considered correct if all the nodes of the idiom were present and attached to the correct governor. Table 7 summarizes the number of correct outputs for each part of the evaluation.

Overall, **97.8%** of the SSyntRs had the expected configuration, with only 11 structures deemed problematic out of all 500. Cohen's κ (Cohen, 1960) was 0.91, which indicates near perfect inter-annotator agreement; only one structure was not agreed upon.

The problems we encountered stemmed from possibly too vague linguistic patterns (5), weaknesses in our implementation (4) and annotation errors (2).

The problems identified derive mainly from pattern mapping. As we have seen earlier, mapping requires a matching number of items on both patterns. Although LN_{fr}'s linguistic patterns are supposed to represent a single syntactic tree, some describe idioms containing a varying number of constituents.

The first explanation for this is embedded idioms. LN_{fr} does not specify the POS of idioms when they are embedded in another idiom. For example, `V Det N_Idiom` describes both MANGER LA FEUILLE DE MATCH ('fail to score a goal that should have resulted in victory', lit. 'eat the game sheet') and FAIRE LE JOLI CŒUR. Both FEUILLE DE MATCH and JOLI CŒUR are nominal idioms, but the former has three nodes and the latter only has two. The linguistic pattern might thus be too vague.

The second is our handling of amalgams (*du*, *des*, *aux*, etc.). The token *des* is ambiguous in French: it can be a determiner (the plural of UN 'a') or an amalgam of a preposition and a determiner (*des=de+les* 'of the'). Our handling of idioms failed to take this difference into account. This problem is also a consequence of node inflection. For example, the idiom ALLER AUX FRAISES ('make out in the bushes', lit. 'go to the strawberries') contains two inflected nodes (*aux* and *fraises*). The nodes in SSyntR are usually not word-forms; rather, they are lexemes with attached grammatical features specifying the desired inflection. This allows lexical information to be consolidated into entries corresponding to the lexical unit (FRAISE) rather than the word-form (*fraises*). Although the inflection of articles can be quickly processed, that of nouns or verbs would require going over each of the idiom entries.

6. Conclusion

Since idioms shows signs of form flexibility, it is crucial that their handling makes the isolation of specific nodes possible in order to enable the addition of inflections, complements or modifiers. We propose a creative solution to handling MWEs in MNLG, inspired from a generalization of Pausé's (2017) idiom classification. Our data were thus collected from the LN_{fr} (Polguère, 2009; Polguère, 2014; Ollinger and Polguère, 2020), an open resource for French.

We implemented our solution in the multilingual generic deep realizer GenDR (Lareau et al., 2018), which is built on top of the graph transducer MATE (Bohnet and Wanner, 2010). We automatically generated graph transduction rules for GenDR's template lexicalization. These rules were based on generic patterns that use integer partition to list all possible n-node trees. Our generic patterns are dependency syntactic trees with empty slots that will be completed with lexical data. We thus automatically generated a lexical dictionary encoding 452 linguistic pattern that describe the mapping of 2846 French idioms. We then manually mapped generic and linguistic patterns onto each other.

As a result, we covered 97.5% of the idioms in LN_{fr} excluding only idioms that contain seven lexemes or more. Our implementation also features a precision of 97.8% and a near perfect Cohen's κ of 0.91. The few problems identified stemmed from the pattern mapping caused by vague linguistic patterns and node inflection.

Many of the problems we encountered while implementing our solution originated from our very first decisions regarding our data collection from LN_{fr} data. If we were to start over, we would map each idiom's lexical units to their POS. This would allow us to design a script that fetches the POS describing embedded idioms. This solution would enable us to promptly encode the inflection of the idioms as grammemes and to subtract it from the lexemes' citation form in SSyntR.

Since our handling of idiom is based on data from the LN_{fr}, it would also gain in precision if idioms' lexicographic files systematically described their government pattern (to allow the addition of the proper preposition). Furthermore, these files could include information on the possible coreferences between the idiom's constituents and its actancts. Among other things, this would be relevant for idioms that include a determinative pronoun. For example, the file of the idiom AVALER SON CHAPEAU 'eat one's hat' (`V Det N`) could describe the coreference relationship between the idiom's `Det` and its first actant (X) : *X avala son chapeau* ('X ate his hat').

Our solution is language-agnostic but relies on complex lexical resources that are currently only available for French. The team behind LN_{fr} is also developing resources for English and Russian. Thus, we expect to be able to extend our solution to these languages fairly easily in the near future. Concretely, porting our grammar to a new language could easily be done without modification if the dictionary used to describe this language is in the same format as ours. All that would be required to do would be mapping language-specific idiom patterns to our generic patterns. This mapping can be done by a trained linguist in a matter of days. Obviously, the hard part is to write the dictionary itself (years of work by a whole team of highly trained lexicographers), but this is independent of our implementation.

Appart from handling idioms in MNLG, one of the purposes of our system was to check the accuracy of lexical resources. Accessing the internal structure of idioms in order to regenerate them proved a good way of highlighting errors and inconsistencies in LN_{fr}. In particular, besides the occasional errors one would expect to find in a large lexical database, we found that the linguistic patterns used in LN_{fr} were not explicit enough with regards to the inflection of the words within an idiom. For example, compare the two synonyms À FOND LA CAISSE ('at full throttle', lit. 'all the way (with) the car') and À FOND LES MANETTES ('at full throttle', lit. 'all the way (with) the controls'). In the first case, *caisse* is singular, but in the second *manettes* is plural. This information was not captured by the linguistic patterns used in LN_{fr}.

Finally, our grammar design could be ported to other graph transducers, such as GREW (Bonfante et al., 2018), but this would require significant effort. However, a GREW implementation could be used to apply the rules in reverse, allowing the automatic construction of deep-syntactic corpora from existing surface-syntactic corpora in the SUD format (Gerdes et al., 2018).

7. Bibliographical References

Andrews, G. E. (1998). *The theory of partitions*. Cambridge university press, Cambridge, 2nd edition.

Apresjan, J. D., Boguslavsky, I. M., Iomdin, L. L., and Tsinman, L. L. (2002). Lexical functions in actual NLP applications. In *Computational Linguistics for the New Millennium: Divergence or Synergy? Festschrift in Honour of Peter Hellwig on the occasion of his 60th Birthday*, pages 55–72. Peter Lang, Frankfurt.

Apresjan, J. (2000). *Systematic Lexicography*. Oxford University Press, Oxford.

Basile, V. (2015). *From Logic to Language: Natural Language Generation from Logical Forms*. Ph.D. thesis, University of Groningen.

Bateman, J. A., Kruijff-Korbayová, I., and Kruijff, G.-J. (2005). Multilingual resource sharing across both related and unrelated languages: An implemented, open-source framework for practical natural language generation. *Research on Language and Computation*, 15:1–29.

Bateman, J. A. (1996). *KPML Development Environment*. GMD/Institut für Integrierte Publikations- und Informationssysteme, Darmstadt.

Bohnet, B. and Wanner, L. (2010). Open source graph transducer interpreter and grammar development environment. In *Proceedings of LREC'10*, pages 211–218, Malta.

Bonfante, G., Guillaume, B., and Perrier, G. (2018). *Application of Graph Rewriting to Natural Language Processing*. iSTE/Wiley, London/Hoboken.

CoGenTex, (1998). *RealPro: General English Grammar*. User manual.

Cohen, J. (1960). A Coefficient of Agreement for Nominal Scales. *Educational and Psychological Measurement*, 20(1):37–46.

Constant, M., Eryiğit, G., Monti, J., van der Plas, L., Ramisch, C., Rosner, M., and Todirascu, A. (2017). Survey: Multiword expression processing: A Survey. *Computational Linguistics*, 43(4):837–892.

Danlos, L. (2000). A lexicalized formalism for text generation inspired by tree adjoining grammar. In Anne Abeillé et al., editors, *Tree Adjoining Grammars: Formalisms, Linguistic Analysis, and Processing*, chapter 15. CSLI Publications, Stanford.

Daoust, N. and Lapalme, G. (2015). JSREAL: A text realizer for web programming. In Núria Gala, et al., editors, *Language Production, Cognition, and the Lexicon*, pages 361–376. Springer, Zürich.

de Marneffe, M.-C., Manning, C. D., Nivre, J., and Zeman, D. (2021). Universal dependencies. *Computational Linguistics*, 47(2):255–308.

Dubinskaitė, I. (2017). Développement de ressources lituaniennes pour un générateur automatique de texte multilingue. Master's thesis, Université Grenoble Alpes, Grenoble.

Elhadad, M. and Robin, J. (1996). An overview of SURGE: A reusable comprehensive syntactic realization component. In *Proceedings of INLG'96*, pages 1–4, Brighton.

Elhadad, M. (1993). FUF: the universal unifier. User manual version 5.2. Technical report, Computer Science, Ben Gurion University of the Negev, Beer Sheva, Israel.

Gatt, A. and Reiter, E. (2009). SimpleNLG: A realisation engine for practical applications. In *Proceedings of ENLG'09*, pages 90–93, Athens.

Gerdes, K., Guillaume, B., Kahane, S., and Perrier, G. (2018). SUD or Surface-Syntactic Universal Dependencies: An annotation scheme near-isomorphic to UD. In *Proceedings of the Universal Dependencies Workshop 2018*, Brussels, Belgium.

Kahane, S. (2003). The Meaning-Text Theory. In Vilmos Ágel, et al., editors, *Dependenz und Valenz: Ein internationales Handbuch der zeitgenössischen Forshung/ Dependency and Valency: An International Handbook of Contemporary Research*, volume 1, pages 546–570. Walter de Gruyter.

Lambrey, F. and Lareau, F. (2015). Le traitement des collocations en génération de texte multilingue. In *Actes de la 22e conférence sur le Traitement Automatique des Langues Naturelles (TALN)*, pages 579–585, Caen.

Lapalme, G. (2020). The jsRealB text realizer: Organization and use cases. arXiv:2012.15425v2 [cs.CL].

Lareau, F. and Lambrey, F. (2016). GÉCO. Technical report, OLST, Université de Montréal.

Lareau, F. and Wanner, L. (2007). Towards a generic multilingual dependency grammar for text generation. In *Proceedings of the GEAF07 Workshop*, pages 203–223, Stanford. CSLI Publications.

Lareau, F., Lambrey, F., Dubinskaitė, I., Galarreta-Piquette, D., and Nejat, M. (2018). GenDR: A generic deep realizer with complex lexicalization. In Nicoletta Calzolari, et al., editors, *Proceedings of LREC'18*, pages 3018–3025, Miyazaki.

Lavoie, B. and Rambow, O. (1997). A fast and portable realizer for text generation systems. In *Proceedings of ANLP'97*, pages 265–268, Washington.

Le, H., Vial, L., Frej, J., Segonne, V., Coavoux, M., Lecouteux, B., Allauzen, A., Crabbé, B., Besacier, L., and Schwab, D. (2020). FlauBERT: Unsupervised language model pre-training for French. In *Proceedings of LREC'20*, pages 2479–2490, Marseille, France.

Mel'čuk, I. A., Clas, A., and Polguère, A. (1995). *Introduction à la lexicologie explicative et combinatoire*. Duculot, Louvain-la-Neuve.

Mel'čuk, I. A. (1988). *Dependency syntax: theory and practice*. State University of New York Press, Albany.

Mel'čuk, I. A. (1995). The future of the lexicon in linguistic description and the explanatory combinatorial dictionary. In Ik-Hwan Lee, editor, *Linguistics in the morning calm*, volume 3. Hanshin, Seoul.

Mel'čuk, I. A. (2006). Explanatory combinatorial dictionary. In Giandomenico Sica, editor, *Open Problems in linguistics and lexicography*, pages 225–355. Polimetrica, Monza.

Mel'čuk, I. A. (2012). *Semantics: From Meaning to Text*, volume 1. John Benjamins, Amsterdam/ Philadelphia.

Mel'čuk, I. A. (2016). *Language: From Meaning to Text*. Ars Rossica, Moscow/Boston.

Mel'čuk, I. A. (2012). Phraseology in the language, in the dictionary, and in the computer. *The Yearbook of Phraseology*, 3:31–56.

Meunier, F. and Danlos, L. (1998). FLAUBERT: A user friendly system for multilingual text generation. In *Proceedings of INLG'98*, Niagara-on-the-Lake, Canada.

Mille, S. and Wanner, L. (2017). A demo of FORGe: the pompeu fabra open rule-based generator. In *Proceedings of INLG'17*, pages 245–246, Santiago de Compostela, Spain. Association for Computational Linguistics.

Mille, S. (2014). *Deep stochastic sentence generation: Resources and strategies*. Ph.D. thesis, Universitat Pompeu Fabra, Barcelona.

Molins, P. and Lapalme, G. (2015). JSrealB: A bilingual text realizer for web programming. In *Proceedings of ENGL'15*, pages 109–111, Brighton.

Ollinger, S. and Polguère, A. (2020). Distribution des systèmes lexicaux, ver. 2.0. Technical report, ATILF-CNRS, Nancy, France.

Pausé, M.-S. (2017). *Structure lexico-syntaxique des locutions du français et incidence sur leur combinatoire*. Ph.D. thesis, Université de Lorraine, Nancy.

Polguère, A. (2009). Lexical systems: graph models of natural language lexicons. *Language Resources and Evaluation*, 43(1):41–55.

Polguère, A. (2014). From writing dictionaries to weaving lexical networks. *International Journal of Lexicography*, 27(4):396–418.

Ramos-Soto, A., Janeiro-Gallardo, J., and Bugarín, A. (2017). Adapting SimpleNLG to Spanish. In *Proceedings of INLG'17*, pages 144–148, Santiago de Compostela.

Sag, I. A., Baldwin, T., Bond, F., Copestake, A., and Flickinger, D. (2002). Multiword expressions: A pain in the neck for NLP. In *Proceedings of the International Conference on Intelligent Text Processing and Computational Linguistics*, pages 1–15, Mexico.

Vaudry, P.-L. and Lapalme, G. (2013). Adapting SimpleNLG for bilingual English-French realisation. In *Proceedings of ENLG'13*, pages 183–187, Sofia.

Wanner, L. and Lareau, F. (2009). Applying the Meaning-Text Theory model to text synthesis with low- and middle-density languages in mind. In Sergei Nirenburg, editor, *Language Engineering for Lesser-Studied Languages*, volume 21 of *NATO Science for Peace and Security*. IOS Press, Amsterdam.

Wanner, L., Bohnet, B., Bouayad-Agha, N., Lareau, F., and Nicklaß, D. (2010). MARQUIS: Generation of user-tailored multilingual air quality bulletins. *Applied Artificial Intelligence*, 24(10):914–952.

Leo Wanner, editor. (1996). *Lexical functions in lexicography and natural language processing*, volume 31 of *Studies in language*. John Benjamins, Amsterdam/Philadelphia.

Weißgraeber, R. and Madsack, A. (2017). A working, non-trivial, topically indifferent NLG system for 17 languages. In *Proceedings of INLG'17*, pages 156–157, Santiago de Compostela.

White, M., (2008). *OpenCCG Realizer Manual*.

Žolkovskij, A. K. and Mel'čuk, I. A. (1965). O vozmožnom metode i instrumentax semantičeskogo sinteza. *Naučno-texničeskaja informacija*, 5:23–28.

Author Index

Association for Computational Linguistics
209 N. Eighth Street
Stroudsburg, Pennsylvania 18360

ISBN 978-1-7138-6128-7

CURRAN ASSOCIATES INC.
proceedings.com